Preface

A series of biennial conferences of historians was inaugurated in Dublin by the Irish Committee of Historical Sciences in July 1953. Since then the 'Irish Conference of Historians' has been circulating among the universities and university colleges of Ireland, and papers read at each meeting (usually lasting three days) since that of 1955 have been published as *Historical Studies: papers read before the Irish Conference of Historians*, as follows:

volume	conference	editor	date of publication
I	Trinity College and University College, Dublin, 11–13 July 1955	T. D. Williams	1958
II	The Queen's University of Belfast, 22–3 May 1957	Michael Roberts	1959
III	University College, Cork, 27–9 May 1959	James Hogan	1961
IV	University College, Galway, 25–7 May 1961	G. A. Hayes-McCoy	1963
V	Magee University College, Londonderry 30 May–1 June 1963	J. L. McCracken	1965
VI	Trinity College, Dublin, 2–5 June 1965	T. W. Moody	1968
VII	The Queen's University of Belfast, 24–7 May 1967	J. C. Beckett	1969
VIII	University College, Dublin, 27–30 May 1969	T. D. Williams	1971

volume	conference	editor	date of publication
IX	University College, Cork, 29–31 May 1971	J. G. Barry	1974
X	University College, Galway, 23–6 May 1973	G. A. Hayes-McCoy	1977
XI	Trinity College, Dublin, 28–31 May 1975	T. W. Moody	1978

Till 1975 the subjects of papers read before the conference depended on the choice of speakers, which in turn was governed by the concept of a combination of historians from the host college, other Irish historians, and visiting historians. The result has been that volumes I–X each exhibit a wide spectrum of subjects and scholars, but lack any distinctive theme. A new principle was established for the 1975 conference: while aiming at the traditional variety of home and visiting speakers, the Irish Committee of Historical Sciences accepted a proposal that the conference to be held in Trinity College, Dublin, should have a single theme, 'The pursuit of national independence', and that papers read at the conference should be published under a corresponding title. The conference was organised accordingly, and the present volume reflects its proceedings, which, it is considered, have successfully set a precedent.

T. W. Moody

August 1977

HISTORICAL STUDIES

PAPERS READ BEFORE THE IRISH CONFERENCE OF HISTORIANS

VOLUME XI

NATIONALITY AND THE PURSUIT OF NATIONAL INDEPENDENCE

(PAPERS READ BEFORE THE CONFERENCE
HELD AT TRINITY COLLEGE, DUBLIN,
26–31 MAY 1975)

NATIONALITY AND THE PURSUIT
OF NATIONAL INDEPENDENCE

Donnchadh Ó Corráin   Leon Ó Broin
Michael Richter   Wolfgang J. Mommsen
Aidan Clarke   David Harkness
Rosalind Mitchison   John Blake
                  edited by T. W. Moody

BELFAST
THE APPLETREE PRESS
*For the Irish Committee
of Historical Sciences*
1978

ISBN 0 904651 31 2

CONTENTS

Introduction

T. W. Moody

The papers here published are concerned with two large historical questions: how has nationality expressed itself in the experience of various countries; how has consciousness of nationality been related to political independence? Answers, explicit and implicit, to one or both of these questions are provided or suggested in the experience of Ireland before 1169, in the early seventeenth century, and in the later nineteenth and early twentieth centuries; of Wales in the twelfth and thirteenth centuries; of eighteenth century Scotland; of continental Europe in the late nineteenth and early twentieth centuries; of the British dominions in 1921; and of two British colonial dependencies in Africa, Nigeria and Botswana, that achieved independence in the 1960s.

The Irish experience as presented in this volume shows trends that are part of a general European pattern. Mr Donnchadh Ó Corrain, challenging an established view among Irish historians, shows that for centuries before the Anglo-Norman invasion the Irish, though fragmented politically, were 'conscious of themselves as a larger community or *natio*', and that this sense of Irish identity, expressed in a common culture, religion, and social institutions, was cultivated in genealogies and origin legends by a mandarin class of privileged scholars. It both helped to promote the idea of a kingship of Ireland and was promoted by the efforts of the great provincial kings of the eleventh and twelfth centuries to dominate the whole island. The growth of a national self-consciousness was thus related both as cause and effect to a movement of political unification. That this process was frustrated by the Anglo-Norman invasion is one of the master facts of Irish history; so too is the persistence of a self-conscious Gaelic culture and Gaelic feudal lordships in an Ireland that became an English lordship, ruled from Dublin in the name of the English king, but never completely subjected to his authority till the end of the sixteenth century; and so too is the establishment of an English colony in Ireland, with an identity of its own, that of a 'middle nation'—English to the Irish, Irish to the English— and a parliament on the English model as one of its most distinctive institutions.

A radically changed situation is illustrated by the emergence in the early seventeenth century of the colonial interest identified by Dr Aidan Clarke as the Old English. This has to be seen against the background, first, of the

Tudor conquest and the rise of a new English colony, and, second, of the imposition of the English reformation on an Ireland whose rejection of it gave a religious dimension to Gaelic resistance while creating for the loyalist colonial element an excruciating dilemma. The Old English were a self-conscious community, distinct from both the Gaelic or Old Irish and the New English. Tracing or claiming descent from the medieval English colony, they were fervently loyal both to catholicism and the English crown, and dedicated to the doctrine that these loyalties were compatible, though the march of events proved the contrary. This Old English nation, distinctively of the landowning and professional classes, failed disastrously to make good its claim to a major share with the New English in the political life of the kingdom of Ireland, and eventually, after making common cause with the Old Irish in the rising of 1641 and the Jacobite war of 1689–91, shared a common ruin with them. When a new colonial nation arose in the late eighteenth century, it did so as a dissident element within the 'protestant ascendancy'; and its triumph in 1782 was quickly negated and finally destroyed in 1800 with the extinction of the Irish parliament. So long as that ancient institution, however corrupt and unrepresentative, existed, there remained the possibility of a peaceful transition to responsible national self-government. But the 'protestant nation' of the late eighteenth century failed no less disastrously than the Old English 'catholic nation' of the early seventeenth century; and in each case the failure of a national movement committed to constitutional action was succeeded by recourse to revolution.

Throughout the period of the union of Ireland with Great Britain (1801–1921) national self-government was pursued both by constitutional and by revolutionary methods. The 'nation' in whose name self-government was sought was defined in a European idiom as a fraternal union of Irishmen of all classes, creeds and traditions, sharing a common pride in an Irish past and resolved to work together for an independent Ireland of the future. But in practice this new, democratic Irish nation, first aroused to political consciousness by the gigantic personality of Daniel O'Connell, was a distinctively catholic community, comprising three-quarters of Ireland's population and confronted by a protestant minority, mainly located in the north-east, determined to maintain the union with England and to resist incorporation in a self-governing Ireland. Between the constitutional and the revolutionary levels of nationalist action there were obscure and ambiguous but effective connections, especially from the 1860s, when a secret society, the I.R.B. (Irish Revolutionary, or Irish Republican, Brotherhood), also known as the Fenian organisation, was established under middle-class inspiration and leadership among working-class Irishmen not only in Ireland but also in Great Britain and

America. This organisation, whose sole purpose was to prepare for a war of independence with Britain, claimed to be the government of an Irish republic 'virtually established', but never commanded the allegiance of more than a small minority of Irishmen. The great majority of the nation after 1870 supported the home rule movement—moderate, constitutional, and relying on the pressures that could be exerted on England through Irish representation in the parliament of the United Kingdom. But these two movements interacted significantly on one another, especially under Parnell's leadership of the parliamentary party; and though the independence eventually won for twenty-six counties in 1921 (the six north-eastern counties remaining within the United Kingdom) was the immediate outcome of rebellion, that result could scarcely have been achieved without the long-sustained work of the home rule movement in mobilising Irish, and moulding British, public opinion in favour of Irish self-government. The eventual achievement of national independence was, moreover, inseparable from a social revolution, the conversion of the tenant farmers into owner-occupiers through state-aided land-purchase, which attached the whole farming class firmly to home rule. For this enormous change in the social system of Ireland after 1879 was the result of mass agitation, largely conducted without violence, by a combination of agrarian radicals, opportunist Fenians, and parliamentary home-rulers, directed by Parnell in the interests of constitutional, not of revolutionary, nationalism. The revolutionary aspect of nationalism is exemplified in the present volume by Dr Leon Ó Broin in his survey of the unique career of the I.R.B., which, having apparently spent itself in the futile rising of 1867, recovered and survived for half a century to play a part in the Easter rising of 1916 and its aftermath.

The case of medieval Wales resembles that of Ireland before the Norman invasion. Dr Michael Richter shows that Wales in the twelfth and thirteenth centuries experienced a growing awareness of national identity not unlike that shown by Mr Ó Corrain to have been characteristic of Ireland in the eleventh and twelfth centuries. As in Ireland this development expressed itself not only in cultural and institutional terms, and in the writing down of local tradition about common origins, but also in a movement of political unification that culminated in the supremacy of the northern principality of Gwynedd over nearly all Wales. This process was in part the response of the independent Welsh rulers to aggression from Norman England, but, ironically, it helped to ensure the ultimate success of that aggression: just as political fragmentation, combined with the nature of the terrain, had been a protection against a foreign takeover, so political integration meant that the defeat of the 'prince of Wales' by Edward I in the wars of independence (1267-7, 1282-3) entailed the conquest of the whole country by the English. In this context Dr Richter discusses the 'transition from a tribal to a feudal society' as an aspect of the growth of national consciousness in medieval Wales that has been neglected, and that parallels developments in continental Europe.

Wales retained its cultural identity after the Edwardian conquest but lost its political identity, and was eventually incorporated administratively with England in 1536. This union, which established a shire system and parliamentary representation for the whole country on the English model, though conceived in a benevolent spirit by an English king, Henry VIII, who was of Welsh descent, was imposed on a powerless Wales by an act of the English parliament. In marked contrast, the union of England and Scotland in 1707, was a negotiated settlement, which, though it left many Scotsmen angry and resentful, left Scotland with her own legal system and her own church-establishment. Scotland had had a long history as a separate kingdom, which, on the whole, had successfully resisted English aggression, when she was joined to England in a parliamentary union. What became of her long-established national identity under that union? Mrs Rosalind Mitchison's answer to that question is that, while an intransigent minority of Scotsmen, with its stronghold in the highlands, attached themselves to Jacobitism and separation, the great majority of the 'political nation'—landowners, merchants, industrialists, and professional men—turned their backs on the past and expressed their sense of national identity by making the most of the present. They did so in efforts to improve agriculture and industry, modernise society, and extract for themselves as much advantage as possible from the English connection. They succeeded so well that, instead of being 'second class Englishmen', many of them became 'super first-class citizens of Great Britain'. By the nineteenth century such patriots could look back with pride to a century of Scottish achievement under the union, and were unwilling to concern themselves with the remoter past of Scotland lest they should 'disturb the accepted myths'. The contrast with the union of Ireland with Great Britain—the situation in which it occurred, the means by which it was effected, the ways by which it was operated, and the reactions of Irishmen to it—has much to say to the differences between national identity in Scotland since 1707 and in Ireland since 1800.

We have been considering manifestations of nationality in three parts of the British Isles, each vitally affected by conflicts of interests with a fourth, England, which in national solidarity and wealth was the strongest of the four. In each case the growth of the state tended to promote, and to be promoted by, the growth of a sense of national identity, but the nationalism of the strongest nation tended, in relation to the weaker nations, to merge into imperialist domination. A more complex situation is opened up by Professor Wolfgang Mommsen, who surveys a Europe between 1870 and

1914 in which the pursuit of national independence was a dominant force. Before the French revolution national self-consciousness, as distinct from the objective elements of nationality—language, religion, culture, common economic and social interests, a common political inheritance—flourished only among the upper and middle classes. Under French revolutionary influence the idea of nationality came to include the principle of democracy, and in the early nineteenth century prophets of national emancipation such as Mazzini looked forward to a peaceful world of democratic nation-states, each devoted to the progress and well-being of its citizens and contributing its own distinctive gifts to the common stock of mankind. Self-determination became an accepted political principle, which could be used to justify the violent overthrow of established states by self-conscious and militant nations subject to non-national governments, as in Italy and Germany. But after 1870 the liberal element in nationality became stunted by the preoccupation of nation-states with power politics and imperialist expansion, and their resulting violation of the interests of rival nations. This, Professor Mommsen concludes, had two effects. (1) In new nation-states, the advance of democracy through the gradual extension of active participation in politics to the working classes was halted, and national ideology was perverted into a means of justifying aggressive foreign policies. (2) The prospects of emancipation for nations still subject to non-national governments (for example the Poles and the Irish) were greatly diminished through the determination of such governments to make no concessions that might conflict with their imperialist interests, and through the spread of the imperialist spirit to national revolutionary movements, as in the Balkans. The first world war appeared to change all this: the Versailles settlement redrew the map of Europe on the principle of national self-determination, and endeavoured to make Europe safe for democracy, and to secure international peace by establishing the League of Nations. But disillusionment quickly set in; and over a quarter of a century culminating in a second world war was needed for Europe to learn the lesson that 'national independence . . . must be accompanied by intensive international cooperation in order to be successful in the long run'.

The two remaining papers in this volume are concerned with aspects of nationality as exported to the British overseas empire. The American colonies in the late eighteenth century had set a sensational example to the world of what could happen when colonies that had developed a sense of national identity were denied essential attributes of self-government. The lesson was not lost on the British empire that emerged from the British defeat in the American war of independence; and one of the main themes of British imperial history in the nineteenth century was the gradual progress to responsible self-government of the dominions of Canada, South Africa,

Australia and New Zealand—developing colonial nations of white European settlement. Professor David Harkness examines the constitutional advance of these dominions in the early twentieth century from the stage of political adolescence they had reached before the first world war to the recognised sovereign status they acquired between 1918 and the outbreak of the second world war. The question of the relations of the dominions to Great Britain was brought to a head by the war of 1914–18, when all of them supported her and took part in the direction of the war through the imperial war cabinet. Two broad approaches to the problem emerge in 1921, that of a centralised imperial authority and that of progressive dominion status leading to full sovereignty. Dr Harkness identifies 1921 as a crossroads on the way to full sovereignty because at that point the Irish situation critically impinged on the imperial debate then in progress. In accepting dominion status instead of full national independence as a basis of settlement of the Anglo-Irish war, the Irish delegates to the peace negotiations were strongly influenced by spokesmen for the dominions; and in making it clear that the dominion status they accepted was a dynamic concept that would develop into full independence they prepared the way for combined action between Ireland and the other dominions in bringing about such a development ten years later, in the statute of Westminster.

Nigeria and Botswana (formerly Bechuanaland) afford contrasting examples of national self-determination on the European model in two of Great Britain's African dependencies. Nigeria was a large, populous, and potentially rich country, Botswana, not much smaller in size but with only half a million people, was one of the poorest and most sparsely populated countries of the world. Nigeria was an artificial entity, created by British wars of conquest over many ethnic groups, differing in language, religion, and culture, who inhabited the territories west, east and north of the River Niger, whereas the tribes of Botswana, nearly all of the same stock, language, and culture, combined to place themselves voluntarily under British protection, in face of encroachments from Boer farmers of the Transvaal and the Orange Free State. Nigeria had a long, bloody, and complex history of resistance to British domination from the 1860s down to 1919 as the background to a movement of constitutional but troubled nationalism that began in the late 1930s and only achieved independence in 1961. In Botswana national self-consciousness did not emerge till the late 1950s, but quickly attained fulfilment, the transition from protectorate to republic being completed with little difficulty by 1966. In Nigeria national identity was in part the outcome of that British rule against which nationalism was directed, and in part the product of nationalist leaders bent on building up the necessary popular pressure behind the independence movement. But the unity thus achieved was far from complete, as the civil war that soon followed independence was so tragically to show. These developments are expounded by Professor John Blake, who was formerly vice-chancellor of the University of Basutoland, Bechuanaland and Swaziland.

The word nation and its derivatives have undergone profound changes of content during the long time-span of the studies in this volume. But these studies, though not conforming to any agreed structure or principle of selection, suggest that there are elements, social, cultural, and political, in the phenomena historians describe as national that have had a certain continuity in European history over the past thousand years and in the history of European expansion for the past two centuries. The purism that would confine the use of 'nation' to the period since the French revolution is not without some justification: the subjective, romantic nationalism of the nineteenth century was a development inseparable from the revolutionary doctrine of the sovereignty of the people. But nineteenth-century nationalism in all its forms harked back to national entities, partly real, partly mythological, of earlier ages, and cannot be explained without reference to these antecedents. And while the concept of the nation as an absolute, and of the nation state as the only legitimate state, has flourished only since the French revolution, national identity was a fact of European life, and the pursuit of national independence a factor in the relations between states for many centuries before 1789.

I

Nationality and kingship in pre-Norman Ireland

Donnchadh Ó Corráin

In undertaking to discuss nationality in pre-Norman Ireland I am well aware that I am laying myself open to objection on a number of counts not least perhaps being that of excessive revisionism. Twice in this century the question of the existence or non-existence of a pre-Norman Irish nation has been a matter for public debate, a debate which has left its marks as much on Irish historiography as on political pamphleteering past and present.[1] It has been charged that the romantic historians of the nineteenth century saw a nation and nationality where there was none and this charge is generally regarded as proven. However, this does not close the debate nor does it dispense the historian of today from the duty of giving critical consideration to those elements of nationality present in the society which was evolving in Ireland in the century or two preceding the Norman attack. Since most if not all these elements expressed themselves in monarchic guise, discussion of them cannot be divorced from a consideration of kingship and Irish political institutions.

Historians have delivered themselves of many and varied judgments concerning the Irish and their institutions in the last few centuries of the

[1] For the earlier debate on this point, see F. X. Martin and F. J. Byrne (ed.), *The scholar revolutionary, Eoin Mac Neill 1867–1945* (Shannon, 1974); Eoin Mac Neill, *Early Irish laws and institutions* (Dublin, [1935]). The nationalistic interpretation of early Irish history finds full expression in the works of Alice Stopford Green: *The making of Ireland and its undoing* (Dublin, 1920); *The Irish state to 1014* (London, 1925); *Irish nationality* (London, 1911). For a sympathetic consideration of Mrs Green, her work and background, see R. B. McDowell, *Alice Stopford Green: a passionate historian* (Dublin, 1967). At the present moment, largely as a result of the political crisis in Northern Ireland, the medieval origins of the modern Irish nation, or, as some would have it, nations, are a matter for intense ideological debate in certain quarters. On this matter, see British and Irish Communist Organisation (henceforth BICO), *Aspects of nationalism* (Belfast, 1972); Workers Association, *One Ireland: two nations* (Belfast, 1973); BICO, *On the 'historic Irish nation'* (Belfast, 1972). A journal entitled *The Two Nations*, dedicated to the proposition that there are two separate nations in the island of Ireland, has been published by BICO in Belfast since 1972. For a commentary on these ideas, in somewhat the same polemical style, see *The Socialist: Monthly Magazine of the Northern Ireland Labour Party Left*, no. 8 (Aug. 1973), pp 10–15. Some of the ideas expressed in these works are echoed by politicians of varying shades of opinion and with varying degrees of conviction both in the north and in the south. Only one thing can be said with certainty of the pamphleteers and the politicians: all are equally innocent of any critical knowledge of Irish history in the period in question.

native polity. For Orpen writing in 1911 Ireland was an anarchic country still in 'a tribal state'.[2] He rightly rejects the symmetrical pyramid structure of political authority depicted in the Book of Rights and similar texts. In his view, the *ard-rí* or 'high-king' held no real political power: 'if the authority of the provincial kings was frequently defied, that of the *ard-rí* or supreme king of Ireland if acknowledged at all was little more than nominal'.[3] Rather, in Orpen's view, must we 'regard the country as split up into 185 tribes of which some were grouped together in comparative permanence and some were generally subordinate to the principal groups'. The reason for this state of affairs was that Ireland lay outside the march of events in Europe; outside the *pax romana*, beyond the barbarian invasions, which might have roused the Gael from his slumbers, and Christianity itself came peacefully to the land only to be absorbed and tribalised.[4] Further, the law was archaic and there was no regular machinery in Ireland for the enactment of laws or for the judicial enforcement of customs normally observed. The reason again is clear:

Until the coming of the Normans, Ireland never felt the direct influence of a race more advanced than herself. She never experienced the stern discipline of Roman domination nor acquired from the law-givers of modern Europe a concept of the essential condition of a progressive society, the formation of a strong state able to make and above all enforce the laws.[5]

Much of what Orpen has said is clearly marked with the political preoccupations of his own time and the received ideas of his own social milieu. Others of his ideas have borne more recent repetition. In a recent work, Professor Lydon has stated that the Irish king

could not depose kings, set up puppet kings subject to himself or impose his will on territories outside his ancestral *túath*. Like everyone else in Ireland, he was subject to the law. He could not therefore legislate. The sort of progression which occurred in Anglo-Saxon England from small tribal kingdoms to a kingdom of England was impossible here.[6]

Evidently the archaism of the law and the weight of its dead hand contrived to keep Irish society in a primitive or tribal state which promised no political change or development.

Professor Warren has advanced a more speculative and indeed sophisticated explanation of this state of affairs: that, since the Celtic conquest of Ireland had been effected by a military caste, the integration of Celtic and pre-Celtic Ireland was achieved by means of elaborate compromises which continued to affect the law and social mores of Irish society. These com-

[2] G. H. Orpen, *Ireland under the Normans*, i (Oxford, 1911), p. 20.
[3] Ibid., pp 23–4.
[4] Ibid., p. 26.
[5] Ibid., p. 105.
[6] James F. Lydon, *The lordship of Ireland* (Dublin, 1972), p. 15.

promises account for the immutability of the law and for Ireland's being rather a cultural association, conformity to which achieved social order at the expense of social conservatism. Irish society had thus achieved an equilibrium that could find little room for progress. In this Celtic world of internally sovereign local lordships, political ambition could be given free play, for society's strength and stability depended not on the state and its institutions but on a generally diffused body of social customs and laws enforced entirely within the context of closely integrated neighbourhood units. This state of the law hindered the advance of monarchy.[7] According to Professor Warren, 'pressure for change was resisted by giving [the law] a religious sanction'; and he proceeds to quote in support of this view the well-known legal dictum: 'this then is Patrick's law and no mortal jurist of the Irish is competent to rescind anything he shall find in the *Senchas Már*'.[8] As we shall see later, this is a very unfortunate choice of text. The Irish king was further handicapped by a three-fold division of authority in Irish society. The king was without peer in the politico-military aspects of the community's life, but its religious life was exclusively controlled by the tribal (and frequently hereditary) abbot, whilst the brehons, through their guardianship of the law, controlled its social and economic structure. The Irish king then, much more than his European peers, was encumbered by 'a fundamental social conservatism and deeply entrenched vested interests'.[9]

Orpen could see no *natio*, no wider community in Ireland than the tribe:[10]

The allegiance of the free born Irishman was given in the first place to the head of his family, kindred or sept, and through the family head to the chief of the tribe of which his family formed an element. . . . The Irishman's country was the *túath* or territory belonging to his tribe.[11]

One is not surprised then that for Orpen the struggle of the half century before the arrival of the Normans was 'a maze of interprovincial and intertribal fighting', through which one could 'glimpse the anarchy that revelled throughout Ireland up to the coming of the Normans'.[12] Eoin Mac Neill attempted the rebuttal of Orpen's arguments by stressing the reality of the high-kingship of Ireland and the existence of many of those institutions of government which Orpen found wanting. He claimed that Irish law

---

[7] W. L. Warren, 'The interpretation of twelfth century Irish history' in J. C. Beckett (ed.), *Historical Studies*, vii (London, 1969), pp 1–19. On Professor Warren's curious notions concerning blood-groupings see now, J. Bernard and J. Ruffie, 'Hématologie et culture' in *Annales E.S.C.*, 31° année—no 4 (July–Aug. 1976), pp 661–76.

[8] Warren, op. cit., p. 6. The quotation is from *Anc. laws Ire.* i, 18. .

[9] Warren, op. cit., p. 7.

[10] Orpen leaves this word undefined; for a discussion of the term, see D. A. Binchy, 'Secular institutions' in Myles Dillon (ed.), *Early Irish society* (reprint, Cork, 1969), pp 54–5; Francis John Byrne, 'Tribes and tribalism in early Ireland' in *Ériu*, xxii (1971), pp 128–66.

[11] Orpen, *Normans*, i, 20.

[12] Ibid., p. 39.

had a national character and further that the king was supreme judge and law-giver.[13] It is perhaps ironic that Orpen and Mac Neill should both be prisoners of their own times for, as Professor Binchy points out, each 'started from precisely the same suppressed premise, that law and order were impossible in any society where the state had not substantially the same functions as the late Victorian era in which they both grew up'.[14] Further, drawing on the legal evidence, Binchy has shown that the law-tracts themselves afford no support for Mac Neill's claims concerning the king of Ireland or *ard-rí*, and has concluded that 'the claim of the king of Tara to be "king of Ireland" has no more basis in law than in fact'.[15] In the period of the canonical law-tracts, there was no king of Ireland; *a fortiori* there were no 'national' institutions associated with that kingship.

It is against this background of social organisation, laws and institutions, relevant to the earliest documentary period, that the political history of Ireland in the tenth, eleventh, and twelfth centuries is most often presented to us, especially by those who feel it incumbent upon themselves to provide some account of native Irish institutions as a prologue to the history of the Normans in Ireland. I shall attempt to show that this stage furniture is for the most part anachronistic. I believe, for example, that the Irish were profoundly conscious of themselves as a larger community or *natio*, that their learned classes were preoccupied with this very notion, and that in the eleventh and twelfth centuries the greater kings attempted to turn that consciousness to political advantage. There are indications, too, that the Irish were not as far out of the mainstream of European life as might at first be imagined. The extreme political fragmentation implied in Orpen's division of the country into a multiplicity of small independent tribes can, I think, be shown to be untrue of the twelfth as well as of any other century for which we have documentary evidence. The position of the law has to a great degree been misunderstood and it is possible to show that, in the later period at any rate, the king was not as impotent in law or at least in practice as has been alleged. Lastly, I hope to give some indication—sketchy and unsatisfactory as it may be—of the ways in which kingship developed between the era of the classical law-tracts and the twelfth century.

[13] Eoin Mac Neill, *Early Irish laws and institutions*, pp 91–118; these views are implicit also in Mac Neill's other works, *Phases of Irish history* (Dublin, 1919) and *Celtic Ireland* (Dublin, 1921); on Mac Neill's treatment of early Irish legal evidence, see D. A. Binchy, 'Mac Neill's study of the ancient Irish laws' in F. X. Martin and F. J. Byrne (ed.), *The scholar revolutionary*, pp 39–48.

[14] Binchy, 'Secular institutions', p. 62.

[15] Binchy, *Celtic and Anglo-Saxon kingship* (O'Donnell Lectures, Oxford, 1970), p. 33; for a fuller discussion of the evidence for the high-kingship and its 'institutions' see Binchy 'The fair of Tailtiu and the feast of Tara' in *Ériu*, xviii (1958), pp 113–38; for further discussion of the high-kingship and for the view that it was originally sacral and cultic, see F. J.Byrne, *The rise of the Uí Néill and the high-kingship of Ireland* (O'Donnell Lectures, Dublin [1970]) and *Irish kings and high-kings* (London, 1973), pp 7–69, 254–74.

It may be appropriate at this point to outline what I understand by 'nationality' in pre-Norman Ireland. Naturally, we are at a loss to know precisely what consciousness the Irish had of themselves outside the Christian context, for the earliest Irish records in regard to this question—the genealogies, origin-legends and related materials—are a tangled skein of pagan and Christian threads. It is certain that they—or at least their royal dynasties—had some explanation of themselves and their origins.[16] There is some evidence that the earliest Irish dynasties regarded themselves as descended from the gods,[17] but it is probable that such mythological statements of origin concerned themselves with individual dynasties rather than with the origin of the peoples of Ireland as a whole. Christianity both as an historical religion of the Book and as an origin-legend for all mankind—quite apart from the heritage of Judaic and Graeco-Roman historical literature which accompanied it—naturally posed the question of the origin and identity of the Irish and their place amongst the nations. One of the earliest of our secular poems, the *fursunnad* of Laidcend mac Baircheda, concerns itself with precisely that problem.[18] Those portions of the poem which contain a detached list of the nations of the earth and which trace the Leinster royal house back to Míl and thence to Noah and Adam, have been dated by Professor Carney and others to the mid-seventh century.[19] Other portions of the poem are much older and contain pagan elements much at variance with the biblical origin of the Irish. The seventh-century portion elaborates what Professor Carney calls 'the theory . . . [of] the unity of Ireland through Míl and of the world through Adam', and he suggests that Senchán Torpéist, writing about 630, was 'the inventor of the politically, and perhaps theologically, useful idea of the common descent of the Irish from Míl of Spain'.[20] It proved to be a fruitful concept.

The tradition is next evidenced in a much more extensive form in

[16] There are two characteristic types of origin-legend: (1) those which treat the royal dynasty as lineal descendants of the ancestral god(s) e.g. the Anglo-Saxon royal genealogies (Kenneth Sisam, 'Anglo-Saxon royal genealogies' in *Brit. Acad. Proc.*, xxxix (1953), pp 287–348) and (2) those which trace the tribe's ascent to a remote eponymous (historical or non-historical) ancestor, often depicted as an immigrant (I. M. Lewis, 'Historical aspects of genealogies in northern Somali social structure' in *Afric. Hist. Jn.* iii (1962), pp 35–48; Ian Cunnison, *History on the Luapala* (Rhodes-Livingstone Papers, no. xxi, London, 1951); Laura Bohannon, 'A genealogical charter' in *Africa*, xxii (1952), pp 301–15). Both types are in evidence in early Irish sources.

[17] This is at least true of the Laigin who looked to Labraid Loingsech Lorc otherwise Lóegaire or Móen as their common ancestor *(Lóegaire Lorcc is hé senathair Laigin,* Rawl. B 502, 115a16 = O'Brien *Corpus geneal. Hib.*, p 1) and the oldest texts describe him as a god *(scéo deëib / dia óen / as Móen mac Áine / óenríg,* ibid., cf. *Ériu,* xxii (1971), pp 70–71). T. F. O'Rahilly, *Early Irish history and mythology* (Dublin, 1946) deals with this and related problems but his conclusions must be used with caution.

[18] *Corpus geneal. Hib.* i, 4–7; cf. pp 201–2.

[19] James Carney, 'Three Old Irish accentual poems' in *Ériu,* xxii (1971), pp 65–73.

[20] Ibid., p. 73.

Nennius's *Historia Brittonum* which was written in the end of the eighth century.[21] A poem of Máel Mura of Othain (+ 887), who is described as 'royal poet of Ireland' and who was almost certainly a cleric, develops the tradition further. In this poem, entitled *Can a mbunadas na nGaedel?*, he sets himself the scholarly question: what is the origin of the Irish, where do they come from, why did they come to Ireland, and why are they called by various names (*Scuitt, Gáedil, Féni*)? In answer to his question he draws on the legend of Míl of Spain and on the biblical origin of the Irish. The various names are accounted for by ancestral aetiologies cast in a genealogical mould and the various tribes and dynasties of Ireland, of which he gives a most detailed account, are all linked together in one common line of ascent.[22] From such work there developed a wide range of speculations, pseudo-historical constructs and deductions which over the centuries agglomerated into the *Lebor Gabála Érenn*, 'Book of the taking of Ireland', which offered a full explanation of Irish pre-history and provided the Irish with a common identity by way of descent from a single set of ancestors.[23] Van Hamel would date the archetype of the recensions which we possess to the second half of the tenth century though, of course, it continued to be transcribed and enlarged for some centuries to come.[24] Its influence and the influence of the theories enshrined in it proved all-pervasive. Dublittir Ua hÚathgaile (*fl.* 1082), a monastic scholar of some distinction, produced an even more elaborate ethnicon into which he integrates the Irish and their language, for all these texts display a curious interest in language.[25] His description of the discovery of the Irish language should delight any modern cultural nationalist: 'ten years after that there was discovered by Fénius Farsaid the speech which is melodious and sweet in the mouth . . .' [26]

The main genealogical *corpus*, much of which is extremely old, is based on this same origin-legend and it is interesting to note that the later the text the more prominent the legend. Behind this self-conscious antiquarianism is the doctrine that all the people of Ireland derive from one common source (however far removed) and form one *natio*. As the Franks, the Saxons, the Lombards, the Goths, the Greeks are *nationes*, so also are the Irish. The tradition of pilgrimage, of missionary endeavour, such a controversy as the Paschal question of the seventh century in the course of which Irish practices were seen to differ from those of the rest of Europe, and, above all,

---

[21] A. G. Van Hamel (ed.), *Lebor Bretnach* (Dublin, 1932).

[22] J. H. Todd (ed.), *The Irish Nennius* (Dublin, 1848), pp 220–87; *Bk Leinster*, iii, 516–23.

[23] R. A. S. Macalister (ed.), *Lebor Gabála Érenn* (5 vols, Dublin, 1938–56); for comment on the text, Rudolph Thurneysen, 'Zu irischen Handschriften und Literaturdenkmälern', 2nd series, in *Abhl. d. kgl Ges. d. Wiss. zu Göttingen*, Phil-Hist. Klasse xiv/3 (Berlin, 1913); A. G. Van Hamel, 'On Lebor Gabála' in *Z.C.P.* x (1915), pp 97–197.

[24] Ibid., p. 115.

[25] *Bk Leinster*, iii, 563–73.

[26] Ibid., p. 573.

the levelling effect of a church which, in its earliest forms at least, transcended local identities, must have deepened the Irish sense of 'otherness'.

The sense of 'nationality' is present also, after a fashion, in the *corpus* of Irish law, much of which was compiled in the seventh century, itself a troubled century of synods and ecclesiastical controversies largely due to the conflict between nativist and romanising parties in the Irish church. Irish law, however local in application or however much dependent on individual law-schools in fact,[27] regards itself as valid for all the Irish. This is evidenced in a remarkable way in *Bretha crólige*, 'judgments of bloodlyings', which states in regard to sick-maintenance consequent on injury:

Direnar do cach a lanamnus a bescnu inse erenn ciapa lin ciapa n-uaite. (Every one is paid *díre* for his [marital] union according to the custom of the island of Ireland, whether it be manifold or single.)[29]

What is even more interesting, this passage occurs at a point in the tract at which the jurist is implicitly contrasting the customs of Ireland and the universal Christian norm advocated by the romanising party. The same term recurs in *Córus béscna: breithemnus indse hErend,* which is to be translated 'the jurisprudence of the island of Ireland'.[30] While it is clear then that the law was local in application (as are so many medieval legal systems elsewhere) and custom differed from place to place, nonetheless the custom of Ireland as a whole was present to the minds of the jurists and with the growing authority of the *Senchas Már* there may have been a real tendency towards uniformity. The jurists and the other learned classes, cleric and lay, were unrestrained by local boundaries and travelled freely to practice their craft where they wished, and for them, a highly self-aware and deeply respected élite, the whole island of Ireland was the field of their labours. It is scarcely surprising that the sense of nationality should first emerge amongst them and be cultivated by them.

However, this sense of nationality soon spilled over into politics for it is implicit in the political claims of the Uí Néill propagandists. Two examples may suffice. Muirchú, writing in the seventh century speaks of *Temoria que est caput Scottorum* 'Tara which is the *caput* of the Irish',[31] whilst Adomnán describes Diarmait mac Cerbaill as *totius Scotiae regnatorem a deo ordinatum*

[27] Binchy. 'The date and provenance of the *Uraicecht Becc*' in *Ériu* xviii (1958), pp 44–54 suggests that the *Nemed* collection of tracts and the *Cáin Fuithirbe* originated in a southern school, whilst the *Senchas Már* was the product of a school or schools situated in the north; he is also of the opinion that *Críth Gablach* (Dublin, 1941, p. xviii) was written in the northern half, in Meath or Ulster, but probably not in the same school(s) as *Senchas Már*; see further Binchy, '*Bretha Nemed*' in *Ériu*, xvii (1955), pp 4–6.

[29] Binchy, '*Bretha Crólige*' in *Ériu*, xii (1934), pp 1–77; the passage in question is §57; cf. the editor's comments, ibid., p. 74.

[30] *Anc. laws Ire.*, iii, 30.

[31] *Bk. Arm.*, 2 ʀb 28.

7

'the ruler of all Ireland, ordained by God'.[32] These claims are highly tendentious and testify to ambition rather than achievement. Less explicitly, they testify, at least amongst some royal propagandists, to an awareness of the Irish as a *natio*, a wider community, rule over which, in one form or another, was a laudable ambition for an over-king of the Uí Néill in the seventh century. The subsequent expansive activities of these Uí Néill kings, the breakdown of localised petty kingdoms, contact with the Vikings and the emergence of more extensive power-blocs must have served to deepen that awareness. By the eleventh and twelfth centuries the poet-historians had elaborated in full the concept of a monarchy of all Ireland and had projected it into the pre-Christian past so that, for their contemporaries, the kingship of Ireland—the political unity of Ireland in one form or another—took on the character of an immemorial tradition. The work of the poet-historians is the political theory which answered to the activities and ambitions of the greater kings of the eleventh and twelfth centuries and not infrequently provided their inspiration. It is this feeling of identity which I understand by nationality and I think one can feel it in the changing nuances of the annalistic record between the ninth and the twelfth centuries. To take one example, the phrase *fir Érenn*, literally 'the men of Ireland' comes to be used of the followers of the greatest kings and of the lesser kings and nobles under their sway. This phrase is used in reference to Máel Sechnaill mac Máele Ruanaid, Muirchertach Ua Briain and Ruaidrí Ua Conchobair,[33] all outstanding kings in their own time, and implies not only a concept of Ireland as a whole but an identification of some sort of the affairs of Ireland as a whole with the fortunes of the dominant king of the day.

Professor Binchy's stress on the archaism of the law[34] may be said to have been misunderstood by some historians less familiar with the early period. It is, for example, quite true to say with Professor Warren that in Irish law equal status was accorded to the king, the principal abbot, and the *ollam*. The law-tracts, which apparently derive from different schools and vary to a degree in date (none is later than the beginning of the eighth century), are not quite at one as to the honour-price or status which they attribute to a

---

[32] William Reeves (ed.), *The life of Columba . . . by Adamnan* (Dublin, 1857), pp 67–8 = A. O. and M. O. Anderson, *Adamnan's Life of Columba* (Edinburgh, 1961), p. 280; see further F. J. Byrne, *The rise of the Uí Néill*, pp 3–8, and *Irish kings*, pp 254–71.

[33] *A.U.*, s. a. 858, 1102, 1106, 1167, 1168.

[34] Binchy, 'The linguistic and historical value of the Irish law-tracts' in *Brit. Acad. Proc.*, xxxix (London, 1943), pp 195–227; 'Linguistic and legal archaisms in the Celtic law-books' in *Philolog. Soc. Trans.*, 1959, pp 14–24; 'Celtic suretyship: a fossilized Indo-European institution' in *Indo-European and Indo-Europeans: papers presented at the third Indo-European Conference, 1963* (Philadelphia, 1970), pp 355–67.

[35] '*Miadslechta*' in *Anc. laws Ire.*, iv, 362; '*Uraicecht Becc*' in *Anc. laws Ire.*, v, 2–114 = Eoin Mac

bishop and, by implication, to a principal abbot.[35] However, it can be stated with some degree of confidence that the tracts generally equate his status with that of the *rí túaithe*. This is not to say that the king and the abbot exercised equal authority, for one must distinguish sharply between that socio-legal status which is the concern of the jurists and the political authority which was exercised by the kings. The comfortable status which the church had achieved for itself in the seventh and eighth centuries did not make it the political rival of the king. Rather, as we shall see, the church did much to strengthen kingship.

The status of *rí túaithe* or tribal king, with which the *ollam* and abbot are equated in standing, was already in decline, it would appear, even in the period of the canonical law-tracts. One early law-tract states: *niba tuath tuath gan egna gan egluis gan filidh gan righ aracorathar cuir agus cairde do thuathaibh* (a *túath* which has no scholar, no church, no poet, no king who extends(?) contracts and treaties to [other] *túatha* is no *túath*).[36] Here, in this tract we may have an indication of the passing of the *túath*, for the statement implies that some communities, formerly *túatha* in the full sense, no longer retained the characteristics of such a structure. Indeed, it has been suggested that the rise of great dynasties such as the Éoganacht and Uí Néill and their expansion in the sixth and seventh centuries undermined the old system based on the *túath*.[37] This conclusion is adequately borne out, as far as the eighth century is concerned, by the contemporary annalistic entries. In these we find kings who must have been kings of *túatha* or even of large kingdoms *(ruirig)* referred to by the inferior title *dux*. In 756, for example, the king of the petty kingdom of Delbna Ethra is entitled *dux*.[38] In 771 and in 796 the same term is applied to the kings of Luigne and Ciarraige.[39] In the ninth century, this usage is much extended and over-kings of the Laígse, Mugdorna, Cenél Conaill, and Uí Meic Uais bear the lesser title of *duces*.[40] The growth of even more powerful overkingship further reduced these lesser kings, and in the eleventh and twelfth centuries the normal title of the

Neill, 'Ancient Irish law: the law of status or franchise' in *R.I.A. Proc.*, xxxvi sect. C (1923), pp 272–81; *Críth Gablach*, pp 18–19; E. J. Gwynn, 'An Old-Irish tract on the privileges and responsibilities of poets' in *Ériu*, xiii (1940), p. 30; see further, Kathleen Hughes, *Ch. in early Ir. soc.*, pp 134–6.

[36] E. J. Gwynn, 'Tract on the privileges of poets', pp 31, 224. It will be noted that the forms appear to be modern (the transcript is that of Dubaltach Mac Fir Bhisigh) but they may readily be restored to Old Irish. For similar uses of *ar-cuirethar* see *Críth Gablach*, pp 15, 34; *Contributions to a dictionary of the Irish language*, A, fasc 2 (Dublin, 1967), col. 385.

[37] Binchy, *Celtic and Anglo-Saxon kingship*, pp 34–40;Thomas Charles-Edwards, 'Some Celtic kinship terms' in *Bulletin of the Board of Celtic Studies*, xxix (1971), pp 117–22.

[38] *A.U.*, s.a. 756.

[39] *A.U.*, s.a. 771, 796. For contemporary and broadly similar Anglo-Saxon use of *dux*, see Eric John, *Orbis Britanniae and other studies* (Leicester, 1966), pp 24–5.

[40] *A.U.*, s.a. 869, 870, 872, 877, 879, 883, 884, 912 etc.

ruler of an area similar in size to the old *túath* is *tigerna, tóisech* and *tóisech dútchais*, all of which may be translated 'lord'.[41]

The older customs which, as Professor Lydon observes, prevented a king setting up puppet kings over neighbouring kingdoms or annexing the kingdoms of others, had also passed away by the eighth century. One wonders if these customs ever existed outside the polite and schematic speculations of the jurists. In fact, we find frequent annalistic reference to such events in the eighth century. It is probably sufficient to cite two. For the year 744 the Annals of Ulster have the following: *foirddbe Corcu Mu-Druadh don Deiss* (the destruction of the Corcu Modruad by the Déis). The Déis are here identical with the Dál Cais, and from this period dates the occupation of extensive lands in Clare by the Dál Cais and the beginning of their rise to political power. For 752, the same annals record: *foirddbe Brecrige do Cheniul Coirpri i Telaigh Findin* (the destruction of the Brecrigi by Cenél Cairpre in Telach Findin). After this the Brecrigi disappear from history. They were totally absorbed by Cenél Maine, a rising branch of the Uí Néill who invented a pseudo-eponym for them, Breccán mac Maine, and from the grandson of this Breccán the new ruling family of Brecrigi is said to descend.[42] Not only were the lands of lesser peoples appropriated but the conquerors frequently took over their names and even their tribal saints. In the late eighth and ninth centuries a branch of the Uí Chennselaig, the dominant south Leinster dynasty, conquered the Uí Dróna and took to themselves the name of the conquered. The northern branch of Síl nÁeda Sláine who expropriated the Cianachta were themselves known as Cianachta by the mid-eighth century. Irgalach ua Maíl Umai, who died in 816, is entitled *rex Corco Sogain*. In fact, Corco Sogain was a small population group which his branch of the Uí Néill, Caílle Follamain, had conquered. So dim had the memory of such earlier and expropriated peoples become that scholars, working in the eighth and ninth centuries, were already compiling antiquarian lists of them.[43]

Orpen's 185 tribes who flourished in the period after the Viking wars must be sought in antiquarian calculations of a later date. Giraldus Cambrensis gives 176 as the number of cantreds in Ireland.[44] It is, however,

---

[41] On these latter terms, see Gearóid Mac Niocaill, 'A propos du vocabulaire social irlandais du bas moyen âge' in *Études celtiques*, xii (1970–71), pp 512–46; for the use of these terms in a local genealogical setting (twelfth century), see John O'Donovan, *Miscellany of the Celtic Society* (Dublin, 1846), pp 48–56.

[42] *Bk Lec.*, 60 ʀb 17–25 = *B.B.*, 82 a 36–45; see also Paul Walsh, 'Meath in the Book of Rights' in John Ryan (ed.) *Féil-sgríbhinn Eóin Mhic Néill* (Dublin, 1940), pp 511–2.

[43] For such lists and their derivatives, see T.C.D., H.2.7., 156 d 19–163a31; R. I. A. Stowe C 1 2, 40 R 18; *Ériu*, iii (1907), pp 138–40; *Y Cymmrodor*, xiv (1901), pp 122–34; T. Ó Raithbheartaigh (ed.), *Genealogical tracts*, i (Dublin, 1932), pp 69–84, 107–32.

[44] James F. Dimock (ed.), *Giraldi Cambrensis opera*, v (London, 1867), p. 145.

clear that he is latinising the Irish term *trícha cét*.[45] His estimate does not derive from his own calculations but, like the greater portion of this section of the *Topographia*, from Irish literary sources. Therefore, Giraldus's work has no independent value as a contemporary reckoning. Keating, O'Flaherty, and other writers give the number as 184 or 185 but all these, as Hogan has shown, derive from the poem *Ca lin trícha i nErind?* which is preserved in a number of medieval manuscripts and which in style and language is a typical product of twelfth-century antiquarianism.[46] There is a further difficulty: *trícha cét* never seems to mean *túath* or tribe in Irish sources. According to Hogan, it denotes a territory associated with a military muster in the earlier period; later (i.e. from the eleventh century on) it denotes a geographical area. In fact, it is attested in the Annals of Ulster for the year 1106 as a unit of assessment. In that year, Cellach, coarb of Patrick, made his circuit of Munster and received his full due, viz seven cows and seven sheep and half an ounce for each area of a *trícha cét* in Munster *(cech fuind trícha i Mumain)*. Orpen's 185 tribes then are the children of misunderstanding: they never existed. Mac Neill, for his part, estimates that there were about eighty *túatha* in the whole of Ireland.[47] I for one am at a loss to discover the precise means by which he arrived at this estimate and, with Professor Byrne, I prefer to resist 'the temptation . . . of trying to impose a neat and schematic pattern on the fluctuating political boundaries of early Ireland'.[48] What we can say with certainty is that there were no more than a dozen overkingdoms of any political consequence in the tenth century, and these were drastically reduced in number by the mid-twelfth century.

Other legal institutions which many seem to consider relevant to the twelfth century had long become obsolete. During the seventh century, the *derbfine*, the four-generation agnatic kindred group, so important as a legal and property-owning unit in the earlier period, became obsolete and was replaced by the *gelfine*, a simpler three-generation group.[49] Similarly, in the matter of royal succession, it can be shown that eligibility was not ordered by the inheritance customs of the *derbfine*, however near or distant such customs may have been to men's mind as a general ideal of the fitness of things, but by the everyday realities of power-politics within dynasties of

[45] James Hogan, 'The *trícha cét* and related land-measures' in *R.I.A. Proc.*, xxxviii, sect. C (1920), pp 148–235.

[46] Ibid, pp 169–74.

[47] Mac Neill, *Early Irish laws and institutions*, p. 96.

[48] F. J. Byrne, 'Tribes and tribalism', loc cit., pp 159–60; see however, *Irish kings and high-kings*, p. 7, where he states that 'there were probably no less than 150 kings in the country at any given date between the fifth and twelfth centuries'.

[49] T. M. Charles-Edwards, 'Kinship, status and the origin of the hide' in *Past and Present*, lvi (1972), pp 1–33; it is to be noted that Liam Ó Buachalla, 'Some researches in ancient Irish law' in *Cork Hist. Soc. Jn.*, lii (1947), pp 41–54 is mistaken in his explanation of these institutions.

growing strength and self-confidence.[50] However, one still finds the *túath* with its tabus and the *derbfine* with its manifold complexities wending their way wearily across the pages of historians of a much later period. What is even more remarkable, if we accept the views of some historians, these institutions were still alive and flourishing in sixteenth-century Ireland[51]—almost a millenium after they had become obsolete and at least five hundred years after the Irish lawyers had ceased to understand at all clearly what they meant.

Much of the misunderstanding—about the political conservatism, tribalism, and supposed immutability of Gaelic society over many centuries—is the result of a methodological error on two levels. On the more general level, the historians have been deceived by the apparently static picture of Irish society presented them in the sources and, as a result, they have been insensitive to those shifts of emphasis and nuances of expression which indicate change in institutions and political and social innovations in society as a whole. This is particularly true of Ireland where the bulk of the early historical sources are literary and highly conventionalised products of specialist learned classes, retainers of the contemporary holders of power, who were at pains to legitimise all change by giving it the sanction of immemorial custom and who ruthlessly reshaped the past to justify the present.[52] This type of activity is not confined to Ireland and, in fact, finds a close parallel in European legend-building—lay and clerical—in the eleventh and twelfth centuries. Indeed, the unchanging Gaelic Ireland of the modern historical scholars bears silent witness to the effectiveness of their medieval forebears in discharging their duty. For example, the rise to power of Dál Cais led not only to the drastic recasting of their previous genealogy but to a rewriting of the history of the Viking wars in Ireland in the interest of their political aspirations, and offered an example which their rivals were not slow to imitate.[53] In such rewritings of history, fundamental political changes and altered circumstances of recent

---

[50] Ó Corráin, 'Irish regnal succession: a reappraisal' in *Studia Hib.*, xi (1971 [1972]), pp 7–39.

[51] G. A. Hayes-McCoy, 'Gaelic society in Ireland in the late sixteenth century' in G. A. Hayes-McCoy (ed.) *Historical Studies*, iv (London, 1963), pp 45–61; Nicholas P. Canny, 'Hugh O'Neill and the changing face of Gaelic Ulster' in *Studia. Hib.*, x (1970), pp 7–35.

[52] For interesting examples of this process in other societies, see J. H. Plumb, *The death of the past* (Harmondsworth, 1973), pp 11–50; A. H. Shah and L. G. Shropp, 'The Vahīvanca Barots of Guejerat; a caste of genealogists and mythographers' in *American Folklore Jn.*, lxxi (1958), pp 246–76; E. L. Peters, 'Aspects of rank and status among Muslims in a Lebanese village' in J. A. Pitt-Rivers (ed.), *Mediterranean countrymen* (The Hague, 1963), pp 159–200.

[53] Their 'revised' genealogies were first exposed by Eoin Mac Neill in his paper, 'The *Vita Tripartita* of St Patrick' in *Ériu*, xi (1930), pp 34–40, reprinted in Eoin Mac Neill, *St Patrick* (Dublin, 1964), pp 214–20, Compare the legends, deliberately fostered, about the Carolingian associations of Hugh Capet: R. Fawtier, *Capetian kings of France* (London, 1960), pp 55–7. For the Dál Cais-inspired account of the Viking wars, see J. H. Todd (ed.), *Cogadh Gáedhel re*

events are frequently projected back into the remote past and thus the fiction of continuity and changelessness is maintained. On a more particular level, some historians may be said to have mistaken the pedantic archaism of the jurists for the attitude of society at large, and have to a degree taken their legal tracts (which were probably conservative if not out of date at the time of writing) as a true account of the practice. The customary law did in fact change, as can be observed even in the texts of the schools where we see the later glossators attempting, where they understood them, to bring the rules of the older texts into line with the practice of their own day. And, as to the later middle ages and early modern period, Dr Mac Niocaill has pointed out that, though the classical tracts were cited as ever, they had no relevance to actual litigation or the manner in which it was conducted. They were cited for the sound rather than the sense and were a useful window-dressing which lent mystique to the men of the law as they went about their business in a much more mundane and practical way.[54] What the actual practice was must be pieced together (if ever it can) from the later legal literature and from incidental references in non-legal sources. We have no texts, for example, that gratuitously tell us the legal powers of the king, the order of the royal household, or the legal functions of the king's officers in the eleventh and twelfth centuries—and even if we had, we should treat them with the utmost caution. It is equally true to say that the detailed and painstaking work involved in discovering such matters from our all too meagre sources has yet to be done, and I can only offer a few tentative suggestions on the relations of the later kings with the lawyers and the law, their law-making powers, and their rights over the property of their subjects.

Professor Warren's observation that the law was given a certain religious sanction and that this was done to resist pressure for change is perfectly true in its own way but not in the sense in which he intends it. As we have seen, he bases his statement on the prologue of the *Senchas Már*, a document which, as Professor Binchy has shown, was written in the beginning of the twelfth century but which incorporates older materials.[55] In effect, the prologue is the developed form of a legend relating how the Irish brought their native law into consonance with Christianity: those parts of the law

---

Gallaibh (London, 1867); and for examples of the manner in which this latter work continues to impose itself on historians, see Gwyn Jones, *A history of the Vikings* (London, 1968), pp 204–8; Johannes Brøndsted, *The Vikings* (Harmondsworth, 1970), pp 55–8; G. Turville-Petre, 'Poetry of scalds and of the *filid*' in *Ériu*, xxii (1971), pp 2–3.

[54] Gearóid Mac Niocaill, 'Notes on litigation in late Irish law' in *Ir. Jurist*, ii (1967), pp 299–307.

[55] Binchy, 'The pseudo-historical prologue to the *Senchas Már*' in *Studia Celt.*, x–xi (1975–6), pp 15–28. I am deeply grateful to Professor Binchy for a copy of this paper while yet in typescript and for allowing me to cite from it.

which were in conflict with the scripture were discarded; and the revised law is the law of Patrick which no mortal jurist of the Irish may change. An earlier version of the legend occurs in *Corus Béscna*[56] and there it serves the same purpose. As Binchy notes, 'what the compiler of *Corus Béscna* really wanted to emphasise was the perfect compatability of the *Senchas* with Christian teaching; he was, in fact, defending the traditional law against attack'.[57] The most spectacular of these attacks came from the Romanist party in the Irish church in the seventh century and from the twelfth century reformers who found much that was objectionable in the Irish law of secular marriage.[58] The twelfth century prologue to the *Senchas Már*, then, is an apology and a defence of Irish peculiarities in certain limited areas of social life, with which the church reformers concerned themselves, rather than an attempt to invest the whole of ancient legal *corpus* with the highest religious authority in the land, that of St Patrick, in order to resist legal and institutional changes of a general character.

However, it is likely that there is another and more general reason for the legend of Patrician revision of the laws, for a glance at the annals between the ninth and the twelfth centuries reveals a most interesting development amongst the practitioners of law. Very many of them are churchmen and many are of high standing. The following examples may serve to illustrate the trend:

A.U., s.a. 802:
> *Ailill m. Cormaicc, abbas Slane, sapiens et iudex optimus obiit.*[59]

A.F.M., s.a. 884 (=887):
> *Colcu mac Connacáin, abb Cinn Ettich, ollam, aurlabhraidh agus senchaidh as deach ro bhui i nErinn ina reimhes [d'écc]* (Colcu mac Connacáin, abbot of Kinnitty, an *ollam*, legal pleader and the best historian in Ireland in his time, died).

Three frags p. 210 (=908):
> Amongst the slain at the battle of Belach Mugna was Colmán, *ab Cinn*

---

[56] *Anc. laws Ire.*, iii, 28–32.

[57] Ibid.

[58] Rudolph Thurneysen and others, *Studies in early Irish law* (Dublin, 1931); for a deft defence of Irish polygamy by reference to the Old Testament, see '*Bretha Crólige*', p. 44 §57. *Acallam na Senórach*, a twelfth-century literary *Rahmenerzählung*, has an interesting reflex of the contemporary debate on marriage between the reformers and the conservatives: Áed mac Muiredaig, king of Connacht, is depicted as bitterly resenting St Patrick's insistence on monogamy (Whitley Stokes (ed.), *Acallamh na Senórach* in *Irische Texte*, Vierte Serie, i (Leipsig, 1900), pp 176–7), a touch which may reflect the well-earned reputations of Tairdelbach Ua Conchobair (+1156) and his son, Ruaidri (+1189), kings of Connacht and 'high-kings'.

[59] He belonged to an ecclesiastical family which gave abbots to the monasteries of Slane, Louth and Duleek (Hughes, *Ch. in early Ir. soc.*, p. 163).

Etigh ard-ollamh brithemnachta Eirenn (Colmán, abbot of Kinnitty and chief *ollam* of the jurisprudence of Ireland).[60]

A.F.M., s.a. 937 (=939); cf. *Ann. Ult.*, s.a. 939:
Finnachta mac Ceallaigh comharba Doire, epscop agus saoi berla Fene [d'ecc] (Finnachta mac Ceallaigh abbot of Derry, a bishop and a scholar in Irish law, died).

Ann. Inisf., s.a. 1032:
Ailill Hua Flaithim, airchinnech Aird Ferta Brenainn quievit. Ollam Muman a brethamnas hé (Ailill Ua Flaithim, erenagh of Ardfert rested. He was the *ollam* of Munster in jurisprudence).[61]

A.U., s.a. 1041; *Ann. Tig.*, s.a. 1041:
Mac Beathad m. Ainmere, ard-ollam Ard Macha agus Erenn archena (Mac Beathad mac Ainmere chief *ollam* of Armagh and of Ireland besides [died]); *Ann. Tig.* add further: *airdbreatham Aird Macha agus tuile eolais Erenn* (chief judge of Armagh and flood of knowledge of Ireland).

A.F.M., s.a. 1095; *Ann. Inisf.*, s.a. 1095:
Amongst those distinguished persons who died of the plague were *Hua Mancháin .i. an brethem, comharba Caoimhghin . . . agus Augustin Ua Cuinn, airdbreithem Laighen* (Ua Mancháin, i.e. the judge, abbot of Glendalough . . . and Augustín Ua Cuinn, chief judge of Leinster); *Ann. Inisf.* describe Ua Mancháin as being *do muintir Glinne do Lacha* (of the community of Glendalough).

Ann. Inisf., s.a. 1106:
In brethem Hua Rebacháin, airchinnech Mungarat mortuus est (The judge Ua Rebacháin, erenagh of Mungret, died).

A.F.M., s.a. 1158:
An breithemh Ua Dúilendáin, airchindech Eassa Dara, ollamh feineachais agus taoiseach a thuaithe d'écc (The judge Ua Dúilendáin, erenagh of Ballysadare, an *ollam* of Irish law, and lord of his territory died).[62]

These annalistic entries are supported by the proverbial sayings: *Féineachas hÉrenn Cluain hUama; bérla Féine hÉrenn Corcach; brethemnas hÉrenn, Sláine*—namely, that the monasteries of Cloyne, Cork, and Slane were famous centres for the study of Irish law.[63]

[60] It is probable from his title that he was royal judge to Cormac mac Cuilennáin, king of Munster, who was slain in the same battle.

[61] It is possible that he was royal judge to Donnchad mac Briain, king of Munster.

[62] Mr K. W. Nicholls has suggested to me that this man may be the ancestor of the later Mac an Bhreitheamhan, erenagh family of Ballysadare.

[63] Kuno Meyer (ed.), *The triads of Ireland* (Dublin R.I.A., Todd Lecture Series, XIII, 1906), p. 2; the entry on Cork is glossed in MS H. 1. 5: *.i. a n-iomat breithemhuin no cuirt no sgol feinechuis ann* (ibid., p. 36).

It is evident then that the practice of the law was much in the hands of clerics and clerical families at this period, and it may be added that, judging by the language and content of some of the earlier legal tracts—*Uraicecht Becc, Miadslechta,* and others—the churchmen had a powerful influence on legal development at a much earlier date. It is interesting to note the association of cleric and lawyer as late as the fifteenth and sixteenth centuries, for the family of Ua Brесléin held dual office as *brethem* to Maguire and as erenaghs of Derryvullen, though they themselves were relative newcomers to legal practice.[64] It is likely that, given the nature of much of the social content of Irish law and the obvious conflict between it and the Christian norms, some of the clergy at least may have had reservations about practising as secular lawyers. It is most probable that the legend of the Patrician revision also served as a justification for their position, and a defence against the attacks of more reform-minded colleagues.

I am not convinced that the clergy either as churchmen or jurists served as an obstacle to the development of monarchy in Ireland or saw themselves as rivals to political authority. On the contrary they did much to enhance kingship by their introduction of wider political ideas concerning the royal office and by acting as servitors of the great dynasties. Already, the tract *De duodecim abusivis saeculi,* written most probably between 630 and 650, has much to say about kingship though admittedly the writer's notions contain very archaic elements. The results of evil kingship are social and economic ruin and, eventually, the loss of sovereignty. All good things—peace, plenty and social order—attend the rule of the good king whose justice 'is the peace of peoples and the protection of the fatherland'. The Christian king is to judge justly, protect the weak, destroy the wicked, the parracide and the perjurer; he himself is to have wise and sober counsellors and just officials.[65] The *Collectio canonum Hibernensis,* material compiled from scripture, from Irish and foreign synods, papal decretals and Christian fathers, and put together in the first half of the eighth century, has a great deal more to say about kingship.[66] It repeats the section on the *rex iniquus* from the early text but adds much more. The Christian king is to have power of judgment over those who disobey the royal or divine law and condemn them to death or exile, fine or prison, and though there is much pious exhortation to kings, the canonists quote statements attributed to St Jerome that indicate a clear perception of royal authority: 'the word of a king is a sword for beheading, a rope for hanging, it casts into prison, it condemns to exile'. The *Collectio* also

---

[64] *A.U.,* s.a. 1440, 1447, 1495, 1513; Padraig Ua Duinnín, *Me Guidhir Fhearmanach* (Dublin, 1917), pp 27, 105–6.

[65] Kenney, *Sources,* pp 281–2.

[66] Hermann Wasserschleben (ed.), *Die irische Kanonensammlung* (2nd edition, Leipsig, 1885), pp 76–82.

favours the ordination of kings and takes its text from 1 Samuel 10: 'Samuel took a flask of oil and poured it over Saul's head and kissed him and said: "Behold, the Lord has anointed you prince over your inheritance" '.

This attempt to Christianise kingship was never very successful. However, the annals record the *ordinatio* of Artrí mac Cathail into the kingship of Munster in 793, and his Uí Néill contemporary, Áed mac Néill, is known as Áed Oirnide, 'the ordained'. This activity, of course, has its contemporary parallels in Carolingian Francia and Anglo-Saxon England.[67] The conceptualisation of God and the saints in the prologue to the Calendar of Óengus, written about 800, is profoundly royalist and triumphalist, and gives us another indication of the clerical view of kingship. His principal metaphor is the contrasting kingship of of the saints, 'the royal folk of God', and secular rulers; yet, however much we may discount his rhetoric and his striving after literary effect in the contrast which he makes between the pomp of earthly kings (including Irish provincial kings) and the glory of the heavenly kingdom, we cannot easily escape the conclusion that the power and pretensions of the kings of his own day were very much present to his mind and that he was deeply impressed by them.[68] We again see some clerical notions of kingship in a poem of advice to a king, *Cert cech ríg co réil*. From internal evidence, it is certain that it was written by a churchman, and, in date, it is hardly earlier than the tenth century. The king is not to tax the church: 'leave the churches untaxed in your course of clear success, so you may be over all and all may be obedient to you'. He is to esteem the clerics and have contented and wealthy clergy. However, the king is to rule over them and control them and their dwellings; it is his duty to see to it that at all times the clergy and laity are to be confined to their own duties. In contrast to this, the advice given him in regard to secular affairs is that he should be ruthless and effective. He is to place harsh fetters on prisoners, for it is better that they should die rather than escape. He is to billet his troops sternly, and in the matter of food-render, or cosher, nobody who possesses a house, not even the kinsman of a king, is to be exempted. He is to levy his rent to the last penny, because that is the right of a king. Every violent rebel is to be put to death at once.[69] The church apparently had strong views on capital punishment and it is frequently urged on kings. This heady mixture of exhortation to rule rather than reign, to act as supreme judge, to extend

---

[67] Byrne, *Irish kings*, p. 159. Dr Kathleen Hughes quite rightly calls my attention to Adomnán's earlier views on royal ordination. For a discussion of these and their possible influence on eighth-century Anglo-Saxon kings, see John, *Orbis Britanniae*, pp 27–35.

[68] Whitley Stokes, *On the Calendar of Óengus* (Dublin, 1880), pp xiii–xxiv.

[69] Tadhg Ó Donnchadha (ed.), 'Cert cech ríg co réil' in O. J. Bergin and Carl Marstrander (ed.), *Miscellany . . . to Kuno Meyer* (Halle a. S., 1912), pp 258–77. For examples of capital punishment by (or on behalf of) the church, see *A.U.*, s. aa 746, 893; *A.F.M.*, s. a. 889 (=893); *Ann. Tig.*, s.a. 1129.

royal powers and income, and the constant reference to Old Testament kingship must have made a powerful impact on the power-hungry kings of the eighth, ninth, and tenth centuries, who were consolidating those greater lordships that dominated Irish political history until the coming of the Normans.

We may now ask from what groups in society were the cleric-jurists, poets, and royal propagandists recruited. It is evident that the clergy moved easily in legal, poetic, and learned circles, and all seem to derive from one source: the politically unsuccessful segments of the ruling dynasties. This conclusion is amply borne out by the annals and genealogies. The succession to the abbacy of Áth Truim, for example, was dominated from some time before 756 to 846 by a branch of the locally ruling dynasty, the Lóegaire of the Southern Uí Néill. All were descendants or relations of the famous poet, Rumann mac Colmáin (+747), and, on its own admission, the whole group had been displaced from the kingship of Lóegaire in the seventh century.[70] The office of abbot at Lusc was monopolised by the descendants of Colggu mac Máenaig from 702 to 805. He belonged to the politically unsuccessful Cianachta Mide.[71] The well-known scholar, historian, and churchman, Fland Mainistrech (+1056) belonged to a discard segment of the Cianachta Breg. His son, Echthigern, continued the family association with Monasterboice and died as abbot of that monastery in 1067.[72] The cleric-jurists whom we can identify belong to the same class of persons. The judge Ua Rebacháin (+1106), abbot of Mungret, belonged to the Uí Rebacháin of Cland Chuiléin, collaterals of the Meic Conmara and even more remote collaterals of the dominant Uí Briain.[73] In many cases, those recorded in the annals as poets belong to the same type and very frequently they too have close clerical connections. Fínnechta ua Cuill, 'poet of Munster' who died in 960, and his descendant, Cenn Fáelad Ua Cuill (+1048), 'chief poet of Munster', claimed to belong to a discarded segment of the Éoganacht of Cashel.[74] The 'son of Mac Craith the Poet, chief poet of Munster', who died in 1098 is a pertinent example of the relation of poet and dynasty. He is third in descent from Echthigern, brother of Brian Boru and third cousin and contemporary of Muirchertach Ua Briain, whose poet he was.[75] A year before, there died Cairpre Ua Síta

[70] *A.U.*, s. a. 746, 756, 796, 821, 838, 846; their genealogy is preserved in *B.B.*, 87 d 26–88 a 35. They also attempted to take over the monastery of Clonard at the turn of the eighth century and the beginning of the ninth (*B.B.*, 87 d 26–e 3; *A.U.*, s. a. 830).

[71] Hughes, *Ch. in early Ir. soc.*, p. 162; for the genealogical connections see *Corpus geneal Hib.*, p. 168, *B.B.*, 194 b 6, *Bk Lec.*, 222 va 13.

[72] *Corpus geneal. Hib.*, p. 247.

[73] *Bk Lec.*, 227 va 37 = *B.B.*, 185 b 46 = *Bk Uí Maine*, 31 vb 25.

[74] Tadhg Ó Donnchadha (ed.), *An Leabhar Muimhneach* (Dublin [1940]), p. 220; *A.F.M.*, s.a. 958 (=960); *A.U.*, *A.F.M.*, *Ann. Tig.*, *Ann. Inisf.*, s.a. 1048.

[75] *Bk Lec.*, 226 ʀa 21, *Bk Uí Maine*, 30 vb 54; S. Pender (ed.), 'The O'Clery book of

whom the annalist describes as *ollam breithemnuis Erenn* (*ollam* of the juris-prudence of Ireland)—a term which, shorn of its rhetoric, mèans royal judge of Muirchertach Ua Briain, the high king. He, like his cousin, Ua Rebacháin, belonged to a discard segment, Síl Nárgalaig, who were remote collaterals of the ruling family and remarkably prolific in producing ecclesiastical and professional personnel throughout the middle ages.[76]

We may now enquire as to the relationship which existed between the kings and this class of clergy, poets, and jurists. In general, it seems, this mandarin class provided the professional servitors of the greater kings, and, far from being triarchic, Ireland was monarchic in its concepts of political authority. In fact, it was this mandarin class that elaborated the idea of the overkingship of all Ireland and projected it backwards into even the remote past, thus creating what remained for a millenium one of the best-known 'facts' of Irish history. And their influence on the image which the Irish had of their past is all-pervasive. Amongst the most important of these scholars, whom Mac Neill calls the synthetic historians, are Máel Mura of Othain (+887), Cináed Ua hArtacáin (+995), Cúan Ua Lothcháin (+1024), and Flann Mainistrech (+1056). Much of Flann's work survives and a great deal of it is concerned with the glorification of kings—a poem on the *dindshenchas* of Ailech, fortress and symbol of the Northern Uí Néill, a versified list of their kings, another on their victories, and a further poem on the exploits of their kings.[77] A note in Lebor na hUidre allows us a glance at Flann's activity:

Flann then and Eochaid the Wise Ua Céirín gathered this material from the books of Eochaid Ua Flannacán in Armagh and from the books of Monasterboice and other choice books besides, namely, from the Yellow Book which is missing from the strong-room in Armagh, and from the Short Book of Monasterboice and that is the one which the student stole and brought with him overseas and which was never found again.[78]

Here we may at first sight think we are in the presence of the quiet studiousness of bookish men, but the reality is quite otherwise for they were

genealogies' in *Anal. Hib.*, xviii (Dublin, 1951), p. 152, §1999.

[76] *Bk Lec.*, 226 va 9, *B.B.*, 185 b 22, *Bk Uí Maine* 31 vb 1. For further examples of the origin of learned families, see Proinsias Mac Cana, 'The rise of the later schools of *Filideacht*' in *Ériu*, xxv (1974), pp 126–46.

[77] John [Eoin] Mac Neill, 'Poems by Flann Mainistrech on the dynasties of Ailech, Mide and Brega' in *Archiv. Hib.*, ii (1913), pp 37–99; for the *dindshenchas* of Ailech, see E. J. Gwynn, *The metrical Dindshenchas IV* (Dublin, 1924), pp 100–06 = *Bk Leinster* iv, 782–4; for comment on some materials wrongly attributed to Flann see F. J. Byrne, 'Historical note on Cnogba (Knowth)' in *R.I.A. Proc.*, lxvi, sect. C (1968), pp 391–2.

[78] R. I. Best and O. J. Bergin, *Lebor na hUidre* (Dublin, 1929), p. 94. Eochaid Ua Flannacán was erenagh of Lis Oeiged in Armagh and of Clonfeakle in northern Armagh and died in 1004 (*A.U.*, s.a. 1004; *A.F.M.*, s.a. 1003 (=1004)). He was brother of Dubdáleithe, abbot of Armagh and was himself progenitor of eight subsequent abbots (Tomás Ó Fiaich, 'The church of Armagh under law control' in *Seanchas Ardmhacha*, v (1969), pp 111, 124).

deeply concerned with the politics of their own day. In the same way as the feudal lords of contemporary Europe listened to the deeds of their ancestors, in the same way as the poems on Charlemagne served the needs of Capetian propaganda, so too the Irish kings paid attention to the work of the synthetic historians and poets and drew political lessons and support from them.

As an example of the influence of these historians, we may cite the revival of the *óenach Tailten* as a political institution in the eleventh and twelfth centuries. As Binchy has shown, *óenach Tailten* was the early assembly of the overkings of the Uí Néill. After the third quarter of the ninth century it was held with increasing irregularity, and throughout most of the following century it was completely in abeyance. After it had fallen into desuetude, the synthetic historians and poets remodelled it, and it came to be regarded as an asembly of all Ireland and a notable institution of the kingship of Ireland.[79] What is remarkable is that two of the greatest kings of the twelfth century, Tairdelbach Ua Conchobair and his son, Ruaidri, celebrated the *óenach* almost certainly in the belief that in so doing they were exercising the prerogative of the king of Ireland. Tairdelbach Ua Conchobair celebrated it in 1120. A year earlier, Muirchertach Ua Briain, whom the annals unanimously describe as 'king of Ireland', had died, and Tairdelbach had taken his place as the most powerful king in Ireland and chief contender for the 'high-kingship'. Ruaidri celebrated it in 1168 after most successful campaigns in 1166 and 1167, in the course of which he demonstrated his effective authority by summoning a royal council at Athlone and levying a tax on 'the men of Ireland', and led an army of nation-wide composition into Cenél Éogain which extinguished the remaining armed opposition to his rule.[80] This was not the only *óenach* to be revived with a political purpose. In 1033 Donnchad mac Gilla Phátraic, king of Ossory, celebrated the *óenach Carmain* after he had seized the kingship of Leinster. He had no hereditary claim on Leinster and had in fact seized it by force from the Uí Dúnlainge who had ruled the province for centuries.[81] In 1079, it was again celebrated by Conchobar Ua Conchobair Failge, another king who had no hereditary claim on the kingship of Leinster and who took advantage of the weakness of the ruling dynasty, Uí Chennselaig, to advance himself.[82] What is noteworthy about these events is that the *óenach* is held by two kings who clearly regarded its celebration as a prerogative of the king of Leinster, and no doubt considered it to be a means of strengthening and legitimising their dubious claim to the kingship in question. On either one or the other of

---

[79] Binchy, 'The fair of Tailtiu and the feast of Tara', pp 113–27.

[80] *Ann. Tig.*, s.a. 1120, 1166, 1167, 1168.

[81] *A.U., A.F.M., Ann. Tig.*, s.a. 1033; *Bk Leinster* i, 183; Paul Walsh, 'Leinster states and kings in Christian times' in *I.E.R.*, liii (1939), pp 47–61.

[82] *A.F.M.*, s.a. 1079.

these occasions, one of the poet-historians provided a highly dramatic account in verse of the activities at the *óenach*.[83] Clearly, then, the learned classes were not only servitors of the great kings but, after a fashion, played the role of political theorists.

Since it has been argued that the power of the church was one element in the so-called triarchic structure of authority in Ireland, it may be useful to see how the church functioned within one of the major kingdoms, the kingdom of the Uí Briain. To begin with, from 991 all known holders of the abbacy of Killaloe, the central dynastic church, are members of the dynastic families and on occasion the office was held by brothers or other close relatives of the ruling kings. In the case of the surrounding monasteries, there is a conscious policy on the part of the dynasty to intrude its own members. Marcán, brother of Brian Boru, was a grand pluralist who held office as abbot of Killaloe, Terryglass, Inis Celtra and Emly. As the dynasty expanded under the rule of able kings, so did its control of monasteries in the person of its junior segments. The twelfth-century reform did little to change this pattern, and for a century and a half after its inception only members of the dynasty became bishops of the new territorial diocese; of these, two were brothers of the ruling king and all were relatives. Further, with the increased power of the dynasty, there was an imperialism in church as well as in state. Ó hÁilgenáin, abbot of Cork who died in 1106, was a distant cousin of Muirchertach Ua Briain and a member of a group of extensive clerical families to which belonged the reformer, Domnall Ó hÉnna. About 1100, Gilla Pátraic Ua hÉnna, a member of the same group, was abbot of Cork and (possibly subsequently) bishop of Killaloe. All this reflects the power and policy of Muirchertach Ua Briain and his ability to use the clergy of his own dynasty to infiltrate the monasteries of his rivals, the Éoganacht, and gain control of Cork.[84] Similar policies were pursued by other kings with varying degrees of success. It is evident, even from the bald political narrative of the annals, that the great kings of the eleventh and twelfth centuries were deliberately using the church—and the reform movement itself—to further their political ambitions and enhance their prestige. Lastly, given the changed nature of society in this latter period, the statement in the classical laws that the abbot or bishop had the same social status as the *rí túaithe*, if at all applicable, amounts to far less than it appears. All it means is that the bishop and abbot had the same standing in society as their local lord, a situation which can scarcely be said to be far removed from the European norm.

[83] E. J. Gwynn (ed.), *Metrical Dindshenchas*, iii (Dublin, 1913), pp 2–24; Máirín Ó Daly, 'The Metrical Dindshenchas' in James Carney (ed.) *Early Irish poetry* (Cork, 1965), pp 65–8; Mac Neill, *Early Irish laws and institutions*, pp 102–9 (where, however, the historical value of the poem is greatly exaggerated).

[84] D. Ó Corráin, 'Dál Cais—church and dynasty' in *Ériu*, xxiv (1973), pp 52–63.

It has frequently been stressed that the Irish king had no power to make laws, but this is not quite true even of the earlier period. The king could enforce a *rechtge* proclaimed by him at a public assembly, but most of these were special ordinances designed to meet situations of emergency. The term *rechtge* may also have included ecclesiastical regulations issued by individual monasteries *(cána)* and depending on public promulgation for their validity.[85] The promulgation of such ecclesiastical *cána* is frequently mentioned in the annals in the eighth and ninth centuries. They are promulgated by the dominant kings for entire provinces, and it is to be inferred from the annalistic record that these provincial kings were preempting and over-riding any independent decision to which a local king and his assembly might come. It is difficult to imagine that the kings in question did not benefit materially from the promulgation of these *cána*. Fr Felim Ó Briain asserts, I think with some exaggeration, that

the local rulers, in concurrence with the unworthy superiors they had intruded into the monasteries, carried out a commercial exploitation of relics and spiritual favours. . . . By the eighth century the practice seems to have deteriorated to a mere expedient for replenishing the coffers of the king and his monastic relatives.[86]

Whether they followed the example set by the church or not may be a matter for doubt, but it is evident that the Irish kings exercised the right to impose extraordinary taxation on their subjects at will. In 986, for example, Máel Sechnaill mac Domnaill, overking of the Uí Néill, committed an outrage on the community of Armagh. One of the things he conceded the clergy of Armagh as compensation was 'the visitation [by the community of Armagh for taking a cess] of Mide, church and laity as well as refection in every fortress or stead of his own'.[87] In 1007, the same king made a grant to the altar of Clonmacnoise and then levied a hide on every *les* in Mide to pay for it.[88] These instances of extraordinary taxation concerned the churches, and for this reason we have a record of them in the monastic annals. We have little such direct evidence of purely secular taxation, but there are hints that, on a purely secular level, the kings were equally effective in public taxation. In 1166 Ruaidri Ua Conchobair held a great royal council at Athlone at which the kings of Meath, Brefne, and the Ostmen of Dublin were present. On that occasion he levied a tax on 'the men of Ireland' of 4,000 cows, which he required as royal *tuarastal* for the Ostmen of Dublin. The tax seems to have been paid forthwith, for in the same year Ruaidri went on an expedition to Dublin where he was inaugurated king, and, in

---

[85] Binchy, *Críth Gablach*, p. 104.
[86] Felim Ó Briain, 'The hagiography of Leinster' in *Féil-sgríbhinn Eóin Mhic Néill*, p. 457. I hope to show elsewhere that the monastic towns which issued the *cána* were genuinely concerned with the good order of society.
[87] *A.F.M.*, s.a. 985 (=986).
[88] *Chron. Scot.*, s.a. 1005 (=1007).

return, he presented the Ostmen with their enormous endowment.[89] This extraordinary taxation is all the more notable in that it was levied specifically by the king directly for his own aggrandisement. It is reasonable then to assume that such kings levied lesser taxes as time and occasion demanded.

However, kings engaged in legislative activities other than the imposition of public taxes. It is true that the annals do not gratuitously supply us with details of such legislation in the eleventh and twelfth centuries, for the type of incident which they report is in general altogether different. One might point out in this connection that if we were dependent on them for the enactments of the great reforming synods in the twelfth century we should know very little indeed about them. Nonetheless, on three separate occasions the annals record legislation by Donnchad mac Briain, king of Munster, and by his successor, Tairdelbach Ua Briain. In 1040 we find the king of Munster legislating against theft, against 'feats of arms', and manual labour on Sunday, and promulgating a law that cattle should not be brought indoors.[90] The term used to describe the legislation is *cáin agus rechtge,* and it is evident from the tone of the entry that the annalist considered the legislation itself to be innovatory. One further point: it appears that at least some clerical inspiration lies behind these provisions and some of them bear a remarkable resemblance to the demands of the contemporary peace movement in Aquitaine and other parts of France.[91] In 1050, in the course of a famine in which there was much suffering and disorder, and churches and secular buildings were being attacked, the same king summoned an assembly of the Munster rulers and clergy at Killaloe—one of the royal residences—and promulgated a law forbidding injustices great and small. The motive force behind the law seems to have been the king: *cáin mór oc mc Briain* (a great law by the son of Brian).[92] Unfortunately, the annals preserve no details of these enactments. In 1068, we find his nephew and successor, Tairdelbach Ua Briain, promulgating laws, and the remark of the annalist, 'and no better law was enacted in Munster for a long time' surely allows us to infer that royal legislation was not uncommon.[93] These stray pieces of evidence lend themselves to the

[89] *Ann. Tig., A.F.M.,* s.a. 1166. In modern terms such a tax would amount to about £800,000. If we allow for modern productivity and at least a quadrupling of the estimated population of the twelfth-century, the real equivalent in present-day Ireland may be well in excess of £5,000,000. Measure against this the fact that a grant of ten cows per annum in perpetuity by the same king to the lector of Armagh to teach the students of Ireland and Scotland was considered sufficiently important to be recorded in the annals (*A.U.,* s.a. 1169).

[90] *Ann. Inisf.,* s.a. 1040.

[91] Marc Bloch, *Feudal society* (2nd ed., London, 1962), pp 412–20; H. E. J. Cowdrey, 'The peace and the truce of God in the eleventh century' in *Past and Present,* xlvi (1970), pp 42–67.

[92] *Ann. Inisf., A.F.M.,* s.a. 1050.

[93] *Ann. Inisf., s.a.* 1068. I must confess that I cannot grasp the significance of the law in question as it is reported by the annalist.

conclusion that, in certain areas at least, the greater overkings of the eleventh and twelfth centuries had emerged as law-makers.

Further, the rule that the king was not *dominus terrae* and could not grant away either his own hereditary land or the land of others without the consent of the owner's kindred had long become obsolete. Again, I shall cite a few dated examples from the annals. In 1072, Murchad Ua Máelsechlainn billetted his troops somewhat ruthlessly on Clonmacnoise, and in the course of their stay they killed the steward of the mendicants, an important local official. In compensation for this, he granted the mendicants Mag nÚra, identified by O'Donovan with Moynore in the barony of Rathconrath, probably part of his own hereditary lands.[94] In the terror inspired by the falling of St John's day on Friday in 1096, the annalists report that many kings and lords granted lands to the church. Land was also being sold, and in sales or grants we must distinguish between the transfer of land which is encumbered with dues and cess, and land held in *dílse*, a term which seems to imply absolute ownership and perhaps a freedom similar to that freedom *ab omni publico vectigali, a victa, ab expeditione, ab opere regio* of certain Anglo-Saxon book-land. In 1089, Cormac mac Cuinn na mBocht, tanist-abbot of Clonmacnoise, described as 'a prosperous and affluent man', purchased the *dílse* of Ísell Ciaráin from one Ua Flaithnén (probably the local lord) and Domnall Ua Máelsechlainn, king of Meath. What is interesting in this case is that Clonmacnoise already owned this land but it was subject to rents or cess.[95] In 1143 we find Tairdelbach Ua Conchobair granting a townland, apparently in the present parish of Roscommon, to the abbot of Roscommon, who however gives gold to Ua Conchobair and his kinsmen and to the local lord in return for the *dílse* of the property.[96] Our records of such sales relate mostly to the church. The Kells charters record the sale of land by one Ua Rímán, who can only have been petty gentry, to a priest of Kells. A similar document records the purchase of a plot of ground by one Congal Ó Breislén. The document is now damaged but the phrase *unga fon dílse* (an ounce [in addition] for the *dílse*) is still legible.[97]

These grants of townlands or other parcels of land (such units appear to be quite specific and may well be the smaller land-divisions for purposes of assessment) to the church are quite commonplace and frequently such

[94] *A.F.M.*, s.a., 1072.

[95] *A.F.M.*, s.a., 1089; for evidence of the fact that the property already belonged to Clonmacnoise see *A.F.M.*, s.a., 1072; Plummer, *Vitae sanctorum Hiberniae*, i (Oxford, 1910), pp 209–10; *Bk Lec.*, 60 ʀa 5–8 = *B.B.*, 81 b 6–8.

[96] *Ann. Tig.*, s.a. 1143; for the identity of the local lord see *Bk Lec.* 65 ʀa 25 and R.I.A. 23 Q 10, 19 vf 1.

[97] John O'Donovan, 'Irish charters in the Book of Kells' in *Miscellany of the Irish Archaeological Society* (Dublin, 1846), pp 127–58; Gearóid Mac Niocaill, *Notitiae as Leabhar Cheanannais* (Dublin, 1961), p. 22.

grants are made by charter.[98] The granting of land to the church in a newly acquired territory or on the borders of a disputed territory is a characteristic of the age, and, in this case at least, it is clear that the new political authority overrides the proprietary rights of the conquered. Perhaps the most spectacular of these was the grant to the church of Cashel, the hereditary seat of the Éoganacht, by Muirchertach Ua Briain in 1101 on the occasion of the synod of Cashel.[99] To this category also belongs the grant of land by Tigernán Ua Ruairc to the canons regular of St Augustine of Navan. These lands lay along the Boyne between Navan and Dowdstown, on the borders of territory which he had recently made his own and which was still in dispute.[100] It would appear that political authority now also included proprietary right. In 1165, for example, when Muirchertach Mac Lochlainn compelled the king of Ulaid to hand over a townland to the monks of Saul, it is scarcely likely that the immediate lord of the territory, or what would, lower down on the social scale, have formerly been the free commoner families who were allodial owners in severalty, were consulted about the transfer.[101] It is likely that they were simply transferred with the land to their new masters.

On the broader political level, the overkings grant away whole territories. One annalistic entry speaks of a hosting of Tairdelbach Ua Conchobair and his allies 'to contest his own land unjustly with Ua Máel Sechnaill', king of Meath, but the justice of his case did little to protect him.[102] Ua Conchobair granted and re-granted large portions of Meath to Tigernán Ua Ruairc, and despite many set-backs he made a reality of these grants. His obit in 1172 describes him as king not only of his hereditary kingdom of Brefne but also of Conmaicne and the greater part of Meath, and Giraldus Cambrensis, who describes him in the *Expugnatio* as *Medensium rex* is more accurate than his editor allows.[103] In 1095 Muirchertach Ua Briain expelled the ruling dynasty of Connacht from its homeland, and granted the kingdom of Connacht to Ua Ruairc less three large territories—Uí Fiachrach, Uí Maine, and Luigne, which he apparently reserved for himself.[104] The campaigns of Meic Lochlainn against the Ulaid from 1113 to 1165 indicate the growing claims of the overkings. In

[98] Kenney, *Sources*, pp 768–70.

[99] Aubrey Gwynn, *The twelfth-century reform* (Dublin, 1968), p. 9.

[100] Eric St John Brooks, 'A charter of John de Courcy to the abbey of Navan' in *R.S.A.I. Jn.*, lxiii (1933), pp 38–45, where the grant of Ua Ruairc is recited and confirmed.

[101] *A.U.*, s.a. 1165; for the fate of the commoners, dependent on lords in the later period see Gearóid Mac Niocaill, 'The origins of the betagh' in *Ir. Jurist*, i (1966), pp 292–8.

[102] *A.F.M.*, s.a. 1138.

[103] For the extent of his territories in Meath see *Ann. Tig., A.F.M.*, s.a. 1159; it is evident that he also had fortresses in Meath, *A.U., Ann. Tig., A.F.M.*, s.a. 1161; *Ann. Tig.*, s.a. 1172; *Giraldi Cambrensis opera*, v, 225.

[104] *Ann. Inisf.*, s.a., 1095.

1113, Domnall Mac Lochlainn divided up the overkingdom of the Ulaid; he detached two large territories—Dál nAraide and Uí Echach Cobo—and brought them directly under his own suzerainty; and he divided what remained of the kingdom in two along segmentary lines. In 1148, Muirchertach Mac Lochlainn divided the kingdom in four portions. Finally in 1165, at the height of his power, Mac Lochlainn again attacked the Ulaid. He reappointed their king under strict conditions which made him his subject and compelled him to grant land to the church and make over to himself the territory of Bairrche (the Mourne area). Mac Lochlainn then granted that territory to his loyal vassal, Donnchad Ua Cerbaill, king of Airgialla.[105] A further interesting example is recorded in the annals for 1163. Diarmait Ua Máelsechlainn, king of Meath, was deposed by his subjects but in return for one hundred ounces of gold Mac Lochlainn granted him the kingship of Western Meath.[106] It is evident, too, that these kings granted such territories in return for loyalty and military service and that, in the course of these centuries, the relationship of king and overking changed slowly to that of vassal and lord while concurrently *imperium* and *dominium* merged into one. On the less exalted levels of society, the distinction between base and free clientship became blurred and the complex classes of commoners were radically simplified, largely I imagine to their disadvantage.[107]

These new kings who exercised such wide powers had need of some officers of government. Kings such as Tairdelbach Ua Conchobair were frequently absent on campaign for months on end. An entry in the annals for 1111 casually tells us that Muirchertach Ua Briain was in Dublin from 29 September to Christ.nas of that year. It is evident that there must have been some royal ministers, however unspecialised, to carry out the day-to-day business of ruling in the king's absence. Though there is no formal account of these officers, occasional references in the annals give us some indications of their existence. One of the most important of these was the *airrí*. The significance of the term is somewhat obscured by the artificial classification of the meanings attached to it in the dictionary.[108] There the term is given two separate meanings: (a) 'Tributary king or chieftain' in a native context and (b) 'Viceroy, governor' in a foreign context. The term can, I think, be shown to mean governor in some of the native examples and more specifically royal governor. I set out the annalistic examples:

---

[105] *A.U.*, *A.F.M.*, s.a. 1113; *A.F.M.*, s.a. 1148; *A.U.*, s.a. 1165.
[106] *Ann. Tig.*, s.a. 1163.
[107] Rudolph Thurneysen, '*Aus dem irishen Recht II*' in *Z.C.P.* xv (1925), pp 224, 257–9; Mac Niocaill, 'The origins of the betagh', p. 293.
[108] Royal Irish Academy, *Contributions to a dictionary of the Irish language*, A fasc., i (Dublin, 1964), cols 220–21.

A.U., s.a. 962 (cf. *A.F.M.*, *Ann. Inisf.*):
   Eughan m. Muiredaigh, erri Erenn, do marbad do Uib Failgi (. . . *airrí* of Ireland was slain by Uí Failge).

A.U., s.a. 1003 (cf. *Ann. Tig.* for circumstantial detail):
   Sinach .H. Uargussa, ri H. Meith agus Cathal m. Labradha erri Midhe do comtuitim (Sinach Ua Uargussa, king of Uí Meith and Cathal mac Labrada, *airrí* of Mide mutually slew one another).

A.U., s.a. 1021 (cf. *Ann. Tig.*, *Ann. Inisf.*, *A.F.M.*, *Chron. Scot.*):
   Branacan H. Maeluidir, airrí Midhe do bathad dia Belltaine ic Loch Ainninde (. . . *airrí* of Mide was drowned on Mayday in Lough Ennell).

In the case of none of these have I been able to trace their genealogy and thus establish their class or connections with the ruling dynasty. However, two Munster entries on the *airríg* make that relationship clear:

Ann. Inisf., s.a. 1032 (cf. *A.F.M.*):
   Diarmait mc. Echach airrí Muman moritur (=*A.F.M.*: *cend Cloinde Scandláin* 'head of Clann Scannláin').

A.U., s.a. 1103 (cf. *A.F.M.*):
   Amongst the slain at the battle of Mag Coba was *Ua Failbe .i. ridomna Corco Duibhne agus erri* Laighen (. . . *rígdamna* of Corco Duibne and *airrí* of Leinster).

Diarmait mac Eachach can indeed be identified from the genealogies. He was lord of Clann Scannláin, a subsegment of Uí Ailgile, itself a discard segment of the dominant dynastic group, Uí Thairdelbaig.[109] His father, Eochaid, was slain at the battle of Clontarf in 1014. His brother, Tadc, was abbot of Killaloe and died either in 1027 or 1028, and his cousin, mac Craith mac Conduib, lord of Clann Scannláin, died in 1067.[110] His cousins, the Uí Magair, were coarbs of Dromcliffe, near Ennis.[111] The segment to which he belonged was not only out of the running for the kingship but had never possessed it. Under no circumstances could he be regarded as a 'tributary king' of Munster in his own right. It is clear that any importance he had is as a minister of the king, and he belonged, in fact, to that very class from which the great kings drew their learned servitors—jurists, poets and clerics. The position is further clarified by the reference to Ua Faílbe. He belonged to the petty kingdom of Corcu Duibne, a territory corresponding roughly to the present baronies of Corkaguiny and Iveragh, with small

---

[109] *Bk Lec.*, 226 vb 27 = *B.B.*, 184 b 5 = *Bk Uí Maine* 30 Rb 41, 29 vb 35.
[110] *A.U.*, s.a. 1014 = *A.F.M.*, s.a. 1013 (=1014); *A.U.*, 1028, *Ann. Inisf.*, s.a. 1027; *Ann. Inisf.*, s.a. 1067.
[111] A Gwynn, and D. Gleeson, *A history of the diocese of Killaloe* (Dublin, 1962), p. 142. The form and derivation of the name there proposed is in error.

portions of other baronies, in County Kerry. In no way could the *rígdamna* of such petty kingdom have any claim to be regarded as a tributary king of Leinster. In fact, Muirchertach Ua Briain dominated Leinster in these years, and was able to command the forces of Leinster at the battle of Mag Coba. Ua Faílbe can be none other than Ua Briain's governor of Leinster. It is evident that these men were the deputies and governors of the more powerful kings: Domnall Ua Néill (956–80), Máel Sechnaill mac Domnaill (+1022), Donnchad mac Briain (+1064) and Muirchertach Ua Briain (+1119). If the status and relationship to the dynasty of the two I can identify are at all representative, the office was filled by the middling class of lord (either from within the dynasty or from a subject kingdom), who was in no position to challenge the royal authority as greater men might be and who owed his position to royal patronage. Since these men are important enough to be mentioned in the annals, they must of course be men of consequence and it is likely that by the time the office is first recorded in the annals it may have been a well-established part of the Irish overking's administration.

In the early literature, the king's chief officer is his *rechtaire*, his steward or bailiff. He is the majordomo of the king's household and, on occasion, the collector of his food-rents. The word is used to gloss *praepositus* and *villicus* and does have the meaning of royal administrator in some instances. However, the term is absent from the annals until the early eleventh century when the king's *rechtaire* is first mentioned as a person of importance. It is evident that in the early period he was an omni-competent household officer with general duties; in the eleventh and twelfth centuries he becomes a royal official of importance and one not to be identified with the *airrí*. As frequently, the office changes and the name remains the same. It is used in 1031 to describe the commander or keeper of Donnchad mac Briain's important fortress at Dún na Sciath. Since the keeper of the same fortress, Domnall mac Beollán is later referred to as *flaith Dune na Scaich* (lord of Dún na Sciath), it is fair to assume that the *rechtaire* was usually a nobleman.[112] In 1108, the same term is used to refer to Muirchertach Ua Briain's governor of the city of Limerick who died *infeliciter* in that year.[113] Limerick had become one of the royal seats as early as 1058 and it is clearly the most important residence of Muirchertach Ua Briain, for there he held court, kept prisoners, and entertained. However, since he also lived at Kincora (where he had a fortress built of stone and wood) and at Killaloe, and since he was frequently absent on campaign (sometimes for as long as four months) he required somebody to govern the city, particularly since

[112] *Ann. Inisf.*, s.a. 1031, 1095.
[113] *Ann. Inisf.*, s.a. 1108.

the Ostmen of Limerick were occasionally restive.[114] In contrast, the greater dignity of the governorship of Dublin, held by Muirchertach in the reign of his father, and held during his own reign by his son, Domnall, is always referred to as kingship. It is to be noted that the governor of Limerick who died in 1108, Ua Béoáin, again belonged to a remote collateral family of Dál Cais who supplied clergy to the monastery of Tomgraney.[115] When we turn elsewhere, we find that other great kings make use of subject petty kings and discarded segments to fill this office. Domnall Ua Caíndelbáin, king of the petty kingdom of Lóegaire, was *rechtaire* to Máel Sechnaill mac Domnaill—for Lóegaire was a petty kingdom within his dominions—and Gilla na Náem Ua Birn—a remote collateral and local lord—was *rechtaire* to Tairdelbach Ua Conchobair.[116] This latter *rechtaire* is entitled *ríghrechtaire Érenn* (royal steward of Ireland)—an indication that his duties were perhaps coterminous with the territories within the control of his master and were not confined to Connacht.

There are some references too to the *taísech lochta tighe* (head of the [king's] household) or *taísech teglaig,* a term which has the same meaning. In 1100, one Ua hIndredhán is reported as holding this office under Ua Máelechlainn, king of Mide. In 1143, Gilla Brénainn Ua Flaind, *taísech lochta tige* of Tairdelbach Ua Conchobair, was unhorsed in an encounter in Munster.[117] The genealogies show that he again was a remote collateral of the ruling house. We are fortunate that another annalistic entry lists some of the *lucht tige* of an over-king. In 1013, the *lucht tige* of Máel Sechnaill mac Domnaill were drinking together, and in their drunken exuberance they took on a raiding party of the king of Cairpre and some of them were killed. These included Donnchadh mac Donnchada Finn, *rígdamna* of Tara, Cernachán mac Flainn, king of Luigne, and Senán Ua Leocáin, king of Gailenga. In this case, at any rate, the *lucht tige* included some of the most important vassal lords of Mide.

With the growth of kingship came a concomitant development in warfare. Kings employed a standing army, bought the military support of their peers, and hired foreign mercenaries.[118] There was also a great development of the use of cavalry, and the new office of *taísech marcslúaige* (commander of the [king's] cavalry) came into being. This post was also held by the subject lords of the great kings. Such a person was Diarmait Ua hAinbféith, lord of Uí Meith and commander of Mac Lochlainn's

---

[114] *Ann. Tig., Ann. Inisf.,* s.a. 1058; *A.U.,* s.a. 1083; *Ann. Tig.,* s.a. 1084, 1088; *Ann. Inisf.,* s.a. 1093, 1113, 1116, 1125; *Ann. Tig.,* s.aa 1118, 1124.

[115] D. Ó Corráin, 'Dál Cais—church and dynasty', p. 55.

[116] *A.U.,* s.a. 1016; *Ann. Tig., A.F.M.,* s.a. 1133; for the relationship between Ua Birn and Ua Conchobair see *Bk Lec.,* 63 rc 12; *R.I.A.,* 23 Q 10, 20 rb 16, 40 ra 33.

[117] *A.F.M.,* s.a. 1100; *Ann. Tig.,* s.a. 1143.

[118] *Ann. Tig.,* s.a. 976, 1066, 1132; *A.U.,* s.a. 980; *Ann. Inisf.,* s.a. 983, 985.

cavalry.[119] There were rapid developments also in the building and use of castles, fortifications, and military earthworks.[120] The same development took place in the use of ships and boats in warfare, and the inland rivers and lakes and the coastline fairly teemed with vessels of different shapes and sizes. In general, the seafaring peoples of the south and west coast—Ó hEterscéoil, Ó Muirchertaigh, Ó Conchobair Chiarraige, Ó Domnaill of Corcu Baiscind, Ó Flaithbheartaig, Ó Dubda, and others served as commanders of the king's fleets.

Behind the violence and the military campaigns is a world of claim and counter-claim, of historical fabrication and political propaganda, which helps to flesh out the bare bones of the annalistic record. The great kings and their supporters, if we may judge from the inscriptions they caused to be placed on the shrines they had made for the churches, were in no doubt as to their own aims. On the shrine of the Stowe Missal, Donnchad mac Briain describes himself as king of Ireland.[121] On the Cross of Cong Tairdelbach Ua Conchobair asks a prayer for himself as *ri hErend.*[122] In the Corpus Christi Missal we find the prayer-formulae: *pro gloriosissimo rege nostro N eiusque nobilissima prole N* and elsewhere *ut regem Hibernensium et exercitum eius conservare digneris.* These formulae are old and may have been introduced to Ireland at an earlier period but on chronological stylistic grounds Dr Françoise Henry considers Tairdelbach Ua Conchobair to be the person most likely to be in the writer's mind.[123] All is grist to the mill. Hagiography is pressed into service in a direct and crude way as it is in continental Europe both for secular and ecclesiastical purposes. Tairdelbach Ua Conchobair could point to Fínnechta mac Tomaltaig (+848), saint and king of Connacht.[124] The Uí Briain could point to Flannán as the saint of their dynasty, and the twelfth-century lives of that saint are highly propagandistic documents.[125] The eponymous ancestor of Uí Briain is

[119] *A.U.*, s.a. 1170; the compiler of the late preface to the *Senchas Már* (see above n. 55) imagined that this office existed in the fifth century (*Anc. laws Ire.* i, 4).

[120] D. Ó Corráin, 'Aspects of early Irish history' in B. G. Scott (ed.), *Perspectives in Irish archaeology* (Belfast, 1974), pp 68–71. Some such permanently fortified places seem to have been secular towns in embryo.

[121] R. A. S. Macalister, *Corpus inscriptionum insularum Celticarum* ii (Dublin, 1949), p. 105.

[122] Ibid., p. 16.

[123] F. Henry and G. Marsh-Micheli, 'A century of Irish illumination' in *R.I.A. Proc.*, lxii, sect. C (1961), pp 101–66.

[124] *Bk Lec.*, 164 ʀa 38–44; see also, K. Meyer, 'Mitteilungen aus irischen Handschriften, Baile Fíndachta ríg Condacht' in *Z.C.P.* xiii (1919), pp 25–7.

[125] There are two recensions of this life: Paul Grosjean (ed.), 'Vita sancti Flannani' in *Anal. Bolland* xlvi (1928), pp 124–41 (R), and W. W. Heist (ed.), *Vitae sanctorum Hiberniae* (Brussels, 1965), pp 280–301 (S). S, the later and more extensive was written about 1162 (§10); R is older and the work of a convinced reformer (§§23, 30, 32, 34). Both probably go back to an archetype redacted by a foreign cleric at Killaloe shortly after the death of Muirchertach Ua Briain in 1119. For evidence that the author was a foreigner see §§1, 7, and the phrases *crimen lese majestatis* (§15), *frequentatio curie regalis* (§20) and *ad regimen rei pupplice* (§12).

deliberately turned into a saint, and a long narrative of his austerities and miracles is provided. In contrast to that, Ailbe, the well-known saint and patron of Emly, a church much favoured by the rival Éoganacht, is dismissed as a demon. One can trace the hand of the ambitious and able Cormac Mac Carthaig in the life of St Finbar, rewritten in the twelfth century as the basis for an enlarged diocese of Cork and the ecclesiastical correlative of Mac Carthaig's secular claims.[126] As in England the sanctity of Edward the Confessor, as in Europe the sanctity of Charlemagne and the sanctity of the Emperor Henry II, who was canonised in 1152, so in Ireland the kings boosted the sanctity of their predecssors and patrons in order to enhance their own dignity and authority.

Two great southern propaganda texts, *Cogadh Gáedhel re Gallaibh* and *Caithréim Chellacháin Chaisil*,[127] allow us to glimpse the notions of kingship which actuated men such as Muirchertach Ua Briain and Cormac Mac Carthaig. Both date from the first half of the twelfth century in essentials. The ideal king of *Cogadh Gáedhel re Gallaibh* is a lover of peace but of course a warrior incomparable when required to be such. He imprisons those who rob and make war; he hangs thieves and brigands; and he maintains excellent public order. He is generous in his endowment of learning and of the church.[128] In the lives of St Flannán, the clerical followers of the Uí Briain give their version of the ideal king. He is a most Christian king who follows in the footsteps of the Saviour and who gives good example to his followers. He rules well, has a care for the poor, and the weak, and is merciful towards his enemies. Above all, he builds churches at his own expense and is generous in granting lands and possessions to the church. *Caithréim Chellacháin Chaisil* is a paradigm in saga-form of the ideal relationship between a king and his vassal lords. They are brave and disciplined in battle, loyal to their lord, prepared to follow him to the ends of the earth and lay down their lives in his service. A northern work, *The circuit of Ireland by Muirchertach mac Néill*,[129] which dates, at least in its present form, from the reign of Muirchertach Mac Lochlainn (1156–66), is more old-fashioned in style but it too is written to glorify kingship. Two of these texts are shot through with a strident patriotism which uses the long-peaceful Norse as a whipping-boy. An example of this is the selfless decision of the rival claimants to the kingship of Munster who retire observing that, if they contested it, only the Vikings would profit from their dissensions.[130] In

[126] Charles Plummer (ed.), *Vitae sanctorum Hiberniae* (Oxford, 1910), pp 65–74; *Bethada Náem nÉrenn* (Oxford, 1922), pp 11–22.
[127] Alexander Bugge (ed.), Christiania (Oslo),1905; D. Ó Corráin 'Caithréim Chellacháin Chaisil: history or propaganda?' in *Ériu*, xxv (1974), pp 1–69.
[128] *Cog. Gáedhel*, pp 136–40.
[129] John O'Donovan (ed.) in *Tracts relating to Ireland* i (Dublin, 1841), pp 24–59.
[130] *Caithréim*, §§5–6.

Cogadh the Vikings are brutal and ferocious tyrants, plunderers of the church and enslavers of the Irish—in all they are the foils to the glory of Dál Cais and the triumph of Brian. The same stress on the glory of victory over the Vikings is present in the work of Flann Mainistrech more than a generation earlier.[131] The sense of triumph also occurs in a late poem (and a clumsy one) in praise of Écnechán mac Dálaig, king of Cenél Conaill (+906) and impossibly fathered on the famous poet Flann mac Lonáin.[132] It is evident that the writers of the eleventh and twelfth centuries drew a remarkably clear line of distinction between the Vikings and the Irish—a distinction which is made with no such clarity by the matter-of-fact contemporary annalists of the Viking wars properly so-called whose records they plundered. For the later writers the Viking age is a remote heroic age of warfare against a foreign invader who was ferocious and barbaric, full of guile, a plunderer of churches and a heartless exploiter of the people of Ireland; and they cast the great kings of their own day as the descendants of the heroes of that past. Paradoxically, never were the Vikings to have more influence on Ireland and never were they less a military threat than in the eleventh and twelfth centuries, when they turned to peaceful pursuits as traders and entrepreneurs. The more advanced Irish kings used the Viking towns to strengthen themselves militarily and economically, for they milked them for men, ships, and taxes while at the same time they used them as the whipping-boy for their growing national aspirations. It is possible too that contact with the Vikings broadened their notions of kingship. Against this background, the use by the synthetic historians of the Norse term *iarla* (earl) as a high honorific term applicable to those whom they considered to be kings of Ireland may more readily be explained.[133]

The type of society that was emerging in Ireland in the eleventh and twelfth centuries was one that was moving rapidly in the direction of feudalism,[134] and indeed bears some striking resemblance—in conservatism as well as in innovation—to European society in the first age of feudalism. This becomes particularly clear from the recent work of the 'prosopographical' school of historians. Here I shall refer briefly to only one

---

131 Mac Neill, 'Poems by Flann Mainistrech', pp 61–2, 72–3.

132 J. G. O'Keeffe (ed.), 'Eulogy of Écnechán son of Dálach' in J. Fraser and others (ed.), *Irish texts*, i (London, 1931), pp 54–62; M. E. Dobbs, 'A poem attributed to Flann mac Lonáin in *Ériu*, xvii (1955), pp 16–34; the story is repeated in a poem in praise of Domnall Ua Domnaill, ibid., ii 1–5.

133 *Bk Leinster* iii, 479, 487 (Gilla Cóemáin); Mac Neill, 'Poems by Flann Mainistrech', pp 84 §24, 85 §37, 95 §33; *B.B.*, 58 a 27, 59 a 6, 7 (Gilla na Náem Ua Duinn).

134 There is nothing much new in this suggestion; see Eoin Mac Neill, *Early Irish laws and institutions*, pp 24, 30, 129–32; F. J. Byrne, *Irish kings and high-kings*, p. 262. In my opinion, Professor Lydon is unduly chary about the existence of pre-Norman 'incipient native feudalism' and his argument *contra* that 'basically the organisation of the *túath* remained unchanged' is unsound (*The lordship of Ireland*, p. 16).

aspect, that of lineage, an area in which Ireland is supposed by many to be peculiar. In the early period, Irish society was a broad-based lineage society, but it appears to have undergone considerable change between the ninth and twelfth centuries at precisely the same time as similar (though not identical) changes took place in Europe. This appears not only from the annals in general but, in a particular way, from the genealogies, for in that period there is a remarkable narrowing of the genealogical record, particularly amongst the lesser dynasts. And this tendency is carried even further in the surviving twelfth-century manuscripts, where genealogical tracts (which we know from the fourteenth and fifteenth century antiquarian movement) are ruthlessly edited. The genealogies of the Ciarraige record thirty-one lines of the ruling house (excluding for the moment twice as many collaterals more distantly removed) about the year 750; by the year 1100, only one line is being recorded, that of the ruling family, Ó Conchobair.[135] In the kingdom of Lóegaire, fifty-one lines are recorded for the eighth century by by c. 1000 these are reduced to four.[136] In Corcu Modruad, there are some fourteen lines in the record for the ninth century, only two are recorded in the eleventh century, those from which the two local lords, Ó Conchobair and Ó Lochlainn, descend.[137]

This tendency is general throughout the genealogical *corpus* except that the narrowing of the lineage takes place earlier and is more rigorous amongst the dominant dynasties. The point of departure seems to be the late eighth and ninth centuries. This should indicate a consolidation of local hereditary lordship and the emergence of a narrower, more powerful, and more exclusive lordly class. It is symbolic, too, that between the tenth and twelfth centuries this class took surnames, thus cutting itself off from that much wider group with which it shared a remoter eponymous ancestor. It is remarkable that what K. Leyser says, summarising recent work on the German aristocracy, can be said of the Irish with only a few verbal changes:

The aristocracies of Carolingian Europe were made up of very large family groups conscious of their nobility by descent from a great ancestor, whose name was perpetuated in their own and by their membership of the group. . . . The transformation of these *Grossfamilien* into small and more circumscribed and close knit families with a much more continuous history was the real significance of the so-called 'rise of the dynasts', which an older generation of historians connected with the long civil wars of the reigns of Henry IV and Henry V and the investiture conflict. The late eleventh and the first half of the twelfth century saw a fundamental change in the structure of the German aristocracy.[138]

---

[135] *Corpus geneal. Hib.*, p. 287; for detail see *Bk Lec.* 117 RC 1–121 Rd 41 = *B.B.*, 155 ac 32–160 a 7.

[136] *Corpus geneal. Hib.*, pp 166–7; for the fuller recension, of which the twelfth century MSS preserve only a tiny part, see *B.B.*, 86 a 1–88 e 36.

[137] *Corpus geneal. Hib.*, pp 315–6; for detailed tracts see *Bk Lec.* 121 Rd 41, *B.B.*, 160 ba 7.

[138] 'The German aristocracy in the early middle ages' in *Past and Present* xlv (1968), pp 31–2.

This process of consolidation had developed in Ireland to the point where the centralising policies of the great twelfth-century 'high-kings' were winning the day against the centrifugal tendencies of the hereditary dynastic kingdoms. In the Rhineland and in northern France the genealogies of the greater princes ascend to the close of the ninth century, those of the lesser lords to the tenth. As one would expect, this lineage society begins when honours become hereditary, and a full-scale lineage society emerges in the tenth and eleventh centuries, with later characteristic narrowing.[139] In regard to this lineage society, Duby says: *il est permit de considérer le renforcement progressif de ces structures proprement lignagères comme un trait spécifique de la société dite féodale.* The narrowing of the lineage takes place at the same time as it did in Ireland or perhaps a little later. In Ireland there is a great deal of learned activity in order to justify and lend authority to these narrower power-holding lineages, further evidence of the novelty of their position.[140] In addition, there is a great deal of eleventh and twelfth century genealogical fabrication devoted to the same end. It would appear that lineage organisation in Ireland differed much less in reality than it appears to do on the surface from such organisation in the feudal lands, and if political authority was segmented in Ireland it was not less so over the greater part of northern Europe.[141]

In the twelfth century Ireland came increasingly into contact with England and Europe, especially through the church-reform movement, the introduction of foreign religious orders, and through pilgrimage. The Uí Briain, for example, were in close touch not only with Canterbury but with Norman Wales and Henry I, while there were foreign clerics (probably Norman) living at Killaloe and involved in producing royalist propaganda. It is clear that influences flowed in many directions and through many channels to a society in rapid change. The example of Anglo-Norman England lay close at hand. In a panegyric in *Cogadh Gáedhel re Gallaibh* the

---

[139] G. Duby, 'Structures familiales dan le moyen âge occidental' in *XIIIᵉ Congrès international des sciences historiques* (Moscow, 1970), pp 1–8; 'The diffusion of cultural patterns in feudal society' in *Past and Present*, xxxix (1968), pp 3–10; 'Structures de parenté et noblesse. France du Nord IXe-XIIe siècles' in *Miscellanea mediaevalia in memoriam Jan Frederick Niemeyer* (Groningen, 1967), pp 149–65.

[140] See for example the poems: *Cuiced Lagen na lecht rig, Bk Leinster* i, 135–44; F. J. Byrne (ed.), '*Clann Ollamon uaisle Emna*' in *Studia Hib.*, iv (1964), pp 54–94; '*Cruacha Condacht raith co rath*' in *B.B.* 58 a 42–59 b 14. These appear to be 'legitimist' poems since all mention the reigning king at the time of writing who in all cases belonged to a ruling family threatened (or threatened within recent memory) by remoter dynasts and bearers of a different surname. Much of the genealogical writing of the twelfth-century conveniently omits contemporary collaterals belonging to the wider old-fashioned structure but records ancient collaterals of little practical consequence.

[141] For some suggestive comparisons see S. L. Thrupp, 'The dynamics of medieval society in *XIII International Congress of Historical Sciences* (Moscow, 1970), pp 1–17, and the literature there cited.

Uí Briain describe themselves as *Frainc na Fotla . . . Meic . . . Israeil na hErend* (the Franks of Ireland . . . the sons of Israel of Ireland).[142] We are to understand *Frainc* as Normans and the terms taken literally must mean that the Uí Briain, regarding themselves as the chosen dynasty, intended to extend their rule over all Ireland as the conquering Normans had recently done in England. It was a high ambition but other dynasties had more success than they, and the prize of overkingship finally passed to Connacht. However, it was a fragile thing and the monarchic structures and the political union which they were bringing about collapsed readily in the face of external attack.

It would appear that the Irish had developed a sense of identity and 'otherness' as early as the seventh century and had begun to create an elaborate origin-legend embracing all the tribes and dynasties of the country. This was the work of a mandarin class of monastic and secular scholars whose privileged position in society allowed them to transcend all local and tribal boundaries. Side by side with this, and in the wake of continued territorial aggrandizement, there came a growth in the political consciousness of the overkings of the Uí Néill which led them to put forward tendentious claims to be kings of Ireland. Such they never were in reality, but the idea of the kingship of Ireland was to have a powerful and abiding political influence especially on the great kings of the eleventh and twelfth centuries who made every effort to turn the idea into a reality. The indications are that tribal kingship, as we know it from the classical law-tracts, fell prey to the expanding provincial kings as early as the end of the seventh century or perhaps earlier and Irish society, far from being static, entered a period of rapid, one might even say convulsive, change in which the old order, so beloved of the jurists, passed away. Larger and more cohesive kingdoms emerged, the powers and pretensions of the kings grew apace, the nature of kingship itself changed and by the eleventh and twelfth centuries rule over the entire island of Ireland had become, for good or for ill, the prize in the political game and the express object of the contenders.

[142] *Cogadh Gáedhel*, p. 160.

II

The political and institutional background to national consciousness in medieval Wales

Michael Richter

The medievalist who is invited to contribute to a discussion of the pursuit of national independence has a feeling of trepidation as well as satisfaction. He takes satisfaction from the assumption that a medievalist has something to contribute, but what he offers is different in substance from the discussion of the modern historian, hence his trepidation. He works in a time when those structures and mentalities which produce the sentiment of nationalism are just appearing in outline, when they can be divined rather than demonstrated. He will have to be contented with less detail and less precision while covering a wider time-span than his modern counterpart. What he can contribute is to indicate that political structures become wider, going beyond the local community, that participation in the running of these political structures begins to broaden. These processes are essential elements in any nationalism, whether medieval or modern. In addition, the medievalist is aware, probably more so than the modern historian, that the modern nations took shape gradually in the course of the middle ages; therefore his contribution is not only to be tolerated but will be a necessary element in any discussion of the subject.[1]

National consciousness requires some kind of framework within which to be expressed, and this can be political, religious, cultural, social, linguistic or a combination of more than one of these elements. It also requires a group of people who express their sense of belonging together. For the study of national consciousness, the historian depends on the survival of written records. In the middle ages, the limits of literacy in every society restricted considerably the circle of those whose awakening national consciousness was recorded and can be studied.

[1] A group of scholars, based at the University of Marburg, West Germany, has started systematically to investigate the origins of the European nations in the middle ages; see *Nationes*, i ('Aspekte der Nationenbildung im Mittelalter', in the press) and the author's contribution therein: 'Mittelalterlicher Nationalismus: Wales im 13. Jahrhundert'. An earlier version of that paper was read to the Irish Historical Society in Dublin in March 1973.

In medieval Wales, literacy was perhaps even rarer than in England, and a great proportion of the written records which were produced in Wales have been lost. What has been preserved, however, does indicate that by the early twelfth century a new era was dawning, heralded by a considerable increase in these records. Older native tradition was written down, and often still shows clearly that it originated in a society based predominantly on oral tradition and transmission of information. The writing down of old traditions, some anthropologists suggest, is a sure sign of growing self-awareness, which in turn is a necessary step towards national consciousness.[2]

The vigorous literary activities that occurred do not indicate the end of a period of isolation, but an important re-orientation of Wales. Prior to the twelfth century, this country was tied to Irish society by links which were probably stronger than those with England; in the wake of the Norman conquest of England, Wales was firmly drawn into the orbit of her neighbour to the east. The country was exposed to military aggression from England as never before, and, after two centuries, it was finally conquered by Edward I and subjected to the English crown. Seven more centuries of English rule have not managed, however, to suppress the spirit of Welsh national consciousness, which has survived, sometimes stronger, at other times in a more muted fashion, the loss of political independence and the strong pressures of linguistic acculturation.[3] In what follows, I propose to comment only on the very first stage of this remarkable phenomenon by analysing some institutional and political changes in medieval Wales, for it was within the process of political unification that Welsh national consciousness found the earliest expressions which can still be traced. The two centuries before the Edwardian conquest were a time when the Welsh people experienced an enlargement of their view of the world, when gradually they came to know each other as fellow-countrymen by being fellow-sufferers.[4]

In the late eleventh century, Wales was still what it had been for some centuries before: a country politically fragmented, where loyalties were intensely local and a sense of identity was found by looking to the past. The people referred to themselves as *Britones,* 'Britons', harking back to the time when their ancestors had ruled over the whole island. The years that brought the first serious advances into Wales from Anglo-Norman England

---

[2] Robert Redfield, *The primitive world and its transformation* (Harmondsworth, 1968), esp. ch. 3.

[3] See, e.g., Glanmor Williams, 'Prophecy, poetry and politics in medieval and Tudor Wales' in *British government and administration: studies presented to S. B. Chrimes,* ed. H. Hearder and H. R. Loyn (Cardiff, 1974), pp 104–16; idem, 'Language, literacy and nationality in Wales' in *History* lvi (1971), pp 1–16.

[4] Redfield, as above, note 2, p. 89.

created a sense of consternation and defenceless grief in the few people who expressed their sentiments:

Now the labours of earlier days lie despised; the people and the priests are despised by word, heart and work of the Normans... One vile Norman intimidates a hundred natives with his command and terrifies them with his look . . . Are you, British people, at enmity with God? O country, you are afflicted and dying, you are quivering with fear, you collapse, alas, miserable with your sad armament; . . . patriotism and the hope of self-government flee; liberty and self-will perish.[5]

The expectation of imminent doom was premature. Wales was too fragmented politically to be taken over by foreign invaders in one fell swoop. Her lack of political unification was her strongest weapon, and the Norman kings did not yet have their hands free to subject Wales. The increasing tendency in Wales to write down the native traditions in history, religion and literature, however, prompted by these strong neighbours, enables the observer for the first time to deal with developments and changes in Welsh society.

If we look at the Welsh scene again a century after Rhigyfarch's Lament, quoted earlier, the country had already changed enormously: by then the low-lying and accessible areas in the south and east of Wales were in the hands of either the English crown or a number of Norman lords who established their own independent rule. To the native rulers was left the upland zone (above 600 ft).[6] But even here substantial changes had occurred. Of the numerous rulers who had existed before, only two dynasties had survived in a recognisable form, those of Gwynedd and Deheubarth. But the strongest indication of change may be taken from the fact that the native rulers had adopted a new name: they no longer referred to themselves as 'Britons', but instead as 'Welshmen' *(Walenses)*. The link with their past history was becoming weaker and lost some of its breadth; they were gradually abandoning their 'retrospective mythology'.[7] Where there had been fragmentation in native Wales before, the signs were now set on nucleation, and this meant that there would be, in future, fewer dynasties in the country, but that these would be more powerful and would command a wider following than their predecessors.

To those observers who measured Wales by European standards, the nucleation had not gone far enough. In the opinion of Giraldus Cambrensis, the Welsh were still too divided to defend their position properly, and it was their weakness that they

---

[5] Michael Lapidge, 'The Welsh-Latin poetry of Sulien's family' in *Studia Celtica.* viii–ix (1973–4), pp 91–3.

[6] See William Rees, *An historical atlas of Wales* (3rd ed., London, 1967), plate 3.

[7] For the term see Redfield, p. 130: 'it is the contact and conflict of differing traditions that brings about the sudden alterations in society, and, among other consequences, the change from a mythology that is retrospective to one that is prospective'.

obstinately refused to be ruled by one king, and be subject to one lord . . . For if they would only be inseparable, they would also be insuperable: for three things work in their favour: a country which is inaccessible; a population that is accustomed to hard life; and a people entirely trained in arms.[8]

The lack of unity, still so noticeable in 1194, showed signs of being overcome in the thirteenth century. At the time when England was weakened by the severe strife between crown and nobility, independent Wales emerged more powerful than ever before under the leadership of a ruler of Gwynedd who styled himself *princeps Wallie* and was recognised as such by the English king in 1267.[9] Prince Llywelyn ap Gruffudd introduced new forms of government at the expense of ancient Welsh customs and traditions. Like his grandfather, Llywelyn ab Iorwerth, before him, he married a foreign noble lady, linking himself to the aristocracy and the royal family of England.[10] Under the younger Llywelyn's rule, the principality of Wales became a feudal state like many others in western Europe, a state, furthermore, in feudal dependence on the English king. When the prince of Wales died in rebellion against his overlord in 1282, the principality escheated to the crown. It is true that Edward I had yet to conquer the country in military campaigns which imposed a great strain on the English finances,[11] but the process of political nucleation in Wales had created the necessary conditions for a complete takeover. As a result of the political changes in thirteenth-century Wales, the fortune of the country was tied to the destiny of one man.

The changes in native Wales thus briefly outlined greatly increased the political awareness of a considerable section of the population. Those who have left records of their feelings show that a strong sense of identity had emerged among the Welsh people. When, shortly before the defeat of 1282, it was suggested by a mediator that Llywelyn should renounce his principality and accept compensation in England, the nobles of Snowdon replied that 'even if the prince would hand over their seisin to the king, they were not willing to pay homage to a foreigner whose language, laws and customs were altogether unknown to them'.[12] It is difficult to penetrate below this class, but here we have a powerful expression of national identity in the terms of common ancestry, language, laws and customs.

The political developments leading up to this growing sense of national

[8] Giraldus Cambrensis, *Opera*, ed. J. S. Brewer and others (Rolls Series, 21, 8 vols, 1861–91), vi, 225–6.

[9] See Richter, as above, note 1, passim, and cf. Rees, *Atlas*, plate 41.

[10] See A. J. Roderick, 'Marriage and politics in Wales, 1066–1282' in *Welsh History Review*, iv (1968–9), pp 1–20.

[11] Michael Prestwich, *War, politics and finance under Edward I* (London, 1972).

[12] *Registrum epistolarum Fratris Johannis Peckham*, ed. C. T. Martin (Rolls Series, 1884), ii, 470–71; cf. also Richter, as above note 1.

identity have been related more than once, and never in more glowing terms than in the impressive study of Sir John Edward Lloyd.[13] What has not been done in equal depth is to analyse the changes that took place. Their result was political unification and—as a by-product to it, so it appears—a growing sense of national awareness. But what did the new structure owe to native tradition, what to foreign inspiration? An attempt will be made here to discuss the gradual transition from a tribal to a feudal society in medieval Wales that took place under the impact of developments in England.

In a widely acclaimed article published nearly twenty years ago, the great constitutional historian, Sir Goronwy Edwards, solved one of the peculiar features of later medieval Wales, that of the independence *vis-à-vis* the crown of the marcher lords. He showed that their comparatively independent position, which included the right to exercise jurisdiction, civil and criminal, high and low, to make war and to build castles, was that same right which the native Welsh rulers had enjoyed before the arrival of the Normans. The marcher lords perpetuated, in the area under their control, the political fragmentation of native Wales; their lordship was, by Welsh law, royal in character.[14] On the basis of this analysis, which has shed a bright light on indigenous political institutions, it is now possible to look at those areas that were not subject to the marcher lords, to independent Welsh Wales and her rulers.

Norman-Welsh relations are very badly documented in the first century after the Norman arrival in England, and we therefore begin our analysis at a point where these relations assume a definable form. This happened in 1177. In that year, King Henry II met the kings and nobility of Wales at Oxford. Rhys ap Gruffudd, king of South Wales, Dafydd ap Owain Gwynedd, king of North Wales, Cadwallan, king of Delwain (ap Madog of Maelienydd), Owain Cyfeiliog (of Powys), Gruffudd of Bromfield and Madog ab Iorwerth Goch are mentioned by name. The historian who reported this meeting, 'Benedict of Peterborough', *alias* Roger Howden, clearly differentiated between various ranks of the Welsh political leaders. This differentiation becomes even more obvious when we hear of the terms agreed at that meeting. 'Benedict' writes:

There the king of England, son of the empress Mathilda, gave Dafydd, king of North Wales, who had married his sister (Emma), the land of Ellesmere, and (Dafydd) there swore to his lord the king of England fealty for it and liege homage henceforth, and swore to keep the peace with the king of England. Likewise, the king of England

[13] John Edward Lloyd, *A history of Wales from the earliest times to the Edwardian conquest* (2 vols, London, 1911).
[14] J. G. Edwards, 'The Normans and the Welsh march' in *Proceedings of the British Academy* xlii (1956), pp 155–77, p. 170ff.

gave to Rhys, the king of South Wales, the land of Merioneth, and (Rhys) swore him fealty and liege homage and promised to keep the peace.[15]

From this report it appears that the kings of North and South Wales both received from Henry II land outside their own territory in exchange for homage and fealty. It must be stressed that they apparently did not perform these acts for North Wales and South Wales but for the other lands mentioned, and we can assume that they were therefore recognised as independent rulers of North and South Wales. There is no reason to assume that the fact that previous Welsh rulers had paid tribute to the Norman kings[16] had in any way diminished their constitutional position within their own territory. Moreover, at Oxford, only Dafydd and Rhys were recognised as independent lords. In his account of the Oxford meeting of May 1177, Roger Howden thus reports indirectly a growing nucleation of political power in Welsh Wales.

For events of such importance, the historian cannot be satisfied with mere narrative accounts, even when they come from respectable and normally reliable contemporaries. Further evidence is not available from England; we have to turn to Wales itself. There, I shall attempt a different approach and analyse the way in which the Welsh rulers in the twelfth century interpreted their own position. This appears in its clearest light when we consult legal documents that these rulers issued, and when we look at the way in which they referred to themselves. The charters of the Welsh rulers which contain such references are legal documents; most of them record gifts of land that these rulers handed over to Welsh monasteries. In some of the charters it is explicitly stated that they were written, not by a chancery clerk of the ruler, but in the monasteries that received these gifts,[17] and even when this is not recorded we can assume that this was the

---

[15] Benedict of Peterborough, *Gesta Regis Henrici Secundi*, ed. W. Stubbs (Rolls Series, 1867), i, p. 162. In his *Chronica*, ed. W. Stubbs (Rolls Series, 1869), ii, p. 134, Howden reports, more briefly, the same event but adds: 'et omnes devenerunt homines regis Angliae patris, et fidelitatem ei contra omnes homines et pacem sibi et regno suo servandam juraverunt'. See also Lloyd, ii, 552–3, who fails to see the significance of this arrangement. My interpretation also differs from that of W. L. Warren, *Henry II* (London, 1973), p. 168. The Welsh *Brut y Tywysogyon* ('Chronicle of the Princes') does not mention the Oxford meeting. Unless otherwise stated, the *Brut* will be quoted hereafter in the Red Book of Hergest version (hereafter cited as R.B.H.), ed. Thomas Jones (Board of Celtic Studies, History and Law Series, no. xvi, Cardiff, 1955). On this see also Thomas Jones, 'Historical writing in medieval Welsh' in *Scottish Studies*, xii (1968), pp 15–27.

[16] J. G. Edwards, as above (note 14), p. 161.

[17] See, for example, a charter of Madog ap Maelgwn for the abbey of Cwm Hir: 'Datum litterarum per manum domini Riredi abbatis, mense Maio' (Gildas Tibbot, 'An Abbey-Cwmhir relic abroad' in *Transactions of the Radnorshire Historical Society* v (1936), p. 65); a charter of Llywelyn ab Iorwerth, *c.* 1208, to Strata Marcella: 'In manu G. prioris de Stratmarchel'; a charter of Dafydd ap Owain, 1215, to Strata Marcella: 'in manu Dauid abbatis', for both of which see E. D. Jones, N. G. Davies, R. F. Roberts, 'Five Strata Marcella charters' in *National Library of Wales Journal* v (1947), pp 52, 53. No attempt is made here to assemble all the charters

procedure. Nevertheless, in these legal instruments 'it was the issuer himself who said the decisive last word about the phrasing and contents of the *intitulatio* formula', for 'we have to ask what a given ruler says of himself; we have to seek what one might label his "self-manifestation" *(Selbstaussage)*, if we want to obtain a methodologically reliable answer to the question "what is a ruler?" '.[18] This new approach of the Viennese historian, Herwig Wolfram, to early medieval concepts of rulership helps, so I believe, to illuminate the situation in twelfth-century Wales.

Only few charters are extant from twelfth-century Welsh rulers, but they tell an interesting tale. We must distinguish at this point those charters in which the ruler expresses his self-manifestation by the traditional Welsh names from the others, all later, where the territory under his rule is referred to otherwise. Of the former type, we have a document issued by *Howell rex Argwestli* and one of *Madawc rex Powyssentium*,[19] both from the first half of the twelfth century. All other relevant charters come from the second half of the twelfth century or a later time. Many of these are undated, but the documents issued on behalf of Owain Gwynedd, who died in 1170 and who styled himself in his documents *Walliarum rex, Walliae rex, Wallensium princeps, princeps Walliae*, are certainly pre-1177.[20] His successor Dafydd occurs (probably before 1174) as *David rex filius Owini* and later as *David filius Owini princeps Norwalliae*.[21] The form *N. princeps Norwalliae* became the standard form used by the Gwynedd rulers until the mid-thirteenth century, when the title *princeps Walliae* was adopted. A similar development can be seen in Deheubarth. From the 1160s onwards, Rhys ap Gruffudd used the following titles: *princeps Wallie, Walliarum princeps, Sudwall' proprietarius princeps*.[22]

When looking at these charters, we notice two important changes which

and letters of the native Welsh rulers. This task is at present undertaken, for Gwynedd, by Mr David Stephenson, to whom the author is greatly indebted for a number of references.

[18] Herwig Wolfram, 'The shaping of the early medieval principality as a type of non-royal rulership' in *Viator* ii (1971), pp 34, 33. For a full appreciation of Wolfram's approach, however, reference should be made to the detailed work published in German: Herwig Wolfram, *Intitulatio I. Lateinische Königs- und Fürstentitel bis zum Ende des 8. Jahrhunderts* (Mitteilungen des Instituts für Österreichische Geschichtsforschung, Erg. Band 21, 1967), and H. Wolfram (ed.), *Intitulatio II: Lateinische Herrscher- und Fürstentitel im 9. und 10. Jahrhundert* (Mitteilungen des Instituts für Österreichische Geschichtsforschung, Erg. Band 24, 1973).

[19] Robert Williams, 'Wynnstay MSS—charters of Trefeglwys' in *Archaeologia Cambrensis* (hereafter cited as *Arch. Camb.*) 3rd series, vi (1860), pp 331, 330.

[20] *Materials for the history of Thomas Becket*, ed. J. C. Robertson and others (7 vols, Rolls Series, 1875–85), v 229; M. Bouquet, *Recueil des historiens des Gaules et de la France*, xvi (1878), nos 357, 358, p. 116ff. See also J. B. Smith, 'Owain Gwynedd' in *Caernarvonshire Historical Society Transactions*, xxxii (1971), pp 8–17.

[21] *Arch. Camb.*, 1860, p. 332.

[22] For *princeps Wallie* (shortly after 1165), see E. M. Pritchard, *Cardigan priory in the olden days* (London, 1904), pp 144–5; for the other two items (of 1184) William Dugdale, *Monasticon Anglicanum*, new edition (6 vols in 8 parts, London, 1846–9), v, 632.

must have occurred in the second half of the twelfth century. The first is this: the traditional Welsh names were no longer used to describe the territory under the control of a ruler, but instead a name was adopted which had long been used in England to describe the country on the western border: *Wallia* and components thereof take the place of the indigenous terms. This is truly remarkable. 'Welsh' meaning 'foreign'[23] was the word that had been used for a long time by the English to describe their western neighbours. It is used in the Anglo-Saxon Chronicle,[24] but was also retained by the Normans. It appears in Domesday Book where it is used in recording the land of Gwynedd which the Norman Robert of Rhuddlan had acquired from Gruffudd ap Cynan. There we read: 'Robert of Rhuddlan holds from the king North Wales *(Nortwales)* at farm for £40, besides that land which the king had given him to hold in fee'. Similarly, the term 'Southwales' occurs in Anglo-Norman royal documents to describe the area of the diocese of St David's in the reign of King Henry I.[25]

From an English point of view, the bishopric of St David's appears naturally as 'South Wales', as Gwynedd is most conveniently described as 'North Wales', and the terms on which Robert of Rhuddlan held 'North Wales' are even comparable to those (expressed in non-technical, non-official language), granted to Rhys ap Gruffudd and Dafydd ap Owain in 1177, at least in one point: none of them held the Welsh lands in fee, i.e. by feudal tenure with the ordinary obligations. But the parallel goes further. The occurrence of the Welsh rulers in 1177 as kings of 'North Wales' and 'South Wales' respectively cannot surprise us in the works of an English twelfth-century historian (as *Fremdaussage*). They are quite remarkable, however, in charters of the Welsh rulers themselves. These rulers adopted, in the second half of the twelfth century, the English usage as well as the English terminology and used it consistently to the end of independent Wales. Henceforth, the Welsh rulers referred to themselves as rulers of 'North Wales', 'South Wales', 'Wales', 'the Welsh' or variants thereof, not of *Venedotia* (Gwynedd), *Demetia* (Deheubarth), or 'the Britons'.[26] In their charter formularies, they submitted to English usage, they accepted the identity impressed upon them from outside.

[23] See Gaston Paris, 'Romani, Romania, lingua Romana, Romanum' in *Romania*, i(1872), pp 5–6. For a contemporary assessment see Giraldus Cambrensis, *Opera*, vi, 179.

[24] *Anglo-Saxon chronicle*, ed. Charles Plummer (Oxford, 1892), p. 104: *s.a.* 922 (921): 'The kings of the North Welsh *(North Wealum)*, Hywel, Clydog and Idwal and all the people of Wales gave (Aethelflaed) their allegiance'; *s.a.* 926: 'King Aethelstan . . . brought into submission all the kings of this island: first Hywel, king of the West Welsh *(West Wala cyning)* and Constantine, king of the Scots, and Owain, king of Gwent'.

[25] For 'North Wales' see *Domesday Book*, i, f. 269a; cf. also J. G. Edwards, p. 159f; Lloyd, ii, 387. For 'South Wales' see *Historia et cartularium monasterii Sancti Petri Gloucestriae* (ed. W. H. Hart, Rolls Series, 1865), ii, 76, and cf. ibid., p. 73.

[26] It should be noted that the new terms were not adopted in the *Brut* and only at a late stage in the Welsh laws, for which see below, note 49.

The second change, likewise not precisely datable, went hand in hand with the first: the earlier title *rex* was replaced by the title *princeps*. Never again after the late twelfth century did Welsh rulers refer to themselves as *reges*. According to the native chronicle, *Brut y Tywysogyon*, this change occured around the year 1157; from that date onwards the *Brut* equally never again applied the title *brenin* (king) to Welsh rulers. On the basis of our previous discussion we have to stress that, in the timing of this change, the *Brut* does not reflect accurately the practice of the rulers themselves.[27] Owain Gwynedd, for example, used the royal title repeatedly, at the time of the Becket controversy in England, when he made a spectacular advance in the field of international diplomacy by offering himself as a vassal to the French king Louis VII.[28] Of the rulers of Gwynedd it was Owain's son and successor, Dafydd, who eventually abandoned the title *rex*, probably as a result of a marriage alliance with Henry II's half-sister Emma. To connect the final and consistent substitution of *princeps* for *rex* with the events of 1177 is a not unreasonable conjecture; it cannot be more.

The difference we have noticed between the titles used by the author of the *Brut* and in the charters of the rulers is marginal rather than major, because from the late twelfth century onwards these sources share one important feature: the title *princeps* is only applied to or used by the leading dynasties. Whereas there had been a multiplicity of kings in earlier Welsh society, including the early twelfth century, there were henceforth only princes of North and South Wales. None of the other nobles would in future call themselves princes.[29] We witness here an increased social and political differentiation, a process during which some dynasties rose while others declined to a status of nobility. There had been changes in the importance of various dynasties in Wales before, but these had been of a temporary nature, not affecting the constitutional position of the dynastic families.

What was the significance of the arrangement of 1177? For the first time, the greatest of the Welsh rulers had entered into a relationship with the

[27] This (therefore inconclusive) evidence has been discussed at some length by T. Jones Pierce, 'The age of the princes', in his collected papers *Medieval Welsh society*, ed. J. B. Smith (Cardiff, 1972), pp 28–9. Insufficient attention is normally paid to the fact that the *Brut* was originally written in Latin and that the terms which are of interest are thus the Latin terms *rex*, *princeps*, *dominus* rather than their Welsh equivalents *brenin*, *tywysog*, *arglwyd*.

[28] Bouquet, *Recueil*, xvi, no. 357, where Owain styles himself *Owinus rex Walliae*, and no. 358, where he occurs as *Ouinus Walliarum princeps*, *suus homo et amicus* (as above, note 20).

[29] A good example of this is a charter by Madog ap Gruffudd of Powys for Valle Crucis, where his *intitulatio* does not include the *princeps* title but where in the narrative part he is referred to as *princeps*, see Morris C. Jones, 'Valle Crucis abbey' in *Arch. Camb.* xii (1866), pp 412–17, esp. p. 415. I know of one example of a Powys ruler using the *princeps* title, *c.* 1206: see 'Gwenwynwyn, prince of Powys and lord of Arwistli, to the monks of Strata Marcella' etc. (National Library of Wales, Wynnstay Collection, no. 18), quoted from J. C. Davies, 'Strata Marcella documents' in *Montgomeryshire Collections,* li–lii (1949–52), no. 22, p. 178. A little later, Llywelyn became 'lord of Arwistli', see ibid., no. 29, pp. 182–3.

English king that was a two-sided agreement. In exchange for a recognition of their continued independent position in North and South Wales respectively, they promised peace to the English king, and this promise was further strengthened by the gift of small territories which they received from the king on feudal terms. King Henry II did not impose a new order upon Wales.[30] Instead he recognised developments that had occurred there and that were not of his making. Yet it must not be forgotten that the nucleation of political power in Wales was apparently acceptable to him. To deal with two partners in Wales rather than a dozen made the political game easier, and it was also better to have two rather powerful rulers there than one very powerful man. We are again on the level of conjecture, but we can assume that the order that took shape in Wales was not without advantages for the English king.

A word must now be said about the significance of the title *princeps*. We have seen already that this title was used by the most powerful dynasties only. It also appears to have been used only as long as the ruler in question was powerful. In addition, it was used only by one member of each dynasty at a given time. In short, the title of *princeps* in the legal documents signifies real political power which was indivisible. In this light, the transition from *rex* to *princeps* by some Welsh rulers expresses an increase in political power, not a decrease. *Princeps* signified a position which was higher than that of the earlier Welsh *rex*. In Wales, it denoted a ruler who was considerably more powerful than other Welsh lords, a title which was indivisible within the dynasty. In other words, *princeps* signified a non-royal but autonomous ruler, an institution known in Europe but hitherto unknown in Wales.[31]

While himself gaining in power, the Welsh *princeps* would, of course, thereby deprive other people of their influence. A reaction to this new constellation appears only once, but then in a clear light. In an undated charter, Madog ap Maelgwn, from a noble family of Maelienydd, gave land to the Cistercian abbey, Cwm Hir. At the end of his charter, we find a statement which has a clearly political ring about it: 'Likewise, my nobles *(optimates)* have sworn before many people that they will never tolerate the lordship of any prince over them'.[32] The only prince who could exercise any

[30] To this extent, I agree with Paul Barbier, *The age of Owain Gwynedd* (London, 1908) who writes on p. 96: '[Henry II] was ... a defender of the existing state of things; with this exception, that he aimed at a feudal rather than a tribal tenure'.

[31] For the non-royal ruler, see Wolfram, as above, note 18; for the latest discussion of *princeps* H. H. Kaminsky, 'Zum Sinngehalt des princeps-Titels Arichis II. von Benevent' in *Frühmittelalterliche Studien*, viii (1974), pp 81–92, with further references; also D. C. Skemer, 'The myth of petty kingship and a new periodisation of feudalism' in *Revue Belge de Philologie et d'Histoire*, li (1973), pp 249–70. Further Robert Feenstra, 'Jean de Blanot et la formule "rex Franciae in regno suo princeps est" ' in *Etudes d'Histoire du Droit Canonique dédiées à Gabriel le Bras*, ii (Paris, 1965), pp 885–95.

[32] 'Similiter et optimates coram multis juraverunt se nunquam passuros cuiuslibet super se principis dominium' (Tibbot, as in note 17 above), p. 65.

lordship over them at that time was Llywelyn ab Iorwerth. It is tempting to connect with this defiance of the growing power of that prince a letter that Llywelyn wrote to a number of Welsh noblemen. 'I firmly command that, as you respect me and my position' *(firmiter praecipio, quatinus me diligitis et honorem meum)*, that they should respect also the property of one of his relatives. The letter closes by singling out one man for this exhortation: 'and I say this especially to you, Madog ap Maelgwn, whom I have fed and exalted, not to repay my good deeds with bad deeds, but to respect my position *(honor)* so that I may henceforth as previously advise and help you'.[33] What this *honor* was which Llywelyn defended so eagerly, he expressed with unprecedented clarity in the *intitulatio* of the same letter: *'Lewelinus filius Gervasii Dei gratia princeps Norwalliae'*.[34] It underlines the extent to which the prince of North Wales had risen above the people of his country. Like the European rulers of his time, he interpreted his position to be one 'by the grace of God'.

These sentences were written at the conclusion of a power struggle in Gwynedd that had lasted for three decades and had seen a succession of princes of North Wales, all of whom at some time carried this title: Dafydd ap Owain, Gruffudd ap Cynan, and finally Llywelyn ab Iorwerth.[35] The last of these, who was to dominate Welsh politics for the next three decades, emerged after a fierce struggle which lasted ten years.[36] In the light of our discussion, Sir John Lloyd seems to be wide of the mark in his comment: 'in the north, the Welsh principalities had now attained such a position that the continuance of Welsh institutions and traditions seemed very well assured'.[37] On the contrary, Welsh institutions were readily abandoned, as will be shown later.

We see that, in another area where the Welsh institutions were maintained, the result was quite different. Rhys ap Gruffudd remained as *princeps*

[33] Dugdale, *Mon. Angl.*, vi, 496–7.

[34] Ibid.; for Carolingian parallels see Wolfram (as in note 18 above), p. 49. For an insular parallel of *c.* 1114 *(David Dei gratia comes)* see *Regesta regum Scottorum*, ed. G. W. S. Barrow, i (Edinburgh, 1960), no. 1, p. 131.

[35] For Gruffudd as *Griffinus Kynan filius Northwalliae princeps* see *Register and chronicle of the abbey of Aberconway*, ed. Henry Ellis (Camden series, 1847), pp 7–8; for a more detailed discussion Colin A. Gresham, 'The Aberconwy charter' in *Arch. Camb.* xciv (1939), pp 123–62. For the succession in Gwynedd see Lloyd, ii, 549–50 and 588 ff.

[36] The genealogy was brought into line with this political development, see Giraldus Cambrensis, *Opera*, vi, 167 and n.2, where the earlier genealogy of the North Welsh princes reads: 'David filius Oenei, Oeneus filius Griphini' etc., and the later version 'Leulinus filius Iorwerth filius Oenei, Iorwerth filius Oenei, Oeneus filius Griphini'. It is remarkable how Giraldus justified the victory of Llywelyn and thereby became a spokesman of the new order when he stressed that Llywelyn's father Iorwerth Drwyndwn ('Flatnose') was legitimate, while Dafydd ap Owain and Rhodri were illegitimate sons of Owain Gwynedd; see *Opera* vi, 134. For such changes in genealogies according to political changes, well know to anthropologists, see M. T. Clanchy, 'Remembering the past and the Good Old Law' in *History*, lv (1970), pp 165–76.

[37] Lloyd, ii 582.

South Walliae to his death in 1197. None of his numerous sons, all of whom were by then of a mature age, gained the position of their father, because all of them fought for the position of *princeps* which was indivisible. The nucleation of political power in South Wales came to an end with the death of Rhys, and it was replaced by the traditional political fragmentation. There was no *princeps* of South Wales at any time in the thirteenth century. Those historians who regret this development[38] do not indicate that thereby, in a manner not unlike that of Giraldus Cambrensis, they implicitly reject one of the essential features of the native Welsh society as well. ' "Lordship" in Wales was fully royal, but . . . this "lordship" was [also] easily divisible and readily transferable.'[39]

The death of the Lord Rhys provoked a long and skilful elegy from the author of the *Brut:*

> *Nobile Cambrensis cecidit dyadema decoris*
> *Hoc est Resus obit Cambria tota gemit*
> . . . . . .
> *Wallia iam viduata dolet ruitura dolori.*[40]

The events after his death can be followed in the account of the local native *Cronica de Wallia.*[41] In 1197 Rhys was succeeded by his son Gruffudd who, was, however, dispossessed by his brother Maelgwn soon afterwards.[42] Similarly, Maelgwn was unable to maintain his sole rule.[43] The fight for the hereditary portions continued among the sons, and when Gruffudd ap Rhys died in 1201 he was described by the annalist as *Griffinus magni Resi filius de iure Kambriae princeps et heres.*[44] The *Cronica* here suggests that Gruffudd was

---

[38] A. J. Roderick, 'The feudal relations between the English crown and the Welsh princes' in *History*, xxxvii (1952), p. 206.

[39] Edwards, as above, note 14, pp 169–70; see also *Littere Wallie*, ed. J. G. Edwards (Board of Celtic Studies, History and Law Series, no. v, Cardiff, 1940), pp xxxix–xl.

[40] This elegy occurs only in the *Brut*, Peniarth MS 20 version, ed. Thomas Jones (Board of Celtic Studies, History and Law Series, no. vi, Cardiff, 1941), pp 140–41. It should be noted that the names used for Wales are the new ones, *Cambria* and *Wallia*, not *Britannia*.

[41] Hereafter cited as C.W. See Kathleen Hughes, 'The Welsh Latin chronicles: *Annales Cambriae* and related texts' in *Proceedings of the British Academy*, lix (1973), pp 3–28, esp. pp 17–18.

[42] From him there exists the transcript of a charter which contains at least an echo of his status in his *intitulatio:* 'Mailgun filius Resi principis South Walliae' (National Library of Wales, MS 12362 (Alcwyn C. Evans 7), unpaginated 19th century transcript).

[43] See *Annales Cambriae*, ed. J. W. ab Ithel (Rolls Series, 1860), p. 62, *s.a.* 1200: 'Mailgonus filius Resi, ut vidit quod solus terram patris sui tenere non potuit, quin Francis vel Grifino fratri suo partem daret, elegit potius cum hostibus partiri quam cum fratre'.

[44] *Cronica de Wallia*, ed. Thomas Jones in *Bulletin of the Board of Celtic Studies* xii (1946), p. 32. 'magnus Resus' in this context clearly does not mean Rhys 'the great' but Rhys 'the elder'; see also *C.W., s.a.* 1204, 1215. The same usage of the term 'magnus' in Giraldus, *Opera*. vi, 143: 'Oeneus magnus', translated by Lloyd, ii, 488, as 'the great', and v, 229: 'Nesta magni filia Resi filii Griffini consobrina'. For a general assessment see Walther Kienast, 'Magnus = der Ältere' in *Historische Zeitschrift*, ccv (1967), pp 1–14. Perhaps the Welsh historian will have to learn also to speak of Llywelyn ab Iorwerth no longer as Llywelyn Fawr but of Llywelyn the elder, if the

the man who should have inherited the principality of his father. That he failed was an indication of the strength of the old order in the south, an order well attested in earlier Welsh history, that of the division of the patrimony among all the surviving sons, illegitimate as well as legitimate.[45] When we take note of this tension between tradition and political innovation, we shall have a better understanding of the violence among the rulers about which the Welsh chronicles tell us. Various methods were used to make relatives unfit for succession to their hereditary portions, ranging from imprisonment, blinding, and castration to plain killing.[46]

With the turn of the century, Wales was about to enter a new phase in its political development. The system that had emerged over the past two decades and had won the approval of Henry II in 1177, that of two major native principalities in Wales, did not last. The principality worked out in Gwynedd, but in South Wales the old order prevailed. The events after the death of Rhys ap Gruffudd show clearly that the sense of Welsh identity could as yet be expressed only insufficiently in the political field.

It is all the more important that in those years there emerged another factor which worked more successfully as an integrating element in Welsh native society. I refer to Welsh law. The earliest extant text of the Welsh laws, written in Latin, dates from the closing years of the twelfth century, and in the course of the following century three further versions of the laws were written, both in Latin and in Welsh. It has been customary to distinguish three regional groups in those texts associated with the greater dynasties of the past, with Gwynedd, Gwent, and Deheubarth.[47] It is significant that the two earliest of these law books, one in Latin (Red. A), the other in Welsh *(Llyfr Iorwerth)*, appear to have been written under the auspices of Rhys ap Gruffudd and Llywelyn ab Iorwerth respectively.[48]

thirteenth century historians called him 'magnus' in order to distinguish him from Llywelyn ap Gruffudd. On the succession in Deheubarth see also Lloyd, ii, 568, 577, 585–6.

[45] From the masses of evidence I select the following: *Vitae sanctorum Britanniae et genealogiae*, ed. A.W.Wade-Evans (Board of Celtic Studies, History and Law Series, no. ix, Cardiff, 1944), pp 24, 148, 172; *Brut* (R.B.H.), pp 47, 108, 119, 162, 195–7, 207; Giraldus, *Opera*. vi, 134, 211, 225. This principle is recalled even in the statute of Wales of 1284, xiii, ed. Ivor Bowen, 1908, pp 25–6: 'whereas the custom is otherwise in Wales than in England concerning succession to an inheritance, inasmuch as the inheritance is partible among heirs male . . .'. This as against J. B. Smith (as above, note 20) who wrote: 'historians have burdened us with the view that Wales was a land where there were unalterable rules which provided that the royal estate was subject to partible succession' (p. 13). See also above, n. 39.

[46] Imprisonment: *Brut* (R.B.H.) *s.a.* 1102, p. 47; *s.a.* 1174, 1175, p. 165; *s.a.* 1197, etc.; blinding: ibid., *s.a.* 1187, 1193; castration: ibid., *s.a.* 1131, 1152, 1175, *Annales Cambriae, s.a.* 1128, 1166 (and cf. *The Latin texts of the Welsh laws*, ed. H. D. Emanuel (Board of Celtic Studies, History and Law Series, no. xx, Cardiff, 1967), Red. D, p. 343: 'Exulet a curia illa legis turpitudo, scilicet membri virilis arreptio'); killing: *Brut, s.a.* 1125, 1170 etc.

[47] See H. D. Emanuel, 'Studies in the Welsh laws' in *Celtic Law Studies in Wales*, ed. Elwyn Davies (Cardiff, 1963) p. 84.

[48] Emanuel, *Latin texts* (as above, note 46), passim.

Variations between the different recensions are of a sufficiently minor nature to allow us to speak of one Welsh law, or, as became customary in Wales, of the law of Hywel Dda ('the Good').

The editor of the Latin texts of the Welsh law books assures us that the oldest extant manuscript, National Library of Wales MS Peniarth 28 (Red. A), is probably not more than two stages removed from the exemplar. We have therefore in the legal sector the same transition from the old to the new order as in other sectors, shown in the writing down of native traditions. The date of the compilation makes it very difficult to distinguish in each individual case between what is old and what is more recent, since even very recent changes were woven into the texts, but the eminent position reserved for the kings of both Aberffraw and Dinefwr seems to reflect the political nucleation around the princes of Gwynedd and Deheubarth in the late twelfth century very adequately.[49]

Considerable attention has been paid by scholars to the dating of these compilations. They are associated with the Welsh king Hywel, who died in 949 (950).[50] It is clear, however, that at least the prologues to the law books, which give an account of the motives and methods of their compilation, show signs of composition in the twelfth, not the tenth century.[51] Nevertheless, the laws are always associated, even outside the prologue, with king Hywel,[52] and we must look into this question more closely.

The *Brut y Tywysogyon* commemorates Hywel's obit as follows: 'and King Hywel the Good, son of Cadell, the head and glory of all the Britons, died'.[53] This chronicle exists, however, only in a fourteenth-century translation into Welsh from a Latin exemplar now lost; when we turn to one of its sources, the earliest version of the *Annales Cambriae,* the corresponding entry is more modest: *Higuel rex Brittonum obiit.*[54] Fortunately, we have independent evidence for the *Selbstaussage* of Hywel. On a coin which has been found he occurs as *Hopael rex.*[55] In order to see the entry in the *Annales*

[49] Ibid., p. 110: 'non redditur aurum nisi regi Aberfrau et Dynever', and similarly pp 194, 317, 436. See also the gradual appearance in the laws of the terms *Norwallia* and *Sudwallia* respectively, ibid., index III.

[50] Annales Cambriae, version A, in Egerton Phillimore (ed.), 'The *Annales Cambriae* and old Welsh genealogies from Harleian MS 3859' in *Y Cymmrodor* ix (1888), a manuscript composed in the last half of the tenth century (ibid., p. 144), extant now in an early twelfth-century copy (ibid., p. 146).

[51] J. G. Edwards, 'The historical study of the Welsh law books' in *Transactions of the Royal Historical Society* 5th series, xii (1962), pp 141–55.

[52] Emanuel, *Latin texts,* index III, *s.v.* Hywel Dda.

[53] *Brut* (R.B.H.), p. 13.

[54] Annales Cambriae, loc. cit., as in note 50 above, p. 169. Closely parallel is the entry in the Annals of Ulster: 'Oel ri bretan moritur', *A.U.,* ed. William M. Hennessey, i (Dublin, 1887), p. 466. This reference was kindly supplied by Mr Charles Doherty with whom I had the opportunity to discuss many aspects of this paper.

[55] See W. P. Carlyon-Britton, 'Saxon, Norman and Plantagenet coinage in Wales' in *Transactions of the Honourable Society of Cymmrodorion,* 1905–6, pp 3–4.

Cambriae in its proper proportion, it has to be stressed that an unqualified *rex Brittonum* is a title by which only Hywel is honoured. He also attested one charter of king Eadred of Wessex as *rex*.[56] Clearly, then, Hywel was a man of considerable political power. On the other hand, the epithet 'the Good' *(bonus* or *dda)* does not seem to be contemporary. It occurs for the first time in the prologues to the laws, and is thus itself of twelfth-century date, certainly later than MS A of the *Annales Cambriae*.

By the late twelfth century, Hywel was certainly well known even outside legal circles as Hywel 'the Good', and in this manner he occurs in the genealogies of the South Welsh dynasty in Giraldus's *Descriptio Kambriae*.[57] In assessing the historical fact of the connection between King Hywel and the Welsh laws, as distinct from their compilation, our verdict must remain a cautious 'not proven, but very likely'.[58] On the other hand, we can call the historical belief in this connection, from the late twelfth century onwards, a fact and as such a powerful integrating factor for Welsh society.

The first application of this appears in the year 1201 in a treaty concluded between the English crown and Llywelyn ab Iorwerth, with which we move again to the level of political discussion. In the king's absence, the treaty was concluded between the justiciar, Geoffrey fitz Peter, and the prince of North Wales. The latter swore, together with his nobles *(majores terre sue)* to be faithful to the king. Thereafter, Llywelyn received from the justiciar all the tenements which he then held and promised to perform homage for these tenements to the king later. Should there be in future any disputes concerning these tenements, Llywelyn would have the choice between the law of England and the law of Wales to have his case decided.[59]

From this treaty we can glimpse precisely the constitutional position of Llywelyn towards the English crown at that time. He and the nobles of his land swore fealty to the king. In addition, he himself would be tied by the act of homage to the king for some tenements and, we should add for the sake of clarity, for these tenements only. Apart from them, the area he ruled over was called *terra sua*, and the same term was applied in the same treaty to the king's land, *terra domini regis*. The situation thus resembles that of

[56] P. H. Sawyer, *Anglo-Saxon charters: an annotated list and bibliography* (Royal Historical Society, Guides and Handbooks, London, 1968), no. 550; and see Carlyon-Britton (as in note 55), pp 11–13; for other titles: *rex genedotae, rex demetorum, rex guent, rex pouis, rex cetericiaun* see Phillimore (as above, note 50), pp 155–66.

[57] *Opera* vi, 167: 'Oeneus filius Hoeli da, id est, Hoeli boni, Hoelus filius Cadelh'.

[58] Cf. Emanuel, *Latin texts*, p. 84: 'there seems . . . every reason to accept the traditional connexion between Hywel Dda and the Welsh laws'. The belief that the *codification* dates from the tenth century is, however, still widely held; see most recently Dafydd Jenkins, as well as, earlier, D. A. Binchy in *Celtic law papers. Introductory to Welsh medieval law and government* (Brussels, 1973), pp 17, 27, 94, 113, 120; against, however, see ibid. J. G. Edwards, pp 139, 150.

[59] *Rotuli litterarum patentium* (Record Commission, 1835), I, i, 8b; also Rymer, *Foedera*, I, i (Rec. Commission, 1816), p. 84; cf. also Lloyd, ii, 615.

1177, with the important difference that for 1201 we have the official text, and in this text Llywelyn is not granted the princely title.

On the other hand, after the death of Dafydd ap Owain, Llywelyn received, perhaps in 1205, the lands of Ellesmere 'which had for so long been held by a scion of the house of Gwynedd'.[60] It is tempting to compare Ellesmere with the Honour of Huntingdon, held by the Scottish king from the English crown at various times in the twelfth and thirteenth centuries, as 'subordinate tenures held by a ruler who within his own domains claimed to be sovereign'.[61]

It is an indication of the fundamental changes introduced into Wales when we see that the political development of Gwynedd in the thirteenth century centred on two issues: (1) the extent to which the integrity and indivisibility of the principality could be maintained; and (2) the process of internal feudalisation. These two points, though interrelated, show one essential difference when observed from England: the maintenance of the integrity and indivisibility of the principality would be a maintenance of the *status quo;* internal feudalisation, on the other hand, would introduce a new element.

The process of feudalisation within native Wales seems to have come very quickly. The first evidence for it dates from 1208 when Llywelyn showed his strength against Maelgwn ap Rhys of Deheubarth.[62] Obviously profiting from the difficulties which King John encountered in his own country, Llywelyn was able to assume a position of a more general leadership, and, in 1212, in the words of the *Cronica de Wallia*: 'the Welsh conspired against the king of England, . . . and they chose for themselves one head, namely Llywelyn, prince of North Wales'. Three years later we hear that one of the leading nobles, Gwenwynwyn of Powys, had done homage to Llywelyn in written form. No wonder that the same *Cronica* spoke about Llywelyn as 'then holding the monarchy and leadership of nearly all Wales'.[63]

It cannot be established in all clarity to what extent this situation was changed after John's death and the accession of Henry III. In 1218, Llywelyn as well as all the magnates of Wales performed homage and fealty to the new king. On this occasion, we read for the first time the title *princeps North Walliae* being conceded to Llywelyn in an English official document.[64] It was fully in line with this increasing independence of Gwynedd that

[60] Lloyd, ii, 616–17; also ibid., p. 553 and passim.

[61] G. W. S. Barrow, *Feudal Britain* (London, 1956), p. 243.

[62] *C.W., s.a.* 1207 = 1208: 'Advenientes vero patriotae universi tam sibi quam filiis Griffini homagium fecerunt'.

[63] *C.W., s.a.* 1215: 'tunc temporis tocius Wallie monarchiam fere atque principatum tenente'; on the homage of Gwenwynwyn, ibid., 'cum cyrographis et cartis tenorem confederacionis et homagii sui continentibus'. See also *Brut* (R.B.H.), pp 205–9.

[64] *Foedera*, I, i, 150.

Llywelyn claimed in 1222 that he had 'no less liberty than the king of Scotland'.[65]

Hand in hand with this process went the question of the succession in Gwynedd. Breaking with two Welsh customs at the same time, Llywelyn intended to pass over his elder illegitimate son, Gruffudd, and give the principality to his younger legitimate son, Dafydd, alone. In 1220, he obtained for this the consent of Henry III's regents, and in 1238 'all the princes of Wales swore allegiance to Dafydd ap Llywelyn ab Iorwerth at Strata Florida'.[66] His brother Gruffudd had been imprisoned before, and he went to prison again, probably after Llywelyn's death in April 1240.[67] Under Dafydd, there followed a rapid collapse of the principality. On his first confrontation with Henry III, in May 1240, Dafydd had to perform homage for North Wales (the first time we have undisputed evidence for this), and acknowledge (also for the first time, so it seems) the king as feudal overlord of all Welsh 'barons'.[68] Fifteen months later, after another defeat, he had to submit to even harsher conditions: while Dafydd had to concede once again the points raised earlier, now, in addition, he was forced to hand over to the king his half-brother, Gruffudd; he also had to return to the king, forever, the lands of Ellesmere.[69] The arrangement of 1177 was finally extinguished.

King Henry III, however, worked only for his own convenience; early in August 1241, he had concluded an agreement with the wife of the imprisoned Gruffudd ap Llywelyn, in which she claimed, on behalf of her husband, the hereditary portion to which he was entitled under Welsh law.[70] Henry forced Dafydd to hand over Gruffudd who was not, however, subsequently reinstated in North Wales but again imprisoned, this time by the English king in the Tower of London. There Gruffudd was killed in 1244 in an attempt to escape.

After Dafydd had died in 1246 without heirs, Henry III tried his best to impose Welsh customs on Wales again, to his own advantage. He forced the joint succession in Gwynedd of two (of the four) sons of Gruffudd ap Llywelyn, Owain and Llywelyn, and formally forbade a renewal of the internal feudalisation of Wales.[71] The English king, however, could keep

[65] *Calendar of ancient correspondence concerning Wales*, ed. J. G. Edwards (Board of Celtic Studies, History and Law Series, no. ii, Cardiff, 1935), p. 24.

[66] *Brut* (R.B.H.), p. 235. For more details see M. Richter, 'David ap Llywelyn, the first Prince of Wales' in *Welsh History Review*, v (1970–71), pp 205–19, esp. 207–8.

[67] See Gwyn A. Williams, 'The succession to Gwynedd, 1238–1247' in *Bulletin of the Board of Celtic Studies* xx(1962–4), pp 393–413.

[68] *Littere Wallie* (hereafter cited as *L.W.*), ed. J. G. Edwards (Board of Celtic Studies, History and Law Series, no. v, Cardiff, 1940), pp 5–6; also ibid., pp xlvii–xlviii.

[69] *L.W.*, p. 9.

[70] *L.W.*, no. 78, p. 52.

[71] *L.W.*, no. 3, pp 7–8.

Wales divided only so long as he could effectively impose his authority. The two brothers did not break with the letter of the arrangement of 1247, but certainly with its spirit when, in 1251, they concluded confederacies *(amicitia)* with other Welsh nobles.[72] While England fell victim to the barons' revolt, Llywelyn was able to oust his brother and then again receive the homage of Welsh nobles.[73] By then he had assumed a new title, *princeps Wallie*. He was recognised as such by the crown in 1267.[74] The transformation of native Welsh society was complete. Feudal concepts had overcome the political fragmentation that had been one of the typical features of tribal Wales and had resulted in a nucleation of power with Llywelyn ap Gruffudd, prince of Wales, at the centre. He was to be the feudal overlord in native Wales and tenant-in-chief to the English king. The treaty of 1267 also provided that this arrangement should last beyond Llywelyn's lifetime.

International treaties have at all times tended to use grand words which were forgotten as soon as the political constellation changed. The principality of Wales which had emerged in 1267 was no exception. Only ten years later, a military defeat of Llywelyn by Edward I heralded the approaching end of the principality: it was to last only to Llywelyn's death. This provision of a new treaty (of Conway, 1277) was later actually implemented. Yet before this came about, the spirit of Welsh independence asserted itself strongly once again. It was articulated by a great number of people, and can still be perceived in the replies given by the Welsh nobles and freemen to members of a royal inquiry set up at the command of Edward I. It is impressive to hear how the Welsh on that occasion measured themselves against other European nations in demanding that their own national law be guaranteed to them. The sons of Maredudd ap Owain expressed this idea forcefully when they said that

all Christian peoples have their own laws and customs in their own lands; . . . they themselves and their ancestors had in their lands unalterable laws and customs until these were taken away from them by the English after the last war.[75]

Llywelyn himself applied to the king for a guarantee of Welsh law for Wales when he said before the royal tribunal:

Each province under the rule of the lord king should have its own laws and customs. This should also be granted to Wales, just as all other nations under the rule of the

---

[72] *L.W.*, no. 284, pp 160–61 *amicitia* is clearly a technical term; see Wolfgang Fritze, 'Die fränkische Schwurfreundschaft in der Merowingerzeit' in *Zeitschrift für Rechtsgeschichte, Germanistische Abteilung*, lxxi (1954), pp 74–125.

[73] *L.W.*, no. 68, p. 45.

[74] First evidence for his own use of the title: *L.W.*, no. 317, p. 184; official recognition in treaty of Montgomery, *L.W.*, no. 1, pp 1–4.

[75] *Reg. Peckham* (as above, note 12), p. 454.

lord king have their own laws and customs according to their own language.[76]

More unanimously than ever before, the free Welsh expressed their sense of belonging together in the terms of living under their own native law. Political unity was accepted more reluctantly, but it was accepted in preference to rule from England, by the majority of the nobles. Those who had suffered harm in their personal status in the process of feudalisation of native Wales which we have described were faced with a choice between two evils, and the lesser of these was the rule by a Welsh prince. In this manner, their identification was more legal-cultural than political.

In this paper I have applied some gentle European breeze to the Celtic mists in Wales. The political structure thereby exposed resembles in some ways that of other European societies at that time. Once the last word has been said about the prince of Wales, the non-royal ruler in a feudalised society, attention should be turned to the aristocracy, a social class of royal stock in Wales as in Ireland, and just as essential to the running of the state as the king or prince. An important theme of later medieval Europe is the growing national awareness of the aristocracy, in fragmented Germany just as much as in the more centralised England and France during the hundred years war. In Wales we have stopped with the first glimpses of this social class. It is a theme that requires much detailed work, but it is a worthwhile objective because it will readjust the historian's outlook. The source-material seduces him anyway into being too 'royal' in his approach, as K. B. McFarlane has so powerfully reminded us.

[76] *The Welsh assize roll, 1277–1284,* ed. J. C. Davies (Board of Celtic Studies, History and Law Series, no. vii, Cardiff, 1940), p. 266. For more detail see Richter (as above, note 1), passim.

III

Colonial identity in early seventeenth-century Ireland

Aidan Clarke

This was conceived as a discussion paper, and it may be described most appropriately in the language of the editor of the *Journal of Modern History* as a 'trial balloon'. It concentrates upon deploying an argument rather than upon parading evidence, and it reports upon thought in process rather than upon work in progress. What I have done has been to pick up certain hints contained in recent work, to explore some of the implications of emerging lines of thought, and to put these together to suggest a revised assessment of the components that made up the identity of the Old English group in early seventeenth century Ireland.

I have two related points of departure. The first of these is what Margaret MacCurtain has described as the gap 'between Dr Edwards' Anglo-Irish of the 1580s and Dr Clarke's Old English of the 1620s'.[1] The second is the gap which I observe between Fr Bradshaw's 'Anglo-Irish political nationalism'[2] of the later sixteenth century and the narrow sectionalism typical of Old English political objectives in the early seventeenth century, a gap which leaves Patrick Darcy in 1614[3] still well short of the position attributed by Fr Bradshaw to Speaker Walsh in the Irish parliament in 1585.

To close those gaps is not my principal concern. I hope that that will be one of the by-products of an attempt to tease out some of the effects of the counter-reformation in Ireland. To sketch the outlines of an explanation, however, will serve to introduce certain themes which are central to my purpose. The exclusion of the colonial community from influence and involvement in the public life of Ireland resulted from two related, but separate, thrusts. One was the introduction of protestantism. The other was the institution of a process of increasingly direct rule, the anglicisation of the Irish governmental system. Colonists were already being superseded

[1] Margaret MacCurtain, *Tudor and Stuart Ireland* (Dublin, 1972), p. 125. The allusions are to R. Dudley Edwards, 'Ireland, Elizabeth I and the counter-reformation' in S. T. Bindoff (ed.), *Elizabethan government and society* (London, 1961), pp 315–39; and Aidan Clarke, *The Old English in Ireland, 1625–42* (London, 1966).

[2] Brendan Bradshaw, 'The beginnings of modern Ireland' in Brian Farrell (ed.), *The Irish parliamentary tradition* (Dublin, 1973), pp 83–7.

[3] Clarke, *Old English*, ch. VIII.

in positions of power, honour, and profit before the oath of supremacy became a statutory qualification for holding office; after it had done so, some catholics nevertheless continued to hold office and many colonists who became protestant failed to secure places against the competition of incoming Englishmen. In the beginning, in short, the source of discrimination was less evidently connected with religion than with a new style of anglo-centric government which relegated the established settlers to an inferior position. Their response was correspondingly politicised. The developing sense of community which Fr Bradshaw has delineated grew from reaction to an external threat which, though it possessed a religious dimension, was more obviously secular.

It is for this reason that Dr Canny, in a recent O'Donnell lecture on the emergence of the Old English in the late sixteenth century,[4] was able to trace a development which rested partly upon a series of calculated political choices in response to government pressures, and partly upon the cultivation of humanism, and was able to dismiss the religious component as a characteristic of the second generation. But it was, of course, precisely this second generation which styled itself Old English. The words 'old English' were used by Spenser in the 1590s, as Dr Canny has noted,[5] but they were always used adjectivally: the collective noun did not appear until the seventeenth century. When it did appear, its signification was so exact that to use it retrospectively merely confuses the issue. The difference between the sixteenth century Anglo-Irish and the seventeenth century Old English was that the former lacked any active principle of self-determination, being simply 'the English of Irish birth',[6] whereas the latter possessed a dynamic coherence which derived from the unifying force of religion. To illustrate the contrast, it is sufficient to consider the example of the two spokesmen of Anglo-Irish political nationalism singled out by Fr Bradshaw, Nicholas Walsh and Richard Hadsor. Both of these men lived into the Old English era, but not as Old English. One became chief justice of the common pleas in Ireland;[7] the other moved to England where he became an official of the privy council, with special responsibility for Irish affairs:[8] both were

---

[4] Nicholas P. Canny, *The formation of the Old English élite in Ireland* (Dublin, 1975).

[5] Ibid., p. 31, note 71.

[6] The term Anglo-Irish was not unknown: on a single occasion, Richard Stanyhurst abandoned his usual locutions—'empaled dwellers', 'descendants of the English', and so on—and wrote of the 'Anglo-Hiberni' *(De rebus in Hibernia gestis libri quattuor* (Antwerp, 1584), p. 30).

[7] Nicholas Walsh: a brief account of his career appeared in C. Litton Falkiner, *Essays*, pp 231–2.

[8] Richard Hadsor, who returned to Ireland as a member of the 1622 commission of inquiry, and was involved in the negotiations which led to the 'graces' in 1628, was last recorded as a member of the English privy council's commission for Irish affairs late in 1632 *(Cal. S.P.Ire., 1625–32*, pp 680–83).

protestants. The transition from Anglo-Irish to Old English was not, in short, a simple progression. It was, rather, a process of differentiation which occurred in response to certain changes, or differences of accentuation, at the outset of James's reign.

At that stage, the principle of exclusion became specifically and explicitly religious. The oath of supremacy was uniformly enforced in the central administration and the long-drawn-out process of dispensing with the services of catholics reached an abrupt and exemplary conclusion when the resolutely catholic Sir John Everard was replaced in the court of king's bench by the ambiguously conformist Dominick Sarsfield.[9] At the same time, direct rule was abandoned, and an increasingly large measure of control, including the lord deputyship itself, was entrusted to locally-based protestants. Both the nature and the direction of the threat altered accordingly: it no longer came from outside, but from within the enlarged community which had been created by Elizabethan settlement, and the source of discrimination was now unmistakably religious.

The Jacobean devolution of power to the colony in Ireland changed the possibilities and the perspectives. It was no longer relevant to develop a view of Ireland as a political unit separate from England, self-regulating, under the same crown. What was now at issue was not the distribution of power between England and Ireland, but the distribution of power within an 'entirely subdued' Ireland, and a satisfactory balance might well depend upon English intervention. The issue resolved itself into a simple sequence of questions. Were political rights derived from English descent, or from protestantism? And if from protestantism, then how was the special position of those of English descent who were not protestant to be defined and preserved? As a political entity, the Old English group was generated by the collective need of the catholic colonists to gain favourable answers to these questions, and by their efforts to do this through the development of a special relationship with the crown. This was a fairly self-conscious process. The catholic colonial community had not previously been united, not even in the nine years war: some of them had perhaps been moving towards a notion, though no doubt a largely rhetorical notion, of Ireland as a distinct unit, rather than towards a sense of colonial identity. But the fact of conquest altered the available options. To survive in the new order, and to counterbalance the impediment of catholicism, an affirmation of Englishry became an essential requisite, if not a sufficient one. At the same time, ironically, the scope of the government's effective competence was such that when it took measures to enforce the act of uniformity, its activities were largely confined to the old colony. Irish areas were almost unaffected. The

[9] Donal F. Cregan, 'Irish recusant lawyers in politics in the reign of James I' in *Irish Jurist*, N.S., v, pt ii (1970), p. 307.

unit of opposition was neatly defined by the area of government operation, and the first mobilisation of the political strength of the catholics of the old colony was induced by the need to resist the enforcement of the 1605 proclamation selectively against colonial catholicism. After success had been achieved, the continued evolution of the Old English group was based upon a general desire to eliminate religious barriers to the retention of some privileges and the recovery of others. Having dealt with the implied proposition that catholicism was more reprehensible in persons of English origin than in others, they set out to establish the proposition that it was less so. In these new conditions, the 'English of Irish birth' ceased to have common interests and priorities: the catholic element in that largely pale and borough-centred group separated out, and made new connections with the rural colonial gentry of Munster and Connacht. There were, of course, distinctions to be blurred. Not all the catholic colonists could reasonably lay claim to the rewards of past good conduct, so the development of the Old English group was associated with the selective appropriation by all of one element in the colonial tradition, that of the 'Queen's loyal subjects'.

The creed of the group was based on the premise that catholicism and loyalty were perfectly compatible. If this were so, it followed that for catholics of English origin to hold property, exercise political and administrative functions, and enjoy religious freedom was in no way contrary to the interests of the state. But problems arose. One was, of course, that recent experience scarcely verified the claim: on the other hand, it did not conclusively contradict it either. More intractable was the fact that the theoretical validity of the premise was open to serious doubt, and this was a matter of critical importance in dealing with a king who was always prone to focus upon the intellectual dimensions of political problems and who enjoyed nothing better than an opportunity to expose the inconsistencies of others.

The point at issue was ushered in dramatically, in the lord deputy's camp outside Waterford in May 1603, when Mountjoy, with the assistance of an oddly convenient volume of St Augustine, engaged in a learned argument with the vicar apostolic of Waterford and Lismore on the subject of catholic teaching on temporal obedience.[10] Their debate was inconclusive, but prophetic. The question remained basic to relations between the new government and the old colony, and became fundamental to the rationalisation of the claims of the Old English. The fact was that the pragmatic willingness of the Old English to entertain dual allegiances to church and state, however accurately it may have reflected their feelings, invited disbelief. It did so for two reasons. First, because it stood in direct and unconvincing contradiction to the common assumptions of English pro-

---

[10] The vicar-apostolic's description of the encounter is conveniently summarised in Frederick M. Jones, *Mountjoy: last Elizabethan deputy* (Dublin, 1958), pp 171–2.

testants, who were brought up to believe that in the catholic church Christianity had degenerated into an erroneous and idolatrous organisation, characterised by lay ignorance and clerical power, which aimed at worldly dominion and forbade its members to give loyalty to a temporal power.[11] Second, because protestants were correct in thinking that the Old English stance was an evasion. The true question was not whether the loyal professions of catholics were genuine, but whether they were free to make them. The truth was that Rome did claim authority to depose rulers for offences against religion and the natural law. The truth was that Pius V had excommunicated Queen Elizabeth and had absolved her subjects from their allegiance to her. And the truth was that the pope was ultimately the sole judge of the validity of professions of loyalty. In short, even those who experienced no difficulty in reconciling their spiritual allegiance to the pope with their temporal obedience to the king could not be confident that their position was doctrinally valid. The willingness of an individual to yield temporal obedience, or even to subscribe to an oath of allegiance and formally deny the pope's power of deposition, though it might attest his personal loyalty, could not exempt him from his ultimate spiritual obligations. In the final analysis, he had no choice but to obey a papal ruling on obedience.

When King James, in 1613, forced three prominent Old English spokesmen to confront their dilemma, and to choose between pope and king in his presence, their responses covered the full spectrum of possible reaction. Patrick Barnewall readily conceded that the pope had no power of deposition; Thomas Luttrell was persuaded to do likewise by three months in the Tower of London; William Talbot stuck fast to his contention that only the pope could answer the royal question. The royal question was a valid question, but it was also a royal obsession. This was a subject upon which James had thought and written extensively in the years since papal opposition had frustrated his early efforts to devise an oath of allegiance for the use of English catholics.[12] It was the king's preoccupation, rather than any anxious crisis of conscience of their own, which created the Old English dilemma. The tension in which they lived came from without, not from within, and the emphasis upon the need to reconcile divided loyalties was imposed upon them. Their difficulties were created by their need for royal support, and by the conditions upon which it might be forthcoming. A failure to recognise that this was the case has distorted the balance of

---

[11] Robin Clifton, 'Fear of popery', in Conrad Russell (ed.), *The origins of the English civil war* (London, 1973), pp 144–67. Carol Z. Wiener, 'The beleaguered isle: a study of Elizabethan and early Jacobean anti-catholicism' in *Past and Present*, no. 51 (1971), pp 27–62.

[12] The difficulties of English catholics, and their responses, have been examined recently by Elliot Rose, *Cases of conscience: alternatives open to recusants and puritans under Elizabeth I and James I* (Cambridge, 1975).

understanding in the past, by creating the impression that the distinctive feature of Old English catholicism lay in the fact that they voluntarily equivocated in this respect to the extent required by their socio-political needs. They were catholic, but politique.[13]

This distortion has been increased by the tendency in some recent works to write of the development of catholicism in Ireland without reference to the differences between the native and colonial sectors of Irish society. It is, of course, only in recent years that we have learned to distinguish between different kinds of catholics in Ireland in this period. When Bagwell and Wilson wrote, catholics were catholics without further refinement. In the same way, in the writings of Fr Jones[14] and Professor O'Farrell[15] catholicism is catholicism. This is an old view: in 1614, it formed the basis of George Carew's celebrated forecast that the interests which separated the Old English from the Irish would prove weaker than the cohesive force of the religion which they shared, and that before long they would find themselves in union against the English.[16] The presumption which underlies this approach is that the distinguishing feature of the Old English was their possession of political attitudes and commitments which stood in unresolved contradiction to their religious beliefs: they shared their ancestry with the English and their religion with the Irish, and were defined by the resultant tension. I have contributed to this formulation myself, while resisting the simplistic attraction of treating the involvement of the Old English in the 1641 rebellion as a verification of Carew's analysis.[17] But that interpretation now seems to me to require reconsideration in the light of the gradual realisation that the divisions which had characterised religion in Ireland for centuries persisted into the seventeenth century and were given a new significance by the counter-reformation. It has become necessary to look more closely at the nature of catholicism in the early Stuart period, and to do so suggests revised conclusions about the identity of the Old English.

Too often, the historiography of the counter-reformation in Ireland has rhetorically invoked the spirit of the movement to the neglect of its substance. In recent years, our knowledge of the detail has proliferated, but the organising principle has tended to remain unaltered. The focus has continued to rest upon the central aim, and the ultimate achievement, of preserving the faith. The ways in which this was to have been done, the ways in which it actually was done, the nature of the faith itself, are matters which are only beginning to receive systematic attention. John Bossy has

[13] Cf. Clarke, *Old English*, pp 21–2.
[14] Frederick M. Jones, *The counter-reformation* (Dublin, 1967).
[15] Patrick O'Farrell, *Ireland's English question* (London, 1971), chs 1, 2.
[16] *Cal. Carew MSS, 1603–25*, pp 305–10.
[17] Aidan Clarke, *The Graces, 1625–41* (Dundalk, 1968), p. 32.

recently reminded us that the aim of the counter-reformation was to preserve the faith by improving its practice, and that this was to be achieved to a marked degree through organisational improvement.[18] The desired model was a tidily hierarchic system, with clear lines of authority, resting on well-defined parish units in which uniform observance of the tridentine decrees regulating attendance at mass and participation in the sacraments could be enforced, in which catechetical instruction could be given, and in which standards of moral behaviour could be supervised. The spirit of the counter-reformation is of course expressed in part in the romantic image of the mendicant missionary conducting outdoor mass on a specially consecrated altarstone, but it is conveyed with greater authority in the busy programme of Francis Kirwan, as vicar general of Tuam, making provision for older priests to be properly instructed in church ceremony, rusticating the sinful clergy, suspending the ignorant from their pastoral duty, reducing the pluralists to a single parish, endlessly adjudicating the disputes of the laity, and arranging to have adulterers publicly whipped.[19]

In Ireland, these two aspects of the counter-reformation were interlocked. They represented successive phases which in practice discordantly overlapped. In the first instance, the movement was in many respects an unstructured, impulsive, missionary thrust, resting upon the continental seminaries, and intruding upon an older tradition of clerical ignorance, laxity and evasion. But it was also part of a wider campaign to make good local deficiencies and suppress local variations in the interests of securing rigorous conformity to new and higher standards of spiritual observance. That task required more than fervour. All the evidence suggests that although there was a great deal of priestly activity in Ireland in the first years of the seventeenth century, it was unevenly distributed, poorly coordinated and inadequately supervised.[20] The bulk of the clergy lacked appropriate preparation to qualify them to introduce change. The supply of new-style clergy was chiefly governed by the haphazard evolution and the individualistic policies of the continental colleges. The secular and regular clergy acted independently of one another; indeed, in rivalry with one another. And the longstanding practice of appointing vicars apostolic instead of bishops left the catholic church in Ireland without effective direction or control. In short, the minimal organisational requirements of

---

[18] John Bossy, 'The counter-reformation and the people of catholic Ireland, 1596–1641' in *Hist. Studies*, viii, 155–70.

[19] John Lynch, *The life and death of the most reverend Francis Kirwan*, ed. C. P. Meehan (Dublin, 1884), pp 55, 63–7, 87–91.

[20] John Brady, 'The Irish colleges in Europe and the counter-reformation', and Patrick J. Corish, 'The reorganisation of the Irish church, 1603–41', in *Ir. Cath. Hist. Comm. Proc.*, iii (1957), 1–8, 9–16. Patrick J. Corish, 'An Irish counter-reformation bishop: John Roche', in *Ir. Theol. Quart.*, xxv (1958), pp 14–32, 101–23; xxvi (1959), pp 101–116, 313–30.

tridentine catholicism were not present in Ireland. Regular mass was not universally available. Neither the laity nor the clergy could be supervised closely enough to ensure continuous observance, or the opportunity for it. The lines of authority were so slack that the reforms of the council of Trent could not be systematically introduced and promulgated, let alone enforced.

In these matters, Rome was not unreasonably inflexible. It recognised the justification for informal structures and loose lines of control in situations of danger and difficulty. And although its true agents were the secular parish clergy, it was intensely aware of the special value of the regulars on the missions. But early in the seventeenth century it became at least arguable that the situation in Ireland was no longer particularly perilous, and that Ireland differed in important respects from the ordinary missionary field. It was a preponderantly catholic country which had survived the initial assault of protestantism, which now required regular spiritual services and was not receiving them. The essential task was regeneration, and no significant improvement could result from the activities of individual missionaries, who might help to sustain Irish catholicism, but could do little to reform it. Indeed, the prominence and vigour of the regular clergy on the Irish mission, with faculties which exempted them from local ecclesiastical jurisdictions, actually tended to impede change by obscuring the importance of both the parish unit and the hierarchy of authority. Despite the apostolic enthusiasm with which the missionary rescue operation was conducted, the results were objectively so unsatisfactory when measured against the tridentine ideal that it became imperative to question the assumptions on which it rested.

In time, it became evident to the absentee primate of Ireland, Peter Lombard, that the exercise of authority by a resident episcopacy would be the most effective means of recovering the detailed control that was essential if systematic reform were to be undertaken. There were obvious difficulties. In effect, it would be necessary to re-classify Ireland, to agree to regard it as a reasonably safe area in which abnormal arrangements were no longer needed. In turn, this required the resolution of certain contradictions in papal policy. Pope Paul, though he was inclined to be conciliatory in principle, was none the less indulgent towards the earl of Tyrone, to whom he allowed considerable influence in the appointment of clergy in Ulster and whose interest in episcopal appointments in Ireland in general he also acknowledged. Paradoxically, it was the execution in 1612 of Cornelius O'Deveney, who had occupied the see of Down and Connor for thirty years and was one of the two bishops resident in Ireland, that presented Archbishop Lombard with his strongest argument for a new policy of moderation. In a memorandum to the pope, the primate interpreted

O'Deveney's death as a direct response to the translation of Eugene Mac-Mahon from the diocese of Clogher to the archdiocese of Dublin at the instigation of Tyrone: contrasting the treatment of O'Deveney with the leniency which was in practice shown towards other clergy, he concluded that the only clergy whom the government found objectionable were those who were or had been associated with Hugh O'Neill. Lombard's analysis was the more convincing since he had himself until recently been one of O'Neill's more influential supporters. He now argued that the safety and freedom of a resident hierarchy would be assured if their loyalty to the king were beyond question, and he urged that a new policy of conciliation should be adopted, within which it should prove possible to reconstitute the indispensable framework of the church and to proceed to the consolidation of its reform with the unwitting connivance of the government.[21]

Already, Lombard was represented in Ireland by David Rothe, who worked closely with the Old English to prevent the enactment of anti-catholic legislation in the parliament of 1613, who summoned and presided over the first of the provincial synods designed to introduce the tridentine reforms to Ireland in 1614, and who was elevated to the diocese of Ossory in 1618. Thereafter, the counter-reformation in Ireland moved gradually into its second phase; at first, piecemeal; then, after the establishment of the Congregation *de propaganda fide* in 1622, more systematically. A resident episcopate was recreated, the exceptional faculties enjoyed by the regulars were revoked, new missions were prohibited, and the renewal of the church in Ireland along normal lines was instituted. But the process was complicated by the attitudes, the habits, the adaptations and the vested interests which had been created in the first phase.

The environment provided by state policy was favourable, as Lombard had judged. He received a curious posthumous accolade when Thomas Wentworth reported to London that the archbishop had been 'the greatest enemy Tyrone ever had and the man indeed that certainly overthrew his credit at the court of Rome'.[22] The change in circumstances can be simply illustrated by two occurrences of the year 1633: the incoming lord deputy met the catholic archbishop of Dublin within three weeks of his arrival,[23] and the Congregation *de propaganda fide* noted that Ireland was now plentifully supplied with both regular and secular clergy.[24] The promotion of

[21] John J. Silke, 'Later relations between Primate Peter Lombard and Hugh O'Neill', and 'Primate Lombard and James I', in *Ir. Theol. Quart.*, xxii (1955), pp 15–30, 124–50.

[22] Thomas Wentworth to Francis Windebank, 28 January 1634 (Strafford MSS, v, ff 51–2).

[23] Thomas Wentworth to William Laud, 28 August 1633 (Strafford MSS, viii). The lord deputy's pen-portrait is perhaps worth recording: 'The archbishop in a black suit with a brown cloth cloak and a blue pair of stockings—a fat well complexioned man, well fed, I think you would have taken him to have been your countryman of Reading if you had seen him stand by a piece of cloth in Leaden Hall'.

[24] *Archivium Hibernicum*, 22 (1959), p. 75.

the counter-reformation was not impeded by government action, but by tensions and divisions within the church itself.

The most obtrusive of these was the conflict between the seculars and the regulars, which has yet to be exactly and frankly studied. In the past, so far as I can discern, their roles in Ireland seem to have been complementary in a rough and ready way. The territorially based parish structure could not fully cope with the complex divisions of Gaelic Ireland, and the more adaptable regulars seem to have plugged the gaps, so that religious provision appears to have been something of a mosaic, with areas of jurisdiction and operation governed by local traditions and accommodations rather than by adherence to theoretical models, and with lines of authority and responsibility correspondingly confused. The customary freedom of action of the regulars was further extended during the missionary period and they became free of most constraints. Well into the seventeenth century, people in many parts of Ireland were accustomed to associate the performance of spiritual duties with the religious orders rather than with the parish clergy. But the numerical facts alone suggest that the contribution of the regulars has been exaggerated.[25] They have been favoured by historians, and by the distribution of the evidence.

The issues in dispute were numerous and confused. They centred upon jurisdictional rivalries, but were extensively complicated by competing claims to the possession of churches and by mutually damaging financial demands upon the laity.[26] The counter-reformation in Ireland was enlivened by an unending succession of disedifying quarrels, often conducted over dead bodies, for funerals were the most frequent triggers of conflict. At times, disagreements led to violence; at times, they led to the ultimate irony of an appeal to the judgement of the civil courts; but usually, of course, they led to Rome. The attitudes of the Congregation *de propaganda fide* were fairly constant, and were most succinctly expressed in the sequel to a celebrated incident in which the vicar general of Leighlin, Matthew Roche, a man well thought of in government circles, 'beat a reverend good abbot with a bat'. When the Cistercian victim complained, he was reminded that Christ had exhorted his disciples to turn the other cheek.[27] But the regulars had strong local support in resisting the dominance of the parish structure which threatened to exclude them from the administration

[25] Reporting to Rome in 1623, Archbishop Eugene Matthews (of Dublin) estimated that there were more than 800 secular clergy and less than 300 regulars in Ireland. (Frank X. Martin, *Friar Nugent* (London and Rome, 1962), p. 245).

[26] The financial point was aptly, if mischievously, made by those (including the local protestant bishop) who ejected a Discalced Carmelite from Kinsale in 1630, inquiring 'what was a friar doing there, depriving the parish priest who lived in the town of his food'. Brendan Jennings (ed.), *Wadding papers* (Dublin, 1953), p. 354.

[27] Corish, 'The reorganisation of the Irish church', loc. cit., p. 12.

of the pastoral sacraments, and they profited from the equivocal attitudes of some regular bishops whose loyalty to their orders was at odds with their official brief. Although the full significance and effects of this rivalry have yet to be elucidated, there can be little doubt of the general result: reform did not triumph and the role of the regulars in Irish religion remained inappropriately large.

Part of the reason for this lies in an ironic disparity. Because of their seminary training and continental experience, the regulars were often better agents of reform than were the secular parish clergy. When the conduct of a funeral was in dispute, for instance, jurisdictional right was likely to be on the side of the parish clergy, but the regulars were more likely to observe the tridentine decrees. Similarly, the organisation of sodalities and fraternities by the regulars disrupted parochial unity while improving the spiritual observance of those involved. In short, the reform of organisation and the reform of practice were by no means always consistent with one another, and the accentuation of the parish might well involve the strengthening of traditional elements against reform. There is no doubt that the ordination of untrained clergy in Ireland was sometimes done to provide them with a means of supporting themselves while they completed their education on the Continent. On the other hand, although Fr Thomas Strange, Guardian of the Order of St Francis, was, in the nature of the case, a hostile source, there is no reason to dismiss entirely his bitter characterisation of the

ignorant beardless priest that is made here, and forthwith set in charge of a parish without having ever quitted Ireland, and whose studies are bounded by his Cato or his Virgil; which His Holiness will do well to consider, since it is the weal of souls that is at stake.[28]

And, though it reads like caricature, there is the pen portrait provided by Patrick Comerford, Augustinian bishop of Waterford, who earned the profound disapproval of his regular colleagues by favouring the parish clergy: 'as most of them are unlearned', he wrote of the clergy,

they make a trade of being ecclesiastical, thereby to live idle, sit among the best, go well clad, and, if I would say it, swagger: a man may not sit at table to a raffe of tripes, but presently one or two clergymen will come in; a man cannot visit a friend in town or abode, but there he shall meet two or three clergymen, and alas! very few spend one hour in a twelvemonth to teach the Christian doctrine or instruct young children.[29]

The division was not simply between the regulars and seculars as such: that distinction was entangled with a further one between the tridentine priests formed in the seminaries and the traditionalist clergy who were content

[28] *H.M.C. Franciscan MSS* (Dublin, 1906), p. 48.
[29] Ibid., pp 52–3.

with local standards, who imperfectly understood the new imperatives, and who did not share the new assumptions and values. The latter were incapable of fulfilling the role of the tridentine priests, not merely because they were insufficiently prepared, but because the role itself was novel and unfamiliar. In the Gaelic community, the priest was a professional functionary who customarily enjoyed respect and status rather than authority. The tridentine priest was required to exercise authority, within a parish: in Ireland, that meant that he was required to challenge the existing distribution of influence, the existing social division, and the accepted social conventions. Men who were accustomed to respect the traditional social nuances; who were used to disregarding strict parochial lines and to living without bishops; who did not expect a disciplined laity; who were unconcerned about catholic uniformity; who did not accept that certain local practices were morally wrong; who were themselves in some cases married; who were, simply, part of the community which they served: such men, though some of them may have had the edges rubbed off a little by crash courses of the kind that Kirwan promoted in Tuam, nevertheless remained a substantial barrier to reform.

Cultural differences constituted another barrier. The disputes between the Irish and Old English clergy usually surfaced in seminary quarrels, often pivoting about allegations of favouritism. They were institutionalised in the sharp distinction between Old English religious orders—Jesuits, Capuchins and Discalced Carmelites—and Old Irish religious orders, particularly the Franciscans and Dominicans. None of the orders was exclusive in its membership, but the identification of each with one or other of the catholic communities in Ireland was a fundamental fact of religious life. The overtones were political, and not merely in local terms, for the Old English orders tended to look to France while the Old Irish looked to Spain. The undertones ran deep. The decrees of the council of Trent laid down minimal standards of practice and conduct which were based upon the assumptions of 'civilised' western European society. The counter-reformation church worked towards a system of conformity which made no concessions to the deviant practices and distinctive customs of areas where separate traditions had produced different norms, as they had in Gaelic Ireland.

The result was that in a culturally divided Ireland the counter-reformation, in its regulations concerning births, marriages and death, as well as in its preoccupation with orderly structures and neighbourhood groupings reflected the assumptions and standards of the anglicised rather than the Gaelic.[30] It was natural that the Old English clergy should

---

[30] There are suggestive comparisons with the situation in England at the same period, as described by Dr Bossy: 'A gap seems to have been widening, within the community, between a

associate their religion with 'civility' and that they should look upon themselves as engaged upon 'this new plantation'[31] of the catholic faith, for in spreading the tridentine gospel they were also affirming the superiority of their own mode of living. Equally, it was natural that the Irish clergy should be sensitive to the implications of this kind of phraseology and should approach their task with some ambivalence. They could not promote spiritual renewal without assaulting the customs and conventions of their families and people. The evidence does not reveal how far this gave them pause. But those who returned to work in Ireland were subject to considerable pressures: they were themselves a part of the society which it was their duty to change, and it cannot have been easy to disregard its standards, its needs, and its tendency to keep the clergy in their place.[32]

These tendencies towards division were confirmed and accommodated at the highest level in the mid-1620s, when the papacy agreed to bring Lombard's appeasement policy to an end and to resume an aggressive policy.[33] The decision was dramatised by the dispute surrounding the appointment of a successor to Lombard in 1625: this brought to the primacy a man who was not only Old Irish, but a Franciscan, and it left a good deal of influence and control in the hands of men whose attachment to tridentine catholicism was qualified by a commitment to the preservation of Gaelic Ireland. In practice, a working recognition of spheres of influence developed, with Irish bishops appointed to Irish dioceses and Old English bishops appointed to Old English ones. As a result, the integrated impulse towards uniform change which had been provided by Lombard, Rothe and the Congregation *de propaganda fide* was diluted, and a form of devolution prevailed as the congruence between the political and pastoral aspects of the counter-reformation in Ireland disappeared. The rigorous requirements of the tridentine church were greatly softened. Novelty was minimised, and a variegated catholicism developed, sensitive to the requirements of particular communities, shaping itself to its immediate environment. An active and well supplied ministry provided an intricate and flexible spiritual presence which allowed the technically proscribed church to consolidate its position among both Old Irish and Old English, accom-

gentry which was being formed by the modernised catholicism of the counter-reformation, and the poorer catholics who largely remained in unreformed ignorance and superstition.' ('The English catholic community, 1603–25', in Alan G. R. Smith (ed.), *The reign of James VI and I* (London, 1973), p. 104.)

[31] Edmund Hogan (ed.), *Ibernia Ignatiana* (Dublin, 1880), p. 161.

[32] The point was made more pithily by Richard Stanyhurst: 'a preacher is sooner by their naughty lives corrupted, than their naughty lives by his preaching amended'. (R. Holinshed, *Chronicles of England, Scotland and Ireland* (London, 1577), i, pt iii, D4v.

[33] Hugh F. Kearney, 'Ecclesiastical politics and the counter-reformation in Ireland, in *Jn. Ecc. Hist.*, ii (1960), pp 202–12. Aidan Clarke, 'Ireland and the general crisis', in *Past and Present*, no. 48 (1970), pp 83–4.

modating itself to their differences, and gaining a general acceptance which in many cases certainly owed more to disregarding tridentine niceties than to observing them.

To assert that the Old Irish and the Old English shared a common religion which pulled them towards one another is to miss the point. The religion which they shared was not an agent of union, but a source of disagreement, and in practice the church did not reconcile their differences; rather, it adapted itself to them. Each group had its own source of pride. The Old English claimed superiority in civilisation and education, the Irish invoked the saintly traditions of Celtic Christianity.[34] But the objective fact was that the counter-reformation was tinged with Old English assumptions. The dictates of politics might prompt the church to support the Irish, right up to the extreme of Rinuccini's relentless partisanship in the 1640s, but the message that the church conveyed at pastoral level remained corrosive, and it was the Old English who conformed to tridentine type, even if they seemed 'a people catholic only in name' to Rinuccini, as they had seemed only 'half-subjects' to James I.[35] The Irishman might be satisfied to tell the Scottish traveller that his religion was 'what his father, his great-grandfather were',[36] which was perhaps not merely an affirmation of catholicism, but of a particular kind of catholicism. The Englishman might despise the Old English for being content to subscribe to the religion of barbarians. The Old English were fortified by the knowledge that theirs was the religion of France, Italy and Spain: that, properly conceived, theirs was the religion of advanced civilisation. They differed from the Irish in the direction of orthodoxy: modern catholicism conformed to and verified their standards, their values, their mode of life, not those of the Irish.

Recognition of this fact was reenforced by the very practice which the government so adamantly and ineffectually opposed, the practice of sending Old English children to Europe to be educated. Far from being seduced from their allegiance, the men and boys who went to the Continent had the opportunity to observe the correspondence between their inherited values and catholic European norms. Where the inheritance had been diluted in

---

[34] The respective claims are summarised (from an Old Irish standpoint) in a memorandum of 1626 (*Franciscan MSS*, pp 88–92).

[35] G. Aiazza, *The embassy in Ireland of Monsignor G.B. Rinuccini*, translated by Annie Hutton (Dublin, 1873), p. 436. Rinuccini's alignment in Ireland does not seem to me to invalidate the argument advanced in this paper. His pronounced ultramontane views, his determination to secure the public exercise of catholicism, and his increasing preoccupation with the need for a catholic viceroy combined to make his choices fundamentally political, as he acknowledged in his first report of the state of Ireland (ibid., p. 132). Moreover, the measure by which he judged groups and individuals was the degree to which they shared his priorities, so that even estimates of spiritual worth rested upon political criteria (ibid., pp 140–44).

[36] William Lithgow, *The total discourse of rare adventures and painful peregrinations* (Glasgow, 1906), p. 375.

the past, the implications were even larger, for the emergence of the Old English group involved the reuniting of colonial streams which had diverged greatly over the centuries, and the mediating force which made it easier to discard Gaelic ways and to assume English ones was tridentine catholicism. If the common bond of the group was descent, the principle of unity and cohesion was provided by a variety of catholicism which conveniently erased the regional deviations of the past. It was, in fact, the spirit of the counter-reformation which made the juncture of catholicism and Englishness a culturally consistent one. In the Irish context, the mixture might seem anomalous: in the European context, it was an appropriate blend.

The gap between Dr Edwards's Anglo-Irish and my Old English is, thus, bridged by religion. At first, this influence acted negatively, in the sense that not-being-protestant became an evident and sufficient cause for discrimination. Before long, it operated positively, in the sense that tridentine catholicism reenforced nationality and descent by enabling the traditional presumption of the cultural inferiority of the Irish to be continued in a new context. The Old English were rescued from provincial backwardness and given access to modernity through their links with a religious movement that allowed them, to their own satisfaction at least, to strip the term 'civility' of its protestant associations. And in this way they acquired the ideological assurance of superiority which is inseparable from colonial identity.

From this argument, a simple conclusion may be drawn: that the religion of the Old English was a fully differentiating characteristic, which set them apart from the Irish as well as from the English. Their Englishness and their catholicism converged to create their identity rather than diverged to threaten it with disintegration.

IV

Patriotism and national identity in eighteenth-century Scotland

Rosalind Mitchison

The title of this paper deliberately avoids the use of the word 'nationalism'. The expressions used instead contain the essence of nationalism: the rest is just froth. 'Froth' is, of course, eye-catching, and usually more noticeable than significant. But in articulate form it was in relative abeyance in the early eighteenth century. Scotland had been engaged in completing amalgamation with England in the 1707 act of union. The passage of union had been noisy and angry: it had produced a considerable literature of rhetoric and analysis. It left a large body of people attached to Jacobitism and separation—in fact incompatible aims—from religious or national feelings, to whom were added in the early years of parliamentary incorporation a larger body of Scottish politicians resentful of the way Scottish issues and Scotsmen were treated at Westminster. Gradually they had discovered that they were not truly equals there: that the top jobs would go inevitably to the English. But though Jacobitism and separation continued to be, for the next forty years or so, alternative policies to whiggery and London in the minds of many Scots, the pursuit of these aims was not particularly active or articulate.

One reason for this was the deep sense of humiliation which national feeling had received in the late seventeenth century and in the revelations of the union debate. Nationalism can be anticipatory or retrospective in its self-congratulatory aspect; that is it can refer back to a splendid past or perceive promise in the future, but it does need some element of self-congratulation. The seventeenth century was not, in the eyes of Scottish politicians, splendid, and the analyses of the situation in 1707 contained further sources of humiliation.

This paper is confined, and has to be confined, to the attitudes of those who could express themselves, to people of means and letters, gentry, merchants and clergy, in Namier's phrase 'the political nation' with its ecclesiastical counterpart. Historians have already charted the opinions of the literary world. For instance Janet Adam Smith and Nicholas Phillipson have gone into the recognition of the ambiguous position held by

73

eighteenth-century Scottish writers.[1] This paper aims, in cultural terms, at a lower stratum. One day perhaps we will have looked far enough into our still unexplored local records, those of sheriff courts, baron courts and the lower courts of the church, to have some understanding of the opinions of really humble people. But till then we have to concentrate on people of some substance, particularly on the dominant class of landowners. It was to these people that the vision of the immediate past was particularly embarrassing. The post-revolutionary settlement in Scotland had produced a church situation which made it impossible for the ministers to represent the nation, and had driven a deep rift between them and the bulk of landed society. Presbyterianism was being forced on the country by a self-appointed group of sixty ministers, the survivors of those ejected after the restoration. Over several years this sixty forced out over two-thirds of the existing ministry and intruded their own nominees; that in so doing they demoralised the church at the local levels of parish and presbytery is probably one of the reasons for the failure of the country to cope with the social problems produced by war and famine in the 1690s. Here it is of more relevance to note that this policy made it impossible for the church to represent the nation. Leadership decisively passed from it to the lairds.

In England, from the late middle ages on, the high court of parliament was regarded as the expression of national identity, the focus of patriotism. It has long been a commonplace of Scottish historians that the Scottish parliament never held such a place in people's minds. Scottish legalism in the seventeenth century did not emphasise the sovereignty of the Scottish parliament because there were other institutions which had a share in lawmaking: the privy council, the convention of royal burghs and, most important of all, the general assembly of the church, a body focussing political as well as religious sentiments. The importance of this assembly was one of the reasons why the country had had to do without it for considerable periods. After the revolution, when it became politically inevitable that it should meet, and when the powers withdrawn from the monarchy were going a-begging for some institution, the extreme partisan control by the sixty of the assembly made sure not only that Scotland would be presbyterian, but also that the temper of the ensuing age would be secular. In no sense could the sixty be looked upon as an expression of national identity. True, the king would send a commissioner to attend the opening of future assemblies, and these meetings would eventually become battle grounds for parties within the church, but not until the evangelical revival gained support, out of fear of radicalism, could the assembly be held

[1] Janet Adam Smith, 'Some eighteenth century ideas of Scotland' and N. T. Phillipson, 'Scottish public opinion and the union in the age of the Association' in N. T. Phillipson and Rosalind Mitchison (eds.), *Scotland in the age of improvement* (Edinburgh, 1970), pp 107–47.

to speak for more than a minority. In one way, too, the church borrowed a secular ethos from the lay world, for the most successful party in it for much of the eighteenth century, the moderates, was dedicated to the idea of cooperating with the lay world, and this cooperation always contained an element of subservience. But generally it was to the law, and the court of session that eighteenth century Scots looked for an expression of national identity.

The Scottish landed class did not like to look back historically to an age when the Church of Scotland had apparently led the nation into a war which had engulfed all three British kingdoms. The failure of the country in the 1690s to feed itself and the unwisdom of its attempts to create a trading colony and produce a rival to the English East India Company were also humiliating. The literature of union was not particularly comforting either. It showed that an independent Scotland would have an insoluble balance of payments problem and, as citizens of modern Britain know, such things are very humiliating. Such was the gloomy message of pamphlets which attempted to show how the country could support itself without trade with England.[2] The country had not been able and would not be able to stop the aristocracy importing foreign luxuries. Moroever, union was followed by the revelation that for many years past the country had not been able to pay the servants of the state. And union, in any case, as has been shown by both economic and political historians in the last fifteen years, merely legalised the way in which London controlled Scotland.[3]

Union masked the continuing problem of balance of payments, but did not solve it.[4] Scottish patriotism was then compelled to have an economic emphasis. The attempt, for instance, of the early 1730s, described by Elizabeth Mure of Caldwell, to make Scottish fabrics fashionable by having a ball attended only by those in home fabrics, was not as footling as it might seem.[5] Paisley muslins and Hamilton edgings were important assertions of economic potential. The sober comments of Clerk of Penicuik took the same line.[6] 'Foreign' luxuries were bad because they were luxuries, of course, but worse because they were imported. The country had not yet developed the

---

[2] An example of this is J. Spreull, *An accompt current betwixt Scotland and England ballanced* (Edinburgh, 1705).

[3] P. W. J. Riley, *The English ministers and Scotland* (London, 1964), pp 1–23; T. C. Smout, 'The Anglo-Scottish union of 1707: 1, The economic background' in *Economic History Review*, 2nd series, xvi (1964), pp 455–67.

[4] This point has been stressed by R. H. Campbell, 'The union and economic growth' in T. I. Rae (ed.), *The union of 1707* (Glasgow, 1974), pp 58–73.

[5] J. G. Fyfe (ed.), *Scottish diaries and memoirs (1746–1843)* (Stirling, 1942), p. 64; see also R. Maxwell, *Select transactions of the Honourable the Society of Improvers . . .* (Edinburgh, 1743), p. 313, for an earlier patriotic decision (Feb., 1724) not to wear foreign linen.

[6] Sir John Clerk, 'Observations on the present circumstances of Scotland' in Scottish History Society, 4th series, ii, *Miscellany* x (Edinburgh, 1965), pp 199–200, 206.

professional approach to law-keeping of later years, and a long, indented coast line and a venal customs service made it impossible to attack the import of luxuries except by propaganda. In any case, not paying indirect taxation was, in the eyes of many, an important element in the Scottish way of life. Smuggling not only brought in luxuries; it also provided the financial foundation of some prosperous businesses. The excess of legal exports of tobacco, gaining drawbacks, over legal imports, shows this use of fraud as a source of capital.[7]

One of the puzzles, all the same, is that after Scotland's basic economic and financial failure had been so powerfully displayed in the years around union, so little was done to rectify it for so long. It is dangerous to speak from negative evidence, but the pamphlet literature on the subject appears to dry up between 1707 and 1724. Even the compensatory arrangements extracted from England in the act of union were not implemented. The 'second equivalent', of article xv, which promised £2,000 of surplus excise receipts first to the coarse woollen industry and then to fisheries and other manufactures, remained a dead letter. No one appears to have tried to put pressure on the governments to act in this matter. No historian has yet advanced any explanation of this failure.

The only explanation I can advance is to make a few points about the governing society of Scotland in this period. It is at this time that there was completed the change of the great noble houses of Scotland from the position of overmighty subjects at home to client politicians in London. The exception to this process was the house of Argyll, which continued to fill both roles. For this house to have taken any other line would have been to leave a vacuum of power, particularly in the southern highlands, where the Campbell vassals and tacksmen were a necessary part of government control. It is a commonplace that the immediate political relationship between Scotland and England rapidly soured in the new imperial parliament, until in 1713 came the attempt of many unionist Scots to destroy this unsatisfactory union. Even the commission of police, a straightforward pensioning system for Scottish politicians, did not prevent this outburst.[8] If politics soured quickly, it took longer for the dream of easy wealth to fade. I think that many in Scotland continued into the 1720s to suffer from what I call the 'Cadillac syndrome': the belief that their new association in Great Britain would, without effort on their part, or adjustment of their society, give them the benefit of a higher standard of living. If it took several decades in our present century for O.P.E.C. (the Organisation of Petroleum Export-

---

[7] T. C. Barker, 'Smuggling in the eighteenth century: the evidence of the Scottish tobacco trade' in *Virginia Magazine of History and Biography* lxii (1954), pp 396–8.

[8] For the commission see Riley, *The English ministers and Scotland*, pp 185–7.

ing Countries) to get going as an organisation, we should not be surprised at this period of inaction in the eighteenth century.

Things changed sharply in the 1720s. The decade produced further shocks to whatever complacency landed society could still indulge in. The issue of customs fraud came to a head. It is true that sometimes Scottish officials had tried to carry out their duties professionally: I found a laconic entry in an exchequer account for 1713: 'Mr John Haldane, surveyor at Montrose, paid him for the loss of his cloathes etc., torn from him by the mobb, £12 13'.[9] But this was rare, and this aspect of the Scottish way of life was endangering the relations between Scotland and England, as well as endangering Scotland's balance of payments. There was also the traumatic experience of the Shawfield riots in Glasgow over the malt tax in 1725. This outbreak was merely the tip of the iceberg of national resentment, and many other sections of Scottish society were ready to protest at increased taxation. The emergency of this year, involving troop movements, arrests and some disciplining of the Scottish bench seems to mark the end of the 'Cadillac syndrome' era for two reasons. The government in London had at last turned its attention to things Scottish, and there was by now a small but vocal movement within Scotland urging 'improvement'.

The eighteenth century improvers were true patriots in every sense of the word, and form one of the main themes of this paper. Improvement meant changing the economy, agricultural as well as industrial, and also the landscape. It meant taking risks, and sometimes even the sacrifice of personal advantage. Often improvers went bankrupt. Through the writings of the improvers runs the note of patriotic self-sacrifice, but the most characteristic theme is angry humiliation at the backwardness of their country. The writers declaim against opportunities missed, bad habits sustained, new ideas spurned. 'Are we of Scotland, that plow over and over our land, without rest or intermission, and that in the dead of winter, the only men in the world wisest and best known in husbandry'[10] asked Mackintosh of Borlum in 1729. 'Our going to Berwick for better meat' he said, 'raised his blood'. 'The manufactured goods we export bear no proportion in value to those we bring in' wrote Patrick Lindesay in 1733, and that this was not the result of the lack of political independence was clear: 'strange, that when we had the power in our hands, to tax ourselves for the improvement of our manufactures, we did it not as the Irish have done'.[11] Anger is a constant element in the writings of the first improver of

[9] Customs accounts, 1713, Scottish Record Office (hereafter S.R.O.) E 502/6/ p. 76.

[10] [W. Mackintosh of Borlum], *An essay on ways and means for inclosing, fallowing, planting, etc. Scotland; and that in sixteen years at farthest*, by a Lover of his Country (Edinburgh, 1729), p. 46 (hereafter cited as *Essay on inclosing*).

[11] [P. Lindesay], *The interest of Scotland considered* (Edinburgh, 1733), pp i, 92 (herafter cited as *Interest of Scotland*). The willingness to borrow ideas and techniques from Ireland is an

all, John Cockburn of Ormiston. 'All the people in Scotland are not so void of taste or their other senses as you incline to think them. It is the not being able to get good things which makes people not have them. . . .' 'Could the lasie man bring himself to more activity or the covetous man to a larger way of thinking, they would both get more business and more money from having more customers'. 'It is commonly our Scots way to do little business but squeese up high prices.'[12]

Anger did not prevent some of these men having a clear understanding of the problems of an undeveloped country. Cockburn was well aware of the way in which poverty reproduces itself, and Mackintosh of Borlum could give an analysis of the price mechanism of undevelopment; how, for instance, lack of feed meant that most half starved calves went as skinny veal to market; when a farmer had something better to offer it was so rare that he charged exorbitantly for it.[13]

Industrial products induced the same angry shame, and this focussed attack on one or two symbols. London porter sold in Edinburgh, a town with numerous breweries of its own and in reach of others in West Lothian. In spite of the cheapness of barley 'our malt drink is the most stupefying stuff ever was contrived', wrote Cockburn.[14] It was still 'a shame and disgrace to us', David Loch wrote in 1774, that such a bulky commodity as porter should be imported.[15] Mackintosh of Borlum had a special bad word for the habits of luxury which led to serving ashets of 'English pickles'.[16] Then there was the issue of English blankets. Scotch blankets were made of coarse wool tightly spun; they were thin and hard, and wore for ever, scratchily. English blankets were light and fluffy; they did not endure as did the Scotch, and probably wore out in a mere twenty years. What was particularly exasperating was that they were both warmer and cheaper than the Scotch. Usually English woollens undersold the Scotch by 10 or 15 percent.[17] Familiarity with testamentary inventories has shown me the thorough way in which English blankets had penetrated the Scottish market: commonly they are to be found on the best beds in a household with Scotch ones kept for the servants and children, who could be expected to suffer urticaria in the interests of the economy. Porter and blankets were particularly sore items because there seemed no inherent reason why the Scotch equivalents should not be competitive. But as the improvers began

interesting feature of improvement literature. See, for instance, R. Maxwell, *Select transactions*, pp 353–9 for an abstract of the Dublin essays on flax treatment.

[12] J. Colville (ed.), *Letters of John Cockburn of Ormistoun to his gardener, 1727–44* (Scottish History Society, 1st series, xlv, Edinburgh, 1904), pp 25, 18, 12 (hereafter cited as *Letters*).

[13] *Essay on inclosing*, pp 134–6.

[14] *Letters*, p. 30.

[15] D. Loch, *Letters concerning the trade and manufactures of Scotland* (Edinburgh, 1744), p. 13.

[16] *Essay on inclosing*, p. 229.

[17] *Interest of Scotland*, pp 107–11.

to see how these equivalents related to the quality of both farming and industry, and to understand the enormous long-term investment of time, skill and specialisation which had to be made to get a domestic textile industry to an advanced state, rage could turn to a hopeless despair. There were no wool staplers in Scotland. There was no fine woolled breed of sheep outside Shetland. (The coarse woolled objects grazing today on most Scottish hills are the 'improved' breeds of the eighteenth century.) Scottish linen was with difficulty bleached into an approximation to white because, once spun by the grubby fingers of Scotswomen, the dirt was engrained, and Scottish cottage housing was so miserable that it was impossible for anyone even to aim at cleanliness.[18] The housing was so little weather-proof that the whole industry stopped in a hard frost. Effort at whitening led to the use of lime which meant that Scottish linen might last a mere seven years before falling to pieces, whereas that bought in Hamburg, says Loch, would give twenty to thirty years' wear.[19]

The improvers had a conspicuous absence of pride in their country. In the mid-seventeenth century the covenanters had seen Scotland as possessed of a special divine mission among the nations of the earth. Other patriots, while rejecting this approach—Sir Thomas Urquhart is an example—had regarded Scotland as higher in the pecking order at least than Ireland, even if only because of 'greater conformity with and proximity to the nation of England'.[20] But the eighteenth century improvers were ready to borrow from either Ireland or England. Borlum wrote: 'Perhaps it will be said, "It is an affront to us, to beg money from another nation to pay our workmen" '. But this was merely asking help of an ally to 'evict an enemy. . . . poverty, inconvenience and ugliness have for . . . years overrun the country'.[21] Lindesay saw the parallel of the Irish economy, and in fact it was from the idea of the Irish linen board that the Scots took the model of the board of trustees for manufactures, of 1727.[22] This was being urged on the government in London by the Scottish burghs at the moment of the Shawfield troubles. Though the board of trustees has come under some fire for its manner of distributing its funds, there is no doubt that its basic idea, borrowed from Ireland, of boosting the linen industry by quality control of the end product was the right policy for Scotland.

[18] A. Durie, The Scottish linen industry, 1705–75, with particular reference to the early history of the British Linen Company (Ph.D. thesis, University of Edinburgh, 1973), p. 13 (hereafter cited as A. Durie, Scottish linen industry).

[19] *Essays on the trade, commerce, manufactures and fisheries of Scotland* (Edinburgh, 1778), i, 165 (hereafter cited as Loch, *Essays*).

[20] S. A. Burrell, 'The apocalyptic vision of the covenanters' in *Scottish Historical Review*, xliii (1964), pp 18–24; Sir Thomas Urquhart, *Works* (Maitland Club, Edinburgh, 1834), p. 190.

[21] *Essay on inclosing*, p. 155.

[22] A. Durie, Scottish linen industry, p. 15.

Improvement was not a party creed. All shades of opinion except one came into this movement. Borlum was an active Jacobite, so unwilling to compromise even his language that he spent the last quarter of his life in prison.[23] But even Borlum could refer to the earl of Islay, lynch pin of the whig establishment in Scotland, as a patriot. Lindesay was enough of an establishment whig to have got into parliament as a protégé of Islay's and to have become lord provost of Edinburgh. Cockburn was a whig placeman until he followed Argyll into opposition. George Dempster of Dunnichen was an erratically independent whig. The most extreme of whiggery in language is that of the anonymous author of the 1727 pamphlet *Reasons for improving the fisheries and linen manufactures of Scotland,* which includes an early version of the whig theory of history applied to Scotland's seventeenth century. The 'party' missing from this list is that of the 'high flyers' in the church, or indeed, after the first secession of the 1730s, out of it. The writings of Robert Wodrow, for instance, show concern over trade recessions and harvest failures, but no desire to change from a situation where such things led to destitution and famine. The better known writings of the evangelical party, the sermons of Ebenezer Erskine, the *Fourfold state* of Thomas Boston, are pitched in generalised terms, with no interest in any aspect of material life except an occasional denunciation of worldly pre-occupations. With the abandonment of the sense of a special mission for Scotland went any close sense of patriotism in material terms. I can think of two partial reasons for this: one is that the exasperation of the improvers with the state of their country stemmed from experience of others: they knew it was not necessary to be poor. The evangelicals rarely went abroad. The other reason was the belief of the evangelical party that any attention to ordinary living was apt to end in preaching what they called 'mere' morality, instead of the divine truths of predestination, election, assurance and the covenant of grace.

The attitude of this outer wing of the church accentuated the secularism of the improvers. These saw the clergy mopping up the pool of ability in the young, encouraging a style of education of no particular economic value. 'The well meaning zeal of our clergy, in pressing honest farmers and tradesmen to send their sons to Latin schools and colleges . . . does a great deal more hurt to the commonwealth than service', wrote Borlum. Children should study agriculture, not obscene Latin authors. The terminology here used was both class conscious and loaded: even more so because Borlum then lapsed into a traditional piece of Scottish Latinist pedantry, pointing out that many ancient authors could not be properly understood without a

---

[23] General Wade to Lord Newcastle, 2 Oct. 1725, and draft reply, 14 Oct. 1725 (S.R.O. RH2/4/320 ff 249, 347).

knowledge of good farming.[24] Lindesay also pointed out that in the vast ecclesiastical clearance after 1689 it had become too easy to get a charge in the church, and now, in 1733, the church was overstocked but still formed the ambition of many.[25]

The improvers thought that it was natural, necessary even, for each country to have its 'staple' product. Here was dangerous ground for unionists, where patriotism was likely to become anti-English. Obviously it was easier in Scotland to rear sheep, some sort of sheep anyway, than to grow flax, and in the case of sheep the natural process went much nearer to producing a raw material for a textile industry in a usuable form than it did with flax. Scotland's coarse woollen industry was therefore more 'natural' and indigenous than her linen. But government pressure and privileges in the 1680s had conspiciously failed in the attempt to raise the quality of this 'natural' staple.[26] In any case there were political facts. English parliamentarians, touchy at best about the presence of Scots, and already inclined to distort the terms of the union, would simply not stand for the use of government money to rear a rival staple. The outcry against Lord Bute was to show, even as late as the 1760s, that the English political world did not accept Scotland as an equal partner. The issue over the staple should have quieted down as it became clear that the £4,000 allotted in 1727 to the coarse woollen industry was being used as feather bedding for Border landowners and not as an aid to improvement.[27] Cockburn in 1744 wrote angrily that the woollens of the Border counties were 'in a great measure useless at home and not fit for exporting abroad'.[28] Yet as late as the 1770s David Loch, though well aware of the deficiencies of the industry, including the persistent use in Scotland of cards already worn out in England, still felt that it was wool that Scotland should be developing, not linen. Loch's writings are the most 'nationalist' of the patriotic literature of improvement.[29]

Loch, though, was one with the other improvers in seeing economic development as an important mechanism for the redistribution of wealth

---

[24] *Essay on inclosing*, pp 195–212, 216–8.

[25] *Interest of Scotland*, pp 123–5.

[26] See for instance W. R. Scott (ed.), *The records of a Scottish cloth manufactory at New Mills, Haddingtonshire 1681–1707* (Scottish History Society, 1st series xlvi, Edinburgh, 1905), pp lv–lxxxiii; C. Gulvin, 'The union and the Scottish woollen industry, 1707–1760' in *Scottish Historical Review*, l (1971), pp 121–4.

[27] C. Gulvin, The Scottish woollen industry, 1603–1914 (Ph.D. thesis, University of Edinburgh, 1969), pp 26–52.

[28] Quoted in C. Gulvin, op. cit., p. 39, from a manuscript in Galashiels Woollen Technical College Library.

[29] See particularly the language in his *Essays*, i, 141, on English penetration: 'an English ·rider (a species of locusts who have long infected poor Scotland) can no longer boast of carrying from this country twelve thousand pounds in a single journey'.

inside the country. He could not bear to see 'the many hundred inhabitants
... in our streets without shoes and stockings ... actually starving for want
of employment'.[30] 'The more equal the distribution of property is, the
better for every country', wrote Lindesay;[31] and Borlum asserted that
'using our commons so hard and keeping them poor, and not giving them
leases, is the cause our country has not improv'd', and added that union
had come about only because of the expectations of 'the commons' that the
'slavish yoke of superiority' would be lifted.[32]

The interesting puzzle here is to find how total was the improvers' sense
of national unity with their lesser folk. Who are these poor commons? There
seems to be a willingness to include all but the inveterately idle: all
improvers felt that there was a substratum of vagrants for whom discipline,
not sympathy, was the right answer. Lindesay envisaged the woollen
industry providing work for the poor in or out of charity workhouses, but he
wished to see the suppression of the numerous beggars, whom he regarded
as embarrassing evidence of Scotland's poverty.[33] All above the beggar
level were, in the eyes of the improvers, to be made industrious and
comfortable. Comfort to Borlum meant the security of leases, to Dempster
also the control of their own time and labour, the end of vexatious services.[34]

There was a resolute refusal of Scottish patriots of this breed to separate
the theme of the good of the country from the good of its inhabitants. A. J.
Youngson in his brilliant analysis of the development of a theory of
economic growth in the eighteenth century indicates, without dwelling on
the point, how none of the Scottish writers express the view that the incomes
of labourers must be kept low. They do not share Arthur Young's well
known and rather crude opinion that 'every one but an idiot knows that the
lower classes must be kept poor or they will never be industrious'.[35] It is
true that in Scotland as elsewhere there were areas of work where a slight
rise in real wages led to a sharp drop in production, but the Scots knew more
than did Arthur Young about the crippling effects of the real poverty of
undevelopment, and could, even in the 1780s, remember a country where
idleness had sprung from the state of the economy, not from high wages.
The improvers forecast the opinion developed further by the Scottish
philosophers and historians of the enlightenment that the trend of
development was towards smaller inequalities in wealth, and that this was

[30] Loch, *Essays*, i, 136.
[31] *Interest of Scotland*, p. 64.
[32] *Essay on inclosing*, pp xxiii, 22.
[33] *Interest of Scotland*, pp 23–6.
[34] *Essay on inclosing*, pp 161–8; George Dempster to Sir John Sinclair, 2 Apr. 1802, Dec. 1809
(microfilm of Sinclair of Ulbster muniments, S.R.O., RH2/49/2/3, ff 273, 319).
[35] A. J. Youngson, *After the fortyfive* (Edinburgh, 1973), pp 51–66.

desirable. They would have agreeed with Adam Smith's remark 'no society can surely be flourishing and happy of which the far greater part of the members are poor and miserable'.[36] When Cockburn wrote 'I shall always have greater pleasure in seeing my tenants making something under me which they can call their own than in getting a little more money myself', he probably meant it.[37] Before the price changes of the 1770s improvement was no guaranteed way of providing wealth for the improver.

In their hostility to the past oppressions of a feudal aristocracy the improvers united with a second stream of patriotic thought, expressed by various politicians and lawyers in the desire to see the union 'compleat'. By this was meant that a Scottish laird should receive all the advantages of an English country gentleman. He should partake in the anarchic local government of the eighteenth century, be answerable to the law but not to the demands of an overlord or the central government, and should have plentiful career opportunities both at home and in England. He should be independent of clerical control, of course, and also should exercise considerable power, by influence and patronage, over his own local minister.[38] In so far that he had, as a landowner in Scotland, a few additional rights and privileges over his tenantry, these were not going to be objected to. There was also a subtle difference in what liberty meant to the gentlemen of the two countries, for in England the stress lay on independence of the central government, in Scotland getting the nobility off their backs. Since Scottish landed society provided about 85 percent of the advocates and all the judges who together shaped the law of Scotland through this formative period, and had, from the relatively primitive state of some branches of law, a pretty free hand in so doing, these people were well placed to get their way.

On the whole the early improvers had paid little attention to the special problems of the existence of a separate culture in highland Scotland. Even Borlum, who was a highlander, had little to say about this except that it was hard on 'subjects' in the highlands to be 'so little protected by the numerous army already raised, that they are forced to raise . . . another army at their own proper cost and charge to protect their goods'.[39] The lawyers were

---

[36] Adam Smith, *Wealth of nations* (London, 1961), i, 88; *Interest of Scotland*, p. 85, gives an instance of the line of thought. I am grateful to Mrs Pauline Moore, research student at Edinburgh University, for information about this strand of thought as developed by the Scottish school of history.

[37] Cockburn's remark is quoted in 'Memoirs of John Cockburn Esq. of Ormiston' in *The Farmers' Magazine*, v (1804), p. 136.

[38] Rosalind Mitchison, 'The government and the highlands, 1707–45' in Phillipson and Mitchison (eds) *Scotland in the age of improvement*, pp 27–8. An instance of this view is the unsigned 'Proposalls concerning the highlands', sent in 1717 to the London government (S.R.O., RH2/4/313, ff 236–7, 244–51).

[39] W. Mackintosh of Borlum, *A short scheme whereby is proposed with the help of the military road made by the Hon Lt Gen Wade . . .* (Edinburgh, 1742), p. 7.

aware that there was more to the highland problem than that. Some would write briskly of 'highland ruffians'.[40] Lord Grange, who like many with a landed base near the highland line, was aware of the difference in culture of the two societies, saw a continuation of clanship as an oppression of the ordinary man (by ordinary he meant someone who would be landowning in lowland society, say a tacksman or greater vassal). He wrote 'things will never be right till the clanship and chieftainrys be abolished and that kindred and name go no further than the common types of relation do or ought to do in civilized countrys'. 'We must consider them' (the highlanders) as 'what the creator and absolute proprietor of nature has made them, and that is MEN—such as we are ourselves. . . .' 'It cannot be agreeable to the use for which God design'd creatures . . . to be slaves subjected to the absolute arbitrary power and pleasure of one or more.'[41] (Part of the fascination of reading Lord Grange on the equality of mankind in the sight of God and the liberty of the subject is to reflect on what happened to Lady Grange.) On a more general level these remarks, besides showing God as the landowner in chief, an interesting manifestation of anthropomorphism, indicate an appreciation of the dual nature of Scottish society. 'Compleating the union' would involve making the highlands subject to the rule of law, and so one with the rest of Scotland. Nobody as yet showed any respect for Gaelic culture.

The attitude to the separateness of the highlands was, of course, accentuated by the '45. Respectably whiggish gentlemen saw this rebellion, which unlike the '15 was almost entirely a highland enterprise, as a disgrace from which they were determined to disassociate themselves. If they had had near kinsmen involved, as most people had in the '15, things would have been different. Whereas today most people in Scotland enjoy singing songs which identify themselves with Jacobitism, the lawyers and gentlemen of the '40s and '50s were particularly anxious to cut the whole issue down to size. This is shown most sharply in the debates over the militia question in 1760. 'It is no more equitable to upbraid the Scottish nation with the universal spirit of rebellion' went a long, front page article in the *Caledonian Mercury* (that a Scottish issue at this date should occupy the front page was itself remarkable) 'because some of her natives were prevailed upon to favour the designs of France, than to accuse every Englishman of bribery and corruption, because some of them make merchandize of their

---

[40] Andrew Mitchell to solicitor general, 9 Nov. 1745 (S.R.O., RH4/15/3, f. 84, microfilm of the Arniston papers).
[41] Memorial by Lord Grange, Apr. 1751, 'concerning H.M. estates of Strowan and Lochgarie in the Highlands of the shire of Perth' (S.R.O. GD124/15/1605/4, p. 2); Lord Grange to earl of Islay, 16 Dec. 1724 (S.R.O., GD124/15/1262/2).

votes'.[42] 'The stale reproach of Jacobitism' complained the *Scots Magazine*, was hackneyed as well as untrue.[43]

Highland issues led to the reduction of what the lawyers complained about most, the long continuance of the rights of feudal superiors in an age when, as Grange said, 'the reasons on which the feudal customs were founded are quite ceas'd'. 'Our feudal law as it now stands, tho much softened beyond what it was formerly, is really grievous, and more and more hated by the generality of the nation'.[44] When Grange wrote these words, in 1724, the law still included rights of superiors over alienation of land, marriage and wardship, which were a genuine handicap to freedom of action, though at least in the case of marriage Grange held that only the 'most barbarous' would exercise such rights. 'The generality of the nation' here obviously means landowners: the peasantry did not come into contact with feudalism, and the merchant classes only in so far as feudal private jurisdictions enabled some highland superiors to be bad debtors with impunity so long as they stayed in the highlands. Legislation, for instance the abolition of feudal franchises in 1747, along with some better mechanisms for inheritance of land, curtailed these rights. But much more appears to have been done by case law.

There is certainly a fascinating story, still largely unacknowledged by Scottish legal historians, in the extension of the privileges and rights of the landowning class in Scotland in the eighteenth century. The legal historians have taken very little trouble to look critically at what was going on, and have been unduly impressed by the great eighteenth century legists and their remarkable capacity for describing what they called the law as if it had always existed. It would be extraordinary if, in the situation where the same lawyers and judges as controlled the courts played a leading part in that study of history and society which was the core of the Scottish enlightenment, there should not be deliberate refashioning of feudal law in the interests of the sub-vassals, that is of property rather than superiority. All students of the recent past were convinced that the powers of some overmighty subjects had been too great in the Scotland of the past (this was not always put in the past, for it formed a useful cover for an attack on the dominance of the house of Argyll in the eighteenth century). Anything that weakened superiority could be regarded as strengthening the authority of the state, as well as increasing the security of landed society. There is a natural tendency to believe in the identity of the interest of one's own sector of society and that of society as a whole, expressed a few years back by a chairman of General Motors in the words 'What's good for General Motors

---

[42] 31 Mar. 1760.
[43] *Scots Magazine*, Jan. 1760, p. 44.
[44] Lord Grange to earl of Islay, 16 and 17 Dec., 1724, ((S.R.O., GD/124/15/1262/2).

is good for the U.S.'. I think this attitude had a parallel in the Scotland of the eighteenth century.

A partial study of the case law of the eighteenth century—I have not been equipped in terms either of intellect or time to make it more than partial—has made me notice several points of interest. Scottish pleading could either be based on careful consideration of minutiae, which it usually was concerning rights in land, or it could base itself simply on broad issues of the good of society. The judges were prepared to considered and take up both types of argument. In some cases even landed rights used the latter type of argument, and we can find in the pleadings remarks of this type: 'when a man purchased land for a full price, it was a natural consequence that he should have more power over it than if he had got it as a gratuity for military service'.[45] Statements like this were an open door to the weakening of feudal rights. In a major discussion of the relationship between superior and vassal in 1752 it was stated 'the feudal law is wearing out, and we have in a great measure lost sight of its principles'.[46] In one sense this was a true statement of fact: in another it merely meant that the lawyers were hurrying on the process of wear and tear. The lawyers were capable even of over-riding the stipulations in feu charters.[47] They took particularly short shrift with ancient privileges that showed themselves handicaps to economic development, whether these privileges were those of landowners in their baron courts or, more often, burghs.[48] In 1762 a judicial decision severely damaged the rights of barons to limit brewing and selling ale in their baronies: such rights were labelled 'oppressive monopolies'.[49] The law lords also took a fairly casual approach to the rights of authors to copyright: 'an author had no property in a book ... further than in the copies remaining in his hands ' was one decision.[50] Another area of particular attack was the privilege of the church.

I have already written about the main attack on the rights of the church,

---

[45] W. M. Morison, *The decisions of the court of session from its institution until the separation of the court into two divisions in the year 1808, digested under proper heads in the form of a dictionary* (Edinburgh, 1811) (hereafter cited as Morison, *Dictionary of decisions*), i, 152; Sir Alexander Cockburn against creditors of Langton, 1747.

[46] Henry Home, Lord Kames, *Remarkable decisions of the court of session, 1736–57* (Edinburgh, 1766) (hereafter cited as Kames, *Remarkable decisions*), pp 279–82; Anne and Margaret Landales *contra* Thomas Landale.

[47] Morison, *Dictionary of decisions*, xvii, 5112–5; Johnston and others against the magistrates of Canongate, 1804.

[48] The section of Morison, op. cit., on Burgh Royal in iii, 1835–2017 and app. pp 1–44, provides numerous instances of restriction on burghal privileges.

[49] Morison, *Dictionary of decisions*, xvii, 15,009–10; Water-Orrock against Michael Bennet etc., 1762.

[50] Sir James Fergusson of Kilkerran, *Decisions of the court of session, 1738–52* (Edinburgh, 1775) (hereafter cited as Kilkerran, *Decisions*), pp 96–8; the booksellers of London *contra* the booksellers of Edinburgh and Glasgow, 1748.

the taking away of the control of the poor law by landowners in the mid-eighteenth century by means of judicial decision.[51] That this was an act of legal piracy is clear from the language used in the pleading: there was no appeal to case law or existing legal practice, since none supported this action. Instead the argument was based on the highest claim of all, that the relief of poverty was part of the 'police of government', and that it would be 'popish' to allow the church as such any say in this. It belonged, as did control over any money raised on their estates, to the landowners, by natural right. Other church rights, or 'assumed rights', were also under attack: in 1776 a legal decision placed restrictions on what a minister might say in church about the morals of members of his congregation. 'There may no doubt be a liberty of the pulpit in the matter of censure necessary to the improvement of the morals of the people. But . . . clergymen have no right to expose the characters and conduct of particular persons'.[52]

Land law did not give the same opportunity for imperialism as did the uncertain areas of ecclesiastical rights and privileges, but even so it is in this subject that the most revealing area for the 'General Motors' approach is found. The objections to the powers of feudal superiors gained force because not only did they limit the liberty of the subject, but they were a handicap to the economic exploitation of land, to the use of it as the landowner judged best. 'It is the privilege of property, that the proprietor can be put under no restraint' was stated as law in 1744, but was more truly an aspiration,[53] (although it informed the liberalisation of the law of entail in 1770). But in one important area of law, preserved and extended in the eighteenth century, the privileges of the landowners were, in practice, restrictions on the rights and enterprise of tenants, and so on the best economic exploitation of the land. This was the law of hypothec, the Scottish variant, in an enhanced form, of the English law of distress. It gave a landowner a prior claim on the goods of his tenantry towards the payment of his rent in any case of failure or potential failure. If that had been all, there would be little to comment about it. Hypothec also gave the labourer a similar lien on the farmer for his wages, but this was not an area for effective action very often.[54] As interpreted by lawyers, hypothec went far

[51] Rosalind Mitchison, 'The making of the old Scottish poor law' in *Past and Present*, lxii (1974), pp 81–8; see in particular Kames, *Remarkable decisions* pp 250–7: heritors of Humbie *contra* Kirk session, 1751.

[52] Morison, *Dictionary of decisions*, iv, app. pp 9–15; John, Robert and David Scotlands *versus* the Reverend James Thomson, minister of Dunfermline, 1776.

[53] Kames, *Remarkable decisions*, p. 80; Fairlie of Fairlie *contra* earl of Eglinton, 1744. It is, though, to be noted that the generalised nature of the principles enunciated suggests a case for which substantive legal support was lacking.

[54] Hypothec was investigated in a somewhat partial manner in the nineteenth century in *Report of the select committee on the law of hypothec in Scotland*, H.L. 1868–9, ix. It was already well established by the time of Stair.

beyond simply preventing a landowner losing his rent. In 1748 it was allowed that 'no mortal is intitled to touch the crop' until the landlord's rent was set aside; and the normal tenancy agreement, that victual rents, that is rents paid in kind, were due between Yule and Candlemas meant that the landowner could arrive at his tenant's farm and take any corn he chose that had been threshed at any time after Yule, and make that his rent.[55] In practice such intereference in the actual process of farming was unlikely to be common, since landowners did not want to come into such intimate contact with the source of their wealth. A more serious infringement of a tenant's rights, with more significant economic consequences, was a decision in 1780 that since a tenant who made his living by acting as a grazier for other men's cattle had no stock of his own which could be distrained for rent, the landowner was entitled to regard the tenancy as void and to evict.[56]

I am not asserting that all significant legal changes in the eighteenth century were in the interests of the landowning class. We can find, for instance, the judges refusing to give sanction to property obtained by fraud, even by the form of fraud most intimately a part of the Scottish way of life, customs fraud. We can find them anxiously preserving the morals of society.[57] But many of their decision do seem inspired by the phrase I have already quoted, that 'when a man has purchased land . . . it was a natural consequence that he should have more power over it' than if it had been given for military service. If he is to have more power, someone else has to have less. There was always a class dimension to the aims of the 'compleat the union' school, and it became more marked as the century went on.

The theme of the patriotic need to 'compleat the union' reached a high point in 1760 in the well-known debate on the issue of a Scottish militia. Gilbert Elliot, who raised this in parliament, had already shown himself a 'compleater' when five years before he had discussed the tenure of sheriffs in Scotland in a whiggish and constitutional manner on 'as high a key as any English member of parliament'.[58] There is a well-known exchange of letters between Elliot and David Hume on what Englishness meant to them, which encapsulates Elliot's patriotism. 'Love the French as much as you will . . .', Elliot had written, 'but above all continue still an Englishman'. Hume wrote back 'I do not believe there is one Englishmen in fifty, who, if he heard that I had broke my neck tonight, woud not be rejoic'd with it.

---

[55] Kames, *Remarkable decisions*, pp 149–51: Sir John Hall of Dunglass *contra* William Nisbet of Dirleton, 1748.

[56] Morison, *Dictionary of decisions*, viii, 6214–5: Ross McKye against Nabony, 1780.

[57] See for instance Kilkerran, *Decisions*, p. 66: Drysdale pursuer, 1752; pp 93–5: Alison *contra* the representatives of Williamson, 1749; Kames, *Remarkable decisions*, p. 181: Elizabeth Linning *contra* Alexander Hamilton, 1748.

[58] G. F. S. Elliott, *The Border Elliots* (Edinburgh, 1897), p. 339.

Some hate me because I am not a tory, some because I am not a whig, some because I am not a Christian, and all because I am a Scotsman. . . . Am I, or are you, an Englishman? Will they allow us to be so?' To this Elliot wrote 'we are both Englishman; that is, true British subjects, entitled to every emolument and advantage that our happy constitution can bestow'.[59] If they were citizens of England at this time, a time when Scots would be unpopular in England because they were Scots, it was of an England only of the mind. This exchange can be contrasted with one after the first world war, when Haig gave a copy of his dispatches to Haldane, inscribing them to the Englishman who had done so much for his country:[60] both men were lowland Scots, but did not meet with hatred on this account in England.

Clearly the union was not complete if theere was an English militia but no Scottish one. A militia was a desirable safeguard against invasion, as well as a way of channelling money and influence through landed families. The themes raised by Gilbert Elliot gained support from the miscellaneous 'representative' institutions of the country: the Edinburgh town council, the commissions of supply of various counties, and freeholders' meetings were called specially to debate and urge the claim. 'Why a people, united under one and the same king, and entitled to the same protection in their laws, religion and property should be neglected in the distribution of arms' was the opening of a long article in the *Caledonian Mercury*.[61] It was, of course, well known why. The issue of a militia had been entangled in the whole issue of disarming the rebel clans and in the problem of whether a government should rely on and accept clanship in the 1740s.[62] However much Scots might point to the fact that lowlanders were loyal and high-landers were now enrolled in the army, and that the '45 would never have got off the ground if there had been a militia in the highlands, the government was unwilling to take a chance on the loyalty of the Scottish upper class and give them this privilege. Even the very real threat of a French squadron off the west coast could not force surrender in Westminster.

The militia debate—heated and voluminous—gave an opportunity for a display of the sort of 'patriotism within the union' theme, but the events of this year (1760) in the Edinburgh press reveal other themes at least as interesting and as important at the time. In spite of the tendency of the Scottish intelligentsia and upper class to be very happy with their existing constitution, there was the beginning of the movement to clean up abuses in

[59] E. C. Mossner, *The life of David Hume* (Oxford, 1970), p. 405; Elliott, op. cit., pp 386–7.

[60] F. Maurice, *Life of Lord Haldane* (London, 1937–9), ii, 172.

[61] 31 Mar. 1760.

[62] Rosalind Mitchison, 'The government and the highlands, 1707–45' in Phillipson and Mitchison, *Scotland in the age of improvement*, pp 24–46.

the electoral system, to get rid of faggot votes and perjury by giving the vote to property.[63] Again the good of society and the good of landed society coincided. There were efforts of the improving societies and clubs to promote economic change by means of 'premiums' for various types of industrial performance. The Edinburgh Society's 1760 list included premiums for raising hawthorns for fencing, for making turkey carpets, and, significantly, for the best hogshead of two-year old porter and for the making of 'imitation English blankets'. The Select Society, that most central of the enlightenment organisations, also put blankets on its list. One of the comments made by the Edinburgh Society about the blankets was that 'the society observes with pleasure, that the manufacturers of blankets have, in a considerable degree, avoided the error which they fell into at first, of using yarn too hard and twisted'.[64] In this year, when assimilation did not go so far as to bring the militia to Scotland, at least it was achieving the end of the Scotch blanket.

But the most significant movement of 1760, in the degree of support and the amount of agitation worked up, a movement that far surpassed the militia question in the heat raised, and that caused more county meetings and declarations from them, was one which also involved these societies as well as other influential groups, the Faculty of Advocates, the Society of Clerks to the Signet, the Grand Lodge of the Scottish Freemasons, the Scots Hunters, etc. The full list would be long and boring, and there is a strong likelihood that many individuals had a say in different organisations, so it would not be of use to quantify the movement. It was a movement of social, but not of constitutional, importance. No reference was made in the declarations to the revolution of 1689, but many to the current state of society, though not usually in the sophisticated language of the great thinkers of the day. What was it that produced an agitation putting the question of the Scottish militia in the shade? The issue of servants' vails.[65]

Vails or tips were extracted by servants from guests to the houses in which they worked. Servants would line the hall and expect departing guests to line their pockets. Failure to comply would mean, on a later visit, systematic bad service. The custom existed in England too, but perhaps not so markedly. It related, it seems likely, to the low level of customary wages in all walks of life in Scotland, as well as to the fact that Scottish upper class houses lacked the organisation of the English at this time: service was directed more personally to a human being than institutionally to the household or the fabric of the house. This meant, in fact, that a fair amount

---

[63] 'Hints concerning the Scots police' in *Scots Magazine*, Dec. 1760, pp 646–7.
[64] *Edinburgh Courant*, 13 Mar. 1760.
[65] This is discussed in David D. McElroy, *A century of Scottish clubs*, (Typescript, Edinburgh, 1969), pp 99–101, and without recognition of the particular Scottish ambience in J. J. Hecht, *The domestic servant class in eighteenth century England* (London, 1956), p. 164.

of servants were simply engaged in hanging about. Certainly the agitation against vails produced the statement (unquestioned) in the papers that if a farm servant, a labourer, would work for his keep and annual wages of £2, then £6 was more than enough for a domestic servant.[66] Later, as vails disappeared, advertisements of footmen seeking places explained that now they would expect higher pay.[67] The meetings and societies, all of course, of upper class or professional people, in the case of the county meetings presumably the same people who had already discussed militia, produced statements binding themselves not to give vails or, as employers, to allow their servants to demand them. The press of 1760 is full of this domestic class war, culminating in this sentence from the *Scots Magazine;* 'men and women born to servitude, have no right to aim at high station. . . . Time was . . . when servants . . . considered their masters and mistresses as parents, and they in return, looked on servants as humble children. . . .'[68] It is not a usual attitude of parents to children to look on them as 'born to servitude', and the remark is a valuable antidote to the general picture of enlightenment society seriously discussing the benefits to society produced by the reductions of inequality. National identity of interest was giving way to a class feeling even this early.

This may be considered as attaching too much weight to what is, in the end, a truly domestic issue. But there was a parallel protest going on in the outside world at the same time, the demand, originating in Stirlingshire, by farmers that something be done to stop farm labourers demanding high wages. Farm servants were said to be leaving their work or insisting on higher pay. The farmers wanted the justices to fix wages. The justices alleged that the trouble was the result of 'concert' among the lower class, and passed the ball to county meetings. The county meeting of Midlothian urged a national system of wage regulation. Actually nothing seems to have happened.[69]

Two other minor features of interest appear in the press in this year. One is almost routine, the prosecution of some collier serfs who had 'withdrawn their labour', that is attempted to change jobs. They had to be taught that the rhetoric about the liberty of the Englishman did not apply to them. The other is the founding of a society in Glasgow to support destitute highlanders who had come to the city. This philanthropic venture justified itself with the words 'the riches and strength of every well-regulated country must depend on the number and industry of its people'.[70]

[66] *Scots Magazine*, Mar. 1760, p. 147.

[67] See for instance *Edinburgh Courant*, 31 May 1760: 'as the servants' vails are taken away, it's expected that the wages will be agreeable to make up the loss'.

[68] *Scots Magazine*, Feb. 1760, p. 81.

[69] Ibid., Aug. 1760, p. 445; Oct. 1760, p. 551.

[70] Ibid., Jan. 1760, p. 48.

Of course all this is small beer, but there is, I think, something significant in the total package of activity of this year. The improvers are becoming a well organised movement, and getting some successes. The 'compleat the union' men have made a big splash. Some people in the central lowland valley are beginning to feel a sense of communal obligation to highlanders. And many of the upper class are trying hard, in a modern phrase, to see differentials perpetuated. The two last features become increasingly apparent as the century went on. Increasingly the highlander, no longer feared, was regarded as part of the community. Encouragement was given to this attitude by the vogue for Ossian, already underway by 1760. But I think it would be true to say that Macpherson's success with his Ossian writings was a symptom of the new attitude, combining sympathy, ignorance, optimism and romance, rather than simply a cause. The new attitude went on to produce plans for promoting highland development, described so well by Youngson,[71] for instance, the British Fisheries Society as a practical attempt to do something, and the Highland Society in the 1780s, in which romantic self-consciousness blended with practical concern. In the earlier part of the century those writers who had treated the highlander as a fellow citizen had been people who were landowners on or near the highland line. Their sympathy was tempered with knowledge. Now we get the beginnings of the modern romantic myth.

While the consciousness of common nationality was being extended to the highlander, it was being withdrawn from the bottom of the social scale. It was, increasingly, class divisions which came to obstruct national consciousness and solidarity rather than political, religious or geographical.

One of the areas where class division showed was the working of the poor law. The take-over of this by the landowning class, already referred to, had at least a logic in operation terms, because in any real emergency only the landowner could raise enough funds to save the situation. Landowners were already acting in this way. Whereas in the famine of the 1690s some landowners had been prepared to ignore their duty in relief, in the crisis year of 1740 there had been a remarkably coordinated effort between the church and the landowners to stave off famine. Sir John Clerk of Penicuik tells in his memoir how the gentry of Midlothian had subscribed £2,000 to buy grain abroad and sell it below cost, and added 'we were so far from receiving thanks from the country people whose lives we had supported, that they were either insensible or ungrateful for the favours we had done them'.[72] His comments reveals a certain amount of social cleavage. A similar action was undertaken in the harvest failure of 1782. In one county

[71] Youngson, *After the fortyfive*, ch. 4.
[72] J. M. Gray (ed.), *Memoirs of the life of Sir John Clerk of Penicuik* (Scottish History Society, 1st series, xiii, Edinburgh, 1892), p. 192.

the landowners called themselves into a committee and collected evidence about the level of shortage, decided how much of this had to be met, and raised the necessary funds. But by then the social attitude to the poor law was hardening, and as a result there had been a change in the accepted definitions of the law. It was argued that the able-bodied had no right to relief, and that even those with entitlement were supposed to receive only marginal support, a small supplement to what they could pick up otherwise. This policy would enable many parishes to continue to run the service on voluntary funds, and in general there was apparent by 1780 the attitude that any system of assessment for relief, which meant of course, assessment of the landowners, was a moral evil, encouraging an attitude of dependency.

Scotland was no longer undeveloped. She was moving into the industrial revolution, though on a narrow front. Farming was being reorganised. The changes meant better incomes for most people, but as always drastic economic and social change meant that there was an increased probability of some people slipping through the net into destitution. So the change in attitude to these was important. One can find instances at the end of the eighteenth century of cases being denied relief who would certainly have obtained it in the seventeenth century.[73] At the same time the tone of commentary on society has changed from that of the early improvers. The note of angry humiliation has gone by the 1790s, and in the *Statistical account* of that decade there is instead one of buoyant achievement.

Possibly if the changes of the 1790s had been purely domestic, the shift of wealth to commercial and industrial activities would have weakened the political and social dominance of landowners, and a more truly fluid society have developed. Possibly not, of course. The evangelical revival had enabled the church to occupy a much more central position in men's allegiance than it had for a century or so, and yet at the same time democratic and radical voices were to be heard in the lay world. There were forces for change which could have softened the rigidities of the social structure. But the clamp down produced by the panic over the French revolution, in and after 1794, made for a further hardening. It became patriotic to be against any change which might weaken the established society. In the later volumes of the *Statistical account* there is very apparent a nervous assertion of the contentment and comfort of the people under their present political system, which is, in fact, a sign of the deep class division of this society.[74]

---

[73] For example, petition of John Brand, weaver, late of Dunnichen, 3 June 1800 (Signet Library, Court of Session papers, 416:56). This was an unsuccessful appeal for help in getting a wet-nurse for a motherless child.

[74] The change seems to occur between vols x and xi, both produced in 1794.

So by the early nineteenth century the nature of patriotism had changed. It had become the patriotism of a class, or of two classes, upper and middle. Scots in the more privileged world now looked to the English connection not as a means of enabling them to improve their own country, and make her more worthy of respect, but to support them in their privilege. The 'compleat the union' school had triumphed over the attitude of the upper classes. The theory had always meant adding the privileges of English landowners, particularly those privileges that related to government, to the already considerable advantages which Scottish landowners had in relation to their peasantry. It had meant gaining liberty under the law with a considerable opportunity to change the law itself. (Typical of this attitude, as is well known, was the movement for the introduction of jury trial, successful in the nineteenth century.) It had meant freeing their property from vexations feudal obligations to those above them while acknowledging very little in the way of tenant right to those below them. By the end of the century the Scottish upper classes were being able to claim it as a sign of superior national virtue that they carried only about a fifth of the burden of poor relief of their English counterparts. Both God and Mammon were on their side.

Janet Adam Smith has discussed the identity problem of the Scots—were they a sort of second class Englishmen? Was the union to be perpetually an 'unfair and uneasy' partnership?[75] It is the argument of this paper that the landed gentlemen of Scotland were managing to be super-first-class citizens of Great Britain. They were getting the benefits of both societies in terms of status and privilege, and adding to it all a touch of 'holier than thou', as seriousness in religion became fashionable. Landed society would accept seriousness: it drew back only when the issue of control of the ministry was raised by the new evangelicalism. The considerable benefits experienced by the Scottish gentry gave a strong vested interest both in a stable, even a static, society, and in close ties with the English landed society from which so much had been borrowed.

The improvers had been possessed of an outward-looking and progressive attitude, and in the long run, often at considerable risk to themselves, had transformed their country. Now by the end of the eighteenth century they had been replaced by a nostalgic and complacent, inward-looking group, which admired the achievements of the country in the past, derived a somewhat unjustified esteem from them, and was determined to keep closely assimilated to England. There was to be a common 'establishment' front between the two countries. The patriotism of the nineteenth century was to be retrospective and, on the whole, unreforming. It is shown

[75] 'Eighteenth century ideas of Scotland' in Phillipson and Mitchison, *Scotland in the age of improvement*, p. 109.

in the attitude to Scotland of both Henry Cockburn and Walter Scott. Cockburn wrote 'my reason is with the modern world, my dreams are with the old'.[76] What he took to be the old, from which he derived both his veneration for the law and the church, and his willingness to see the poor law made purely voluntary, was considerably influenced by the limited historical knowledge then available. Scott's feeling for the past was historically much deeper and more substantiated. It informs his novels, and led to the famous passionate rebuke to Jeffrey over law reform: 'little by little, whatever your wishes may be, you will destroy and undermine, until nothing of what makes Scotland Scotland shall remain'.[77] The essence of national identity now lay in the past This fact has been a major element in the unwillingness of Scots to pay serious attention to their own history, lest they disturb the accepted myths. Phillipson has pointed out how the Scots learnt to assert their 'difference' from the English in outbursts of pedantic antiquarianism, which avoided any likelihood of leading to separation, or in fact, of being taken seriously.[78] The purpose of this paper is to add to this insight a class dimension, and show that this attitude came from nervousness about possible economic or political insubordination.

[76] H. Cockburn, *Journal* (Edinburgh, 1874), ii 91.
[77] J. Lockhart, *Life of Sir Walter Scott* (Edinburgh, 1902), ii, 284.
[78] N. T. Phillipson, 'Nationalism and ideology', in J. N. Wolfe (ed.), *Government and nationalism in Scotland* (Edinburgh, 1969), p. 186.

V

Revolutionary nationalism in Ireland: the I.R.B., 1858–1924

Leon Ó Broin

The reference to revolutionary nationalism in the title of this paper might suggest that, following P. S. O'Hegarty[1], I intended to discuss the many movements in the last century or so in which he found separatist tendencies. The sub-title will, however, make it clear that I had something else in mind, in fact a single organisation that came into being in 1858 and went out of existence in 1924. This organisation was undoubtedly revolutionary in intent—it passed as the Irish *Revolutionary* Brotherhood for a number of years before becoming the Irish *Republican* Brotherhood, but whether revolutionary or republican it was always the I.R.B., or, colloquially, the Organisation, and its revolutionary ambition was to end the British occupation in Ireland, ultimately by physical force.

From the beginning it was an oath-bound secret society, and the form of the oath was altered more than once. An appendix to the constitution of 1869[2] gave 'for the sake of uniformity and simplicity' a short form in which the I.R.B. was not specifically mentioned, as it was in one devised four years later. We cannot be sure what form the oath took before it was shortened, but we do know a good deal about two oaths that were in use in 1858 and 1859. Both of these were drafted by Thomas Clarke Luby. He told Charles Gavan Duffy in 1881 that it had been his good or ill-luck to have figured several times in what he called 'this branch of revolutionary literature'. 'In '52' he said, 'I wrote an oath for another "birth-strangled" conspiracy, and under Stephens's correction [*sic*] I wrote two oaths successively used by the I.R.B. previously to the political trials of 1865'[3]. Luby, of course, was one of the founding fathers of Irish Fenianism, and in one of the letters on which John O'Leary based his published reminiscences, he describes how, in James Stephens's room in a street behind and parallel to Lombard Street, Dublin, where the first I.R.B. meeting was held on St Patrick's day 1858, he drew up the form of what it is fair to regard as the original I.R.B. oath. This,

[1] *History of Ireland under the union* (London, 1952).
[2] T. W. Moody and Leon Ó Broin (ed.) 'The I.R.B. supreme council, 1868–78' in *Irish Historical Studies*, xix, no. 75 (Mar. 1975), pp 306–7.
[3] N.L.I., MS 331–3, p. 8.

to the best of Luby's recollection, committed the person attested to do his utmost, at every risk, while life lasted, to establish an independent democratic republic; to yield implicit obedience, in all things not contrary to the laws of God or morality—he was not sure which—to the commands of his superior officers, and to preserve inviolable secrecy regarding all the affairs of this secret society that might be confided to him.[4]

The inspiration 'to get up [in Ireland] an organisation to win Irish independence'—the phrase is Luby's—came from America, from John O'Mahony principally, who—to quote Luby again—'professed a very romantic strain of friendship for Stephens'. Stephens sent for Luby and the two met for the first time in the timber yard in Lombard Street of Peter Langan, a '48 man who, with a little knot of Dublin and Kingstown friends, had been in the habit of going out to the hills on Sundays to practise military exercises. They had a drill master, a staff-sergeant of the militia, and among themselves they collected money to buy rifles. This was the first group to take the I.R.B. oath, and of Stephens at that time Luby says that he did not seem to think that Ireland could do anything till a revolution occurred in England. He was more interested in the idea of universal philanthropy, whatever that meant precisely, than in Irish patriotism. He gave vent to socialistic theories that Luby did not like. He was affected, dogmatic and arrogant, and it was only later when he threw himself into the organising of the I.R.B. that his ability became apparent.[5]

Stephens and O'Mahony had been together for some time in Paris, in what A. M. Sullivan called the central training school of European revolutionism,[6] and Stephens, in his study of revolutionary societies, paid particular attention to those with ramifications in Italy, for he believed that the Italians had in a certain way perfected conspiracy, and were the best models to follow. He greatly admired Mazzini without wishing to be a servile imitator of him, and he joined the International Workingmen's Association in 1866.[7] However, one need hardly look beyond the preamble to the French constitution of 1848, which Stephens must have known well, to find the allusions to independence, democracy and a republic that were embodied in the first I.R.B. oath and to the spirit of fraternity that one connects with an organised brotherhood.

The oath, such as it was, landed Stephens and Luby in trouble at a very early stage. They discovered in Skibbereen a group like Peter Langan's which since 1856 had been functioning as the Phoenix National and Literary Society, whose members repudiated the queen of England and were

---

[4] Ibid., p. 52.
[5] Ibid., p. 5.
[6] A.M. Sullivan, *New Ireland* (London, 16th edition), p. 192.
[7] Desmond Ryan, *The fenian chief* (London, 1967), p. 51.

committed to taking up arms to fight for Ireland at a moment's notice. Enrolling them in the I.R.B. in the early summer of 1858, Stephens added to this general intention the specific goal of an independent, democratic republic, and sent them out to spread the gospel of revolt; and this they were zealously doing when they were denounced from three different directions, by parish priests and their curates at the Sunday masses, in the popular *Nation* newspaper by A. M. Sullivan and William Smith O'Brien, who had been alerted by David Moriarty, bishop of Kerry, and in a government proclamation that offered rewards for the conviction of persons administering the oath or of being members of the society that imposed it. The government, A. M. Sullivan said, had alerted the bishop but in the opening days of October the government received from Bishop Moriarty's vicar general, the parish priest of Kenmare, an account of an active conspiracy being organised in the parish and copies of oaths that were being administered to 'deluded young men'.[8] In Callan, county Kilkenny, another group 'denominated *democratic*' was similarly uncovered and broken up. There were informers about as usual, both there and in West Cork, and these told the government that the society they were looking for had been formed under the direction of, and in close communication with, a similar one in America which supplied funds.[9]

The government already knew a good deal about the American society. It had evolved in 1858 out of the Emmet Monument Association, which John O'Mahony and Michael Doheny had established two or three years before with the object of invading and liberating Ireland.[10] The Irish Constabulary had a sub-inspector, Thomas Doyle, working for them in the eastern cities of the United States. He was there from 1858 till the outbreak of the civil war and returned when the war ended, and the extracts he sent home from the *Irish News*, the *Irish American*, the *Irish Vindicator*, and particularly from the *Phoenix*, the New York organ of the Phoenix Society, Confederation or Brotherhood—all three descriptions were used—kept the government abreast of what the refugees from the 1848 movement were up to. John O'Mahony was the president of the Phoenix Society with Michael Doheny and Michael Corcoran his lieutenants—there were branches, a military organisation of sorts (Phoenix Brigades etc.), and a Patriotic Defence Fund for the benefit of the Skibbereen prisoners, to one of whom, on his release from gaol, a reception was given by the Fenian Brotherhood which was another name, it was said, for the Phoenix Society. The synonymity of the terms Phoenix and Fenian was confirmed in Dublin Castle on

---

[8] Sullivan, *New Ireland*, p. 201; N.L.I., MS 11187(4).
[9] N.L.I., MS 11187.
[10] N.L.I., MS 7517, p. 86; William D'Arcy, *The fenian movement in the United States, 1858–1886* (1947), p. 6.

the authority of Samuel Lee Anderson who, when he prepared material for an official history of Fenianism, said that he could not trace any real distinction between the Phoenix conspiracy and the Fenian conspiracy that followed it.[11] But while Fenian was a term applicable only to the American Fenian Brotherhood it was, like Sinn Fein in later times, popularly but incorrectly used in Ireland. As late as 1868 the Irish Revolutionary Brotherhood was the name by which what Anderson called the Irish branch of the Fenians was more properly identified; and he distinguished between the Irish Revolutionary Brotherhood and the Fenian Brotherhood by explaining that the Irish Revolutionary Brotherhood was designed to be a secret revolutionary society that could put an army in the field, whereas the Fenian Brotherhood was an auxiliary society whose mission was to provide 'the sinews of war', to supply the army in the field with arms and military stores, with officers, and conceivably with reinforcements of men.[12]

When Stephens and Luby met in the French capital in 1859 and reconsidered the position in the light of the Phoenix trials in Ireland, and, no doubt, of the opposition of the catholic church, they decided that a modified oath was necessary, and Stephens thereupon dictated what Luby called the Paris test. In this test the individual solemnly swore to give allegiance to 'the Irish Republic now virtually established', to defend its independence and integrity, and, as before, to obey his superior officers in all things not contrary to the laws of morality. The changes are noteworthy. The 'democratic republic' has disappeared—the concern now is with a republic *simpliciter*—and gone also are the references to secrecy and to the affairs of 'this secret society'. 'Henceforth', said Luby, 'we denied that we were *technically* a secret body. We called ourselves a mere military organisation with, so to speak, a legionary oath like [what] all soldiers [take]'. He does not say why the word democratic was dropped: like 'secret' it was perhaps in the circumstances of that time, a dirty word.[13]

An odd feature of the Paris test, but one that did not long endure, was the allegation that the republic in that year 1859 was 'virtually established'. This phrase, like what Luby described as the absurd magniloquence that sent him to America in 1863 as 'the Envoy of the Irish republic or Irish nation'—he did not remember which—was a sample of a make-believe to which Stephens and O'Mahony easily succumbed. Stephens's 'virtually established republic' was 'the grand invention' on which, according to Luby, he most piqued himself.[14] It was indeed a grand invention, a myth

---

[11] N.L.I., MS 7517.
[12] Ibid., p. 89.
[13] N.L.I., MS 331–3, p. 15.
[14] Ibid., p. 54.

that made a successful crossing to the United States, and, under Stephens's magnetic influence, was adopted by the Fenian Brotherhood at its first national convention in Chicago in 1863, and it survived down to our own times. There were people still 'recognising' the first Dail long after it had been more than once replaced by the democratic process. Nevertheless, the I.R.B. as an organisation displayed greater realism with the passage of time, and in 1917 the Republic, 'virtually established' in 1859, and provisionally proclaimed in 1867 and 1916, was still just an objective to be aimed at.

Stephens may have deluded himself into thinking that the Republic was just around the corner when he saw how easy it was to get men to join the I.R.B. The numbers rose with great rapidity. Early in 1865 the government were told that the number of drilled Fenians in Ireland exceeded 120,000.[15] The expansion had occurred mainly in the urban areas, and Luby noted in his letters to O'Leary that among the first enrolled in Dublin were men from the patriotic reading rooms or who had worked for T. D. Sullivan's National Petition or in the McMahon Sword of Honour campaign. Later, nearly all the Irish, English and Scottish members of the numerically strong Brotherhood of St Patrick were absorbed.[16] The practice had begun of exploiting open national societies as recruiting grounds, and of changing sometimes the direction in which those societies planned to travel.

After the Skibbereen affair the conduct of the catholic church's opposition to the secret societies he saw around him was taken up by Paul Cullen, the archbishop of Dublin, the most significant figure perhaps on the Irish landscape in the thirty year period between the death of O'Connell and the emergence of Parnell. As a bishop Cullen had a positive obligation to act against secret societies since they were forbidden by the church, but he had also the strongest personal conviction that, in a Europe in which the pope was being stripped of his temporal powers and in which revolutionaries generally were hostile to the church, any threat of successful revolt in Ireland would be bad for the cause of religion everywhere. He fixed his attention in the first instance on the Brotherhood of St Patrick, whose inner circle he believed was oath-bound and Mazzinian—it was 1848 all over again, he said, and decidedly anti-clerical. He was particularly galled by the behaviour of Fr Patrick Lavelle, who was to become the brotherhood's vice-president and who was protected, if not instigated, so Cullen believed, by his bishop, John McHale, of Tuam.[17] Cullen's judgment of the situation

[15] N.L.I., MS 7517, p. 137.

[16] N.L.I., MS 331–3, p. 32; Richard Pigott, *Recollections of an Irish national journalist* (Dublin, 1883), pp 117–19.

[17] Patrick J. Corish (ed.), 'Irish College Rome: Kirby papers' in *Archivium Hibernicum*, xxxii, 52–4; Patrick J. Corish, 'Political problems 1860–1878' in *History of Irish catholicism*, v, ch. 3 (1967).

was broadly accurate. The president of the St Patrick's Brotherhood, Thomas Neilson Underwood, was an I.R.B. man; the secretary in 1863, Charles Guilfoyle Doran, was the secretary of the supreme council of the I.R.B. in 1873; and all the original members of the I.R.B. joined the other Brotherhood in order to maintain a controlling influence over it.[18] They acted similarly and for the same reason when a committee was formed to arrange the funeral of Terence Bellew MacManus.

MacManus had been a Young Irelander, a '48 man, and the surviving Young Ireland leaders, Fr John Kenyon, John Martin, John Blake Dillon, P. J. Smyth and William Smith O'Brien, understandably felt that the funeral arrangements should be left to them. The I.R.B. had other ideas. Seeing themselves as the up and coming party, they were intolerant of the older men who, Luby said, saw plainly that if the physical force movement was allowed full swing, it would destroy their pet fiction that it was idle to attempt to rouse the Irish people to any fresh effort by force of arms to restore Irish national independence. That fiction, ever since '48, had allowed the Young Irelanders to pose as patriots while keeping their precious skins free from all necessity of incurring further risk through any too bold antagonism to British power.[19] The arrogance of that statement was echoed by another of the original I.R.B. men, Joseph Denieffe, who bluntly declared that the MacManus funeral was used by them to demonstrate that they were supreme over the land, and that the Sullivans, the Grays and the prelatists were *hors de combat*.[20] The Sullivans and Grays controlled the popular nationalist newspapers, and outstanding among the prelatists was Archbishop Cullen, who refused a lying-in-state for Mac-Manus, rightly concluding that this was planned as a manifesto in favour of revolution. The government view was rather similar. The remains of the Young Irelander had been brought home from California avowedly to show respect to the 'departed patriot' but really to show the strength of the revolutionary body in Ireland and their chances of success. They were aware of a letter of John O'Mahony's in which he had foreseen the possibility of a great national funeral turning the scales in their favour. The I.R.B., therefore, riposted on Cullen by keeping the body in state in the Mechanics' Institute for what Luby called a week 'of triumph for us and our cause'. 'An endless stream of priest-defiant visitors'—as many as 9,000 a day—passed the catafalque,[21] while Fr Lavelle placarded the city with a remonstrance addressed to the archbishop whom Luby called 'this arch-

[18] Joseph Denieffe, *A personal narrative of the Irish Revolutionary Brotherhood* (New York, 1906; reprint, Shannon, 1969), p. 56.
[19] N.L.I., MS 331–3, p. 99.
[20] Denieffe, op. cit., p. 71.
[21] N.L.I., MS 7517, p. 98.

shaveling, this most baleful of ecclesiastics'.[22] Simultaneously, in another of
his colourful phrases, Luby said that the I.R.B. 'were incessantly spoken of
in the slavish priest-ridden press as a hellish horde of godless infidels and
would-be lawless Jacobin cut-throats'.[23] However, neither the denunciations nor the inclement weather affected the turnout on the day of the
funeral, for the police estimated that some 8,000 men of respectable
appearance followed the remains to Glasnevin.[24] They did this, the
organisers claimed, to prove to the world that they loved the old cause for
which MacManus had suffered.

The archbishop's view, if somewhat cynical, was not dissimilar. The
marching men knew little except that they were pledged to fight for Ireland,
he told his Roman agent. Some of them had said that they would have
nothing more to do with church and clergy, but others had left the banned
St Patrick's Brotherhood, either dreading excommunication or because
they did not know who their leader was; he might be some honest detective,
Cullen suggested, who was out to entrap them all.[25] Looking back on the
episode in later years Luby saw Cullen's action as a reverse for the I.R.B. as
serious as it was unexpected; the breach that then occurred had never been
healed.[26] It was also an occasion when Irish republicans discovered something they have never since forgotten, the exploitable potential of a funeral
for political purposes.

It was 1870 before the bishops obtained from Rome an explicit and
comprehensive condemnation[27] to put an end to the debate on whether the
earlier papal pronouncements about secret societies really applied to
Fenianism, and to still in some measure Fr Lavelle's assertion of the
inherent right of catholics to revolt against a wicked alien tyranny. A weekly
I.R.B. paper, the *Irish People*, which largely concentrated its fire on the
church on the plea of keeping priests out of politics had been suppressed in
September 1865. This, and a police raid on the paper's premises, put the
government in possession of all the information they required about the
extent and character of the conspiracy, and enabled them to have the
leaders convicted and put away. Stephens managed to escape to America
and tried to reunite the rival factions into which the Fenian Brotherhood
had split, but he abandoned, or was driven from, the leadership when the
hopelessness of a rising he had promised to lead dawned upon him. A rising
was nevertheless attempted without him, the initiative and over-all direc-

[22] N.L.I., MS 331–3, p. 97.
[23] Ibid., p. 98.
[24] N.L.I., MS 7517, p. 98.
[25] *Archivium Hibernicum*, xxxii, pp 52–4.
[26] N.L.I., MS 7517, p. 97.
[27] Patrick J. Corish, op. cit., pp 42–4.

tion coming from Irish-American army officers, the principal of whom was Colonel Thomas J. Kelly.[28]

Stephens, as we saw, was an admirer of Mazzini and might well have expected him to be sympathetic to the Irish cause, but when Kelly, urged on by Gustave Cluseret and Octave Fariola, whom he had appointed commander-in-chief and adjutant general respectively of the Army of the Republic and *ex officio* members of a provisional government,[29] approached him and the English Democratic Republicans for support on the eve of the rising—Kelly preferred to call it the revolution—he suffered a double disappointment. According to the government's information Mazzini expressed doubts as to whether the Irish were genuine republicans at all,[30] and the others suspected that the Irish were more anti-English than democratic.[31] Kelly, after the rising, presented the story rather differently. He said nothing about Mazzini: as regards the English reformers, an alliance had in fact been achieved, but by reformers he understood 'those who mean to go radically to the bottom of the movement, and not those who officially assume the direction of it'.[32] And it was to the English working class as a whole that the insurgents of March 1867 especially appealed in a message 'from the Irish people to the world'.

As for you workers of England it is not only your hearts we wish, but your arms. Remember the starvation and degradation brought to your firesides by the oppression of labour . . . Avenge yourselves by giving liberty to your children in the coming struggle for human freedom.

This message printed at the end of the proclamation of an Irish republic, which signalled the start of the rising, emphasised the equality of all men, the determination to replace a cursed monarchical government by a republic based on universal suffrage, the intrinsic value of man's labour, the need to restore the soil of Ireland, held by an oligarchy, to the Irish people, as well as the absolute liberty of conscience and the complete separation of church and state.[33] The appeal to the English people was repeated in the

[28] N.L.I., MS 7517, p. 226.
[29] Leon Ó Broin, *Fenian fever* (London, 1971), pp 89–90 and pp 123–6.
[30] N.L.I., MS 7517, pp 254–5.
[31] Ibid.
[32] *Irishman*, 23 Apr. 1867: reprint of letter, n.d. in *Liberté* (Paris).
[33] *Irishman*, 9 Mar. 1867, copied the proclamation from *Morning Star* (London), 7 Mar. It had been sent to the *Morning Star* on the preceding day, the day of the rising. It was in the form of a large placard headed 'I.R.' and was signed 'The Provisional Government' with a woodcut of a harp. From the *North British Daily Mail*, the *Irishman* of 16 Mar. culled a 'Proclamation of the Provisional Government of the Irish Republic to the Brotherhood of Ireland and the West of Scotland', calling on Irishmen to hasten to their native land. This is signed by General C. Denham, by command of the 'Council of the Irish Republic'. And in the issue of 6 Apr. the *Irishman* reproduced still another proclamation from the 'Headquarters I.R. Army, Limerick Junction, Tipperary' dated 5 Mar. As to what happened at Limerick Junction, see *Fenian fever*, pp 143–6.

proclamation itself, a proclamation which Kelly described as 'the gauge of our republican principles and our social aspirations', and as 'the desire of the Ireland of 1867 regenerated by the stay of its exiles in America'.[34] 'We intend no war against the English people', the proclamation announced, 'our war is against the aristocratic locusts, whether English or Irish, who have eaten the verdure of our fields, against the aristocratic leeches who drain alike our blood and theirs'.

Those blood-stirring phrases would have been lost on the English working class who never showed much sympathy for the Fenians and their ambitions[35] and one is left wondering why they were ever written, and by whom,[36] and whether after 1867 the gross socialist ideology they projected was a burden the I.R.B. were unable or unwilling to bear. Desmond Ryan in *Devoy's post bag* says that there had been certain points of sympathy, dating back to 1864, between Irish revolutionary leaders and organisations—he is no more specific than that—and the International Workingmen's Association, otherwise known as the First International;[37] and from another source we know that towards the end of 1867 a response of sorts to the Fenian appeal to the republicans of the world came from a meeting of the council of the International. 'What is Fenianism?' the French socialist leader Eugene Dupont asked on that occasion.

Is it a sect or party whose principles are opposed to ours? Certainly not. Fenianism is the vindication by an oppressed people of its right to social and political existence. The Fenian declarations leave no room for doubt in this respect. They affirm the republican form of government, liberty of conscience, no state religion, the produce of labour to the labourer and the possession of the soil to the people.[38]

Karl Marx, who had brought the International into being, consistently urged his friends to promote the cause of Irish independence. He did so, believing that by this means they would hasten the social revolution in England, which was the key to the triumph of the workers' movement all over the world.[39] By that time (1870), however, the Irish rising or revolution had already proved to be what we would nowadays call a non-event, and, despite subsequent rumours of Fenian activity and of dates being fixed

[34] *Irishman*, 23 Apr. 1867; reprint of letter, n.d. in *Liberté* (Paris).

[35] David Fernbach, Introduction to Karl Marx, *A First International and after* (Penguin edition, London, 1974), pp 25–30; Norman McCord, 'The fenians and public opinion in Great Britain' in *University Review*, iv, no. 3 (winter 1967).

[36] It was suggested in government circles that Charles Bradlaugh of the Reform League and General Cluseret had more to do with the drafting than the Fenians proper. Cluseret 'a specialist in wars and revolutions', was chief of staff of the Paris Communard forces in 1870. He had earlier, with Bakunin, seized the Town Hall in Lyons and proclaimed the 'abolition of the state', Ó Broin, *Fenian fever*, p. 125.

[37] *Devoy's post bag*, ed. William O'Brien and Desmond Ryan, i (Dublin, 1948), p. 19.

[38] Karl Marx and Frederick Engels, *On Ireland* (London, 1971), p. 369.

[39] Ibid., p. 294.

for a further attempt, the government were satisfied that the Irish revolutionary organisation was seriously in decline. We shall see presently how accurate that judgment was, and as regards association with British and continental radicals, the idea was perhaps now spreading among the I.R.B. that they should be careful of the company they kept. At any rate I.R.B. men, though naturally pleased at the spread of republican ideas, believing that this would help their own cause, were conspicuous by their absence from the public meetings of democratic republicans in England in 1871,[40] and were not noticed to have had anything to do with the completely unsuccessful efforts that were made to establish branches of the International in Dublin and Cork.

A series of documents that Professor Moody and I have published in *Irish Historical Studies*[41] helps to explain the condition and mentality of Irish republicanism at this time. The first of these documents is dated 24 April 1868, thirteen months, that is, after the rising, and is a message to the Irish people from what is called the supreme council of the Irish Republic. Whether this message ever reached the Irish people or a substantial number of them is doubtful. The police found a few copies posted up, and, keeping some of them for the record, they defaced the others as they had done with the proclamation of 1867. This message was prepared with the double object of explaining the circumstances in which the expectations of 1865 and what was admitted to have been 'the disastrous outbreak' of 1867 were frustrated, and of giving an assurance that, despite everything, the revolutionary future could be viewed with optimism.

In the message the supreme council claimed that they had been truly elected by representative men, that is, by men representative of the organisation only, and this they absurdly claimed gave them authority to act in the name of the Irish Republican Army and the Irish people, both those in Ireland and those living in England and Scotland. In explaining what had gone wrong with the rising, the message threw the blame on the American Fenian Brotherhood to whom it said it had been represented that the Irish Republican Army was almost completely equipped, the result being that the Americans entertained other projects and sent wholly inadequate supplies to Ireland. When the real state of affairs became known in the United States, by some unaccountable fatuity time was allowed to pass and the money sent to Ireland was spent on the maintenance of military leaders and on abortive struggles in the courts. *The Irishman* of 27 April 1867 carried a report of 'An Address of centres from Ireland, England and Scotland

[40] S.P.O., C.S.O., R.P., 1871/7903.
[41] 'The I.R.B. supreme council, 1868–78', above, n. 2.

representing the Irish Republican Brotherhood, to Irishmen everywhere and to friends of Irish Liberty'. It begins:'Brothers and friends, for the past three weeks we have worked assiduously to unite the two branches of the Fenian organisation in this country [United States] with a view of sending direct and effective aid to our brothers at home, who are now contending against a tyrannical and wicked government of England'.

The message from the supreme council gave an official view also on two events that were then very much in the public mind, the armed rescue of Fenian leaders at Manchester in September 1867 in which a police sergeant died, and the explosion outside Clerkenwell gaol three months later which killed twelve civilians and maimed one hundred and twenty others. What happened at Manchester, the message claimed, was justified by the law of nations, but the other affair was beneath contempt; were its perpetrators within the council's control, their punishment would be condign indeed. The affair, brutal in the extreme, the council said, was a consequence of the division of the Fenian Brotherhood into rival wings which had paralysed the efforts of the home countries. What, they asked, did the Irish in Ireland, England and Scotland care for Fenian wings and leaders, and their endless accusations and recriminations? Those unhappy party differences were deplorable, and the Irish Republican Brotherhood—now mentioned by that name for the first time in the message and thus explaining who the supreme council of the Irish Republic were—implored their fellow-countrymen in America 'in the name of Ireland, a perishing people, and God' that they should be ended. The message, however, went far beyond an *appeal* to the Irish-Americans. It announced in elaborate terms a rupture of formal relations with the Fenian Brotherhood, and this was to last until 1876 when, with much difficulty, a Joint Revolutionary Directory was formed. Meanwhile, as if to show that they could dispense with American aid anyhow, the message claimed that the army of the Irish Republic numbered 200,000 men and were supported by the sympathies of 7,000,000. The state of discipline in the army was 'more or less perfect', their organisation 'complete', 'their spirit resolute and unsubdued' but, admittedly, their equipment was wholly inadequate. When that deficiency was overcome, as it would be by their own efforts, they would choose their time and command 'a military executive' to strike in the field, which was the only place where England could be successfully combatted and destroyed.

The tory government, who were about to leave office when the message came under notice, were not put off by the claim that a completely organised insurrectionary army of 200,000 still existed. They believed that the Fenian movement was in a state of collapse and their liberal successors, sharing that view, allowed the act suspending habeas corpus to expire and granted a conditional amnesty as part of a general policy of pacification. They would assuredly not have done so were they not reasonably satisfied that Fenianism, as it had begun to be called, had shot its bolt, and that such threat to peace as now confronted them came from an agrarian source. The bishops by this time also believed that the Fenian bubble had been burst, that 'an insane project' had come to an end, and they were greatly relieved. Cullen was especially happy at the passing of the 'villainous' *Irish People* whose leading writers he had seen as the fruit of infidel education.[42] The I.R.B. was not finished, however, and in 1869 a reorganisation was attempted. A constitution was framed in which the supreme council was declared to be the government of the republic and the president of the I.R.B. executive *ipso facto* the president of the republic. This was the Organisation's first constitution; at least we infer as much from a letter John O'Leary wrote to the *Freeman's Journal* on 5 November 1877 in which he stated that under Stephens, that is before 1867, the I.R.B. had no constitution.

In an address issued by the supreme council in January 1870[43] supposedly to the people of Ireland, but really to the rank and file of the Irish Republican Brotherhood, there is a franker admission than before that after 1867 the situation had been 'most deplorable, the once compact and powerful organisation [being] broken up into contemptible fragments, with nothing but discord and disorganisation on every side'. But, like the message of June 1868, this address strove to be optimistic. Reorganisation had been effective, it said, and harmony virtually restored, though to quell faction had not been easy, confidence having been lost and apathy spread through the misapplication of money raised for the purchase of arms. However, without American help, much had been done to procure arms and ammunition and, if only the members would pay their dues regularly, in six months the Irish Republic would occupy a position far exceeding their wildest dreams. Strict discipline was called for and prompt obedience to orders, while the pledge of secrecy would have to be enforced in order to control the mischief being done by loose talk. The members were to abstain from public demonstrations and political agitations of every kind until otherwise directed, but—and this, we think, was an innovation in I.R.B. policy—they were to make persistent efforts to obtain control of local authorities as a means of increasing republican power and influence. Raids for arms, on the other hand, were strictly forbidden: such silly exploits were fit only to excite unthinking boys: they did great injury to the cause, and yielded utterly contemptible results.

[42] Patrick J. Corish (ed.), 'Irish College Rome: Kirby papers' in *Archivium Hibernicum*, xxx, 43–52.
[43] *Irish Historical Studies*, no. 75, pp 307–10.

Despite the claims in that message, it is doubtful if an effective reorganisation had been achieved, but the I.R.B. remained numerically strong, so strong in fact that the viceroy, Earl Spencer, could speak of a vast Fenian organisation covering the whole country and supported from America, which would not fall to pieces until it had made another [insurrectionary] effort.[44] Spencer may have been exaggerating in order to stampede Gladstone into doing something he did not want to do, namely to suspend habeas corpus again. The peace preservation bill then introduced, the threat of a further suspension of habeas corpus, the papal condemnation of the Fenians and Gladstone's church and land reforms quickly and significantly transformed the picture.

A third address in the series of documents I am describing, dated 17 March 1873, is directed by the supreme council specifically and exclusively to the officers and men of the I.R.A.[45] Both sets of initials (I.R.B. and I.R.A.) are employed in the address but we have no reason to think that the I.R.A. at this stage was anything other than the ordinary members of the I.R.B.—to be a member of the Brotherhood was presumably to be a member of the army. What was called 'A solemn convention of the Irish Republic' had just taken place, and the purpose of the address was to explain the convention's *raison d'etre* and what had occurred at it. The organisation had been through a most serious internal crisis: no reference whatever is made to the pressures from *without*. Allegations concerning what were called civil, military and financial transactions had reverberated through the organisation and had induced the supreme council to surrender to the convention the authority it had received—allegedly—from the people. (No mention was made as was done in the previous messages, of authority also deriving from the army.) But following an examination of the allegations, the council's resignation was not accepted and the fullest confidence in it was renewed.

J. F. X. O'Brien's unpublished autobiography[46] sheds some light on the circumstances in which the convention was held and on the civil and financial, if not the military, transactions that were discussed at it. O'Brien, who had achieved senior rank in the organisation—he may for a time have been its president—says that in 1873 there were evident signs of disorganisation and disintegration. Trouble arose within the council over the policy to be followed in regard to what he calls 'the Protestant Home Rule Association'. A document had gone astray, sent by one member of the council to another, containing an incitement to cast out O'Brien and other colleagues, and describing a defence O'Brien had made of the home rulers

[44] Gladstone Papers, B.M., Add. MS 44306.
[45] *Irish Historical Studies*, no. 75, pp 310–13.
[46] N.L.I., MSS 16, 695–6.

as 'tawdry nonsense'. Another serious problem arose from over-indulgence in liquor. It was unavoidable but still regrettable, O'Brien says, that public houses were almost the only places where men could, without suspicion, meet each other, and some men who had given indisputable proofs of their devotion to the cause had made away with money given to them for safe keeping, and had even planned robberies on the plea that the organisation needed the money. He denounced all this in a circular to the rank and file and was threatened for doing so. Subsequently, at council level apparently, he raised the matter in private and at meetings but without success, and he decided to resign his office though he was again warned that it would be better for him to stay where he was. He finally quitted the organisation altogether in December 1874. The I.R.B. had ceased by then to be a useful organisation, he said. 'We were doing no good, while exposing good men to great risks'.[47] What O'Brien says about the condition of the movement is borne out particularly by a report of a meeting of the centres of the north of England division, held early in 1871, which speaks of things being in poor shape in a number of areas. In Liverpool 'disorganisation, insubordination, faction and drunkenness reign almost supreme amongst our supposed brothers there'.[48]

By contrast, and in an obvious attempt to put the best possible face on a poor situation, the document reporting the convention announced that most gratifying reports had been received of the strength and progress of the military side of the organisation. A very substantial quantity of materials of all kinds was held, and the army was capable of enlargement to any extent that equipment would permit. The finances were in a very healthy state despite the defalcations, and the work of accumulating war material would be pushed on energetically.[49]

From the convention there emerged what was effectively a new constitution,[50] one that remained in force until 1917. The organisation was obviously making a fresh start. A preamble to this constitution told of the coming together of Irish patriots representing associations of Irishmen—one wonders who and what these were—to reform the revolutionary movement and to form from it, as if for the first time, the Irish Republican Brotherhood, otherwise the I.R.B., with the purpose of overthrowing English power and establishing an independent Irish republic. This 1873 constitution, unlike that of 1869, was presented in two parts—the first dealt

[47] Ibid.
[48] S.P.O., Fenian papers, 7347. The file contains a similar 'encouraging' statement from the Irish Republic in 1871.
[49] Ibid.
[50] *Irish Historical Studies*, no. 75, pp 313–17.

with the I.R.B. itself as an organisation, the second with a composite entity, the 'supreme council of the I.R.B. *and* government of the Irish Republic', but much of the 1869 document was carried over, with greater emphasis on an independence yet to be won by force of arms. In both constitutions, as in the messages to the Irish people, there was a large element of pretence and a noteworthy omission from them, despite their avowedly revolutionary character, was any indication of social or economic intent, apart, that is, from a clause enshrining the declaration in the 1867 proclamation that in the Republic there was to be no state religion and that every citizen was free to worship God according to his conscience. The constitutions were also undemocratic in authorising the council to alter them as they wished on a month's notice being given and with a two-thirds vote.

What marked the 1873 instrument out from that of 1869 was the commitment to three new, and thoroughly democratic, principles. While always preparing for war the organisation was to confine itself, in time of peace, to exercising moral influence; it was not to resort to war until the time for doing so had been decided by a majority of the Irish nation; and, pending such decision, it was to support every movement calculated to advance the cause of Irish independence consistently with the maintenance of its own integrity. Judged by these principles, quite apart from the dubious fundamental authority of I.R.B. itself, the 1867 rising and the Clerkenwell explosion stood condemned, and the dynamite campaign of the 1880s and the 1916 rising were unlawful.

These principles also indicated perhaps a recognition that the movement was to be one of long-term, that victory was not going to be easily achieved. In deciding to exercise moral influence they became in P. S. O'Hegarty's phrase 'a brotherhood of opinion and principle . . . a sort of bedrock national reservoir'.[51] They were to be 'a small but effective and formidable organisation behind organisations',[52] watching everything; being in everything; and whenever there was an opportunity, however small, of doing anything to forward the separatist cause, being there to do it![53] They made a particular set on the Gaelic Athletic Association from its foundation in 1884 and on the Gaelic League when it was established in 1893, and they considerably influenced the policies of both bodies. But they were themselves influenced by the Gaelic movement, so that when the I.R.B. paper, *Irish Freedom*, was launched in 1910, it preached Fenianism with an Irish-Ireland accent.[54]

The immediate reason for introducing these novel principles into the

[51] *Ireland under the union*, p. 610.
[52] Ibid., p. 634.
[53] O'Hegarty, *The victory of Sinn Fein* (Dublin, 1924), p. 12.
[54] O'Hegarty, *Ireland under the union*, p. 656.

constitution of 1873 was to validate the policy on which the organisation had embarked of supporting Butt's Home Rule League. That was a deviation from I.R.B. orthodoxy that bitterly divided the organisation and left it, during the 1880s far less militant than the quasi-constitutional movement that Parnell led, a movement that was strengthened by defections from the I.R.B., by the transference of what William O'Brien described as the courage, self-denial and glorious madness of the Fenian spirit. On the other hand John Devoy said that in 1879 there was a compact body of 35,000 men which continued to grow during the Land League agitation.[55] The government were well aware of what was happening. They saw the I.R.B. as continuing to decline and its former non-deviant leaders relying on Young Ireland societies of the literary and social type to retain a foothold for them among the people. Charles Kickham and John O'Leary, successive presidents of the supreme council in this decade, deplored the policy of parliamentary agitation that brought fame to Parnell and even more the association of council members of their organisation with it, but at the same time, they could not withhold a considerable admiration from 'this strange and mysterious being of ice and flame'.[56] O'Leary saw Parnell as the only leader who could make a success of constitutional action; in any event he was 'the man on the horse' and should be allowed to take the fence. 'Today', said Luby

Parnell is the accepted representative of the Irish cause. My old comrades and myself are out of the running. Hence, on my own firm principles, I should feel self-condemned if I tried by pen or act to condemn him. Parnell's agitation is not supplicatory like O'Connell's, not to say Butt's; 'tis aggressive; semi-belligerent . . . Parnell seeks no gifts from the bounty of the English parliament. He wrests Irish rights against the will or wish of those forced to concede them. I efface myself for the public good.[57]

Not surprisingly, with such ideas abroad, the syllabus of the Young Ireland Society's central branch in 1884–5 carried an extract from a speech of Parnell's alongside quotations from Tone and Davis.[58] He was almost one of their own. And they postulated that the I.R.B. should have nothing to do with O'Donovan Rossa's dynamiters or with the practice of assassination to which some I.R.B. men had been seduced, they believed, by the Land League. Luby said that he regarded such men as outlaws alike of God and society, as the representatives of the Devil himself in his ugliest aspect, and he would repeat that, even if men of the dynamiter and Invincible stamp were backed by the voice of the whole nation.[59]

[55] Michael MacDonagh, *The life of William O'Brien* (London, 1928), p. 43; John Devoy, *Recollections of an Irish rebel*, (New York, 1929), p. 392.

[56] John O'Leary, *Recollections of fenians and fenianism* (London, 1896), ii, 1142.

[57] Writing to John O'Leary, after Kickham's funeral in 1882 (N.L.I., MS 5926).

[58] Copy in possession of Seán F. Allan.

[59] N.L.I., MS 5926, 7 Jan. 1887.

In June 1886, when the organisation once more claimed to have reached a high pitch of efficiency the supreme council displayed a pragmatic accommodating attitude to Gladstone's home rule bill. In a circular letter then issued, they declared that Parnell had no commission to accept in their name the concession of a parliament such as that outlined in the bill, but the proposals, inadequate though they were, were by no means to be rejected. They represented progress, and should be accepted as such. They were to be seen as a victory for the organisation's policy because it was 'the intensity of Fenianism' that had first enlightened Gladstone and brought to the verge of realisation something that had hitherto been quite outside the region of practical politics. The council then declared that it was the duty of the I.R.B. men not merely *not* to seek to hamper the efforts of the Gladstone-Parnell combination but to assist them as far as they could.[60]

When the split occurred in 1890 over Parnell's entanglement with Mrs O'Shea, committees were formed in many places to ensure the continuance of his leadership, and in these I.R.B. men were always prominent, although some took the anti-Parnellite side. In the Kilkenny by-election Parnell made an inflammatory appeal to the 'men of the hillside' by which he was understood to mean men in the physical force tradition, the Fenians or I.R.B. or by whatever name they were known. He declared himself to be no mere parliamentarian: if he found it useless to continue parliamentary agitation he would return at the head of his party and take counsel with the Irish people as to the next step.[61] More uncompromisingly he told an audience in Navan that someone in the distant future might have the privilege of addressing the men of Royal Meath as the men of Republican Meath.[62] John O'Leary backed him publicly, so did James Stephens emerging from obscurity, so did John Devoy, and, before the bulk of the I.R.B. scarcely knew what was happening, they were engulfed in party politics of a kind they had always abhorred, and in running Parnell's independent newspapers.

They also found themselves openly embroiled with the catholic church once more. Bishops and priests had, like themselves, actively sympathised with Parnell; now individuals among them saw him as a profligate leader, a second Lucifer who would drag the Irish race to perdition. He draws his support, the bishop of Cloyne said, from extremists and remnants of secret societies which were dying out until, for his own selfish and unscrupulous ambition, he sought to revive them, by appealing to the latent hatred of England.[63]

---

[60] I.R.B. Circular, 21 June 1886. Copy in author's possession.
[61] R. Barry O'Brien, *The life of Charles Stewart Parnell* (London, 1898), ii, 304–5.
[62] F. S. L. Lyons, *The fall of Parnell* (London, 1960), p. 255.
[63] *Archivium Hibernicum*, xxxii, pp 27, 31.

It was noticed by the police in the northern counties in the late nineties that the clergy were intervening to thwart the recruiting efforts of the I.R.B. and of a rival American-founded Irish National Alliance or Brotherhood, sometimes identified by the initials I.N.B. A conference in the diocese of Clogher condemned the American importation as well as the Ancient Order of Hibernians, between which and what was said to be the much weaker I.R.B. there had been great animosity.[64] The A.O.H. regarded the I.R.B. as enemies of their country, and lost no opportunity of physically assaulting them. A number of the northern bishops denounced secret societies generally in their lenten letters, and the primate, Cardinal Logue, in one of his, said that he had learned with extreme pain that the promoters of secret societies, taking advantage of the unhappy political confusion, had resumed their efforts to regain a hold on some foolish and unwary members of his community.[65]

The practice of using the lenten pastorals to condemn secret societies continued right down to relatively recent times. That was certainly the case in Dublin, to my own knowledge, and the practice had a deterring effect on the I.R.B. 'Often when after tedious investigation a man was deemed fit in every respect [to be enrolled] . . . the inquisitor found himself up against a stone wall, that of religious scruples . . .'[66] On one occasion, in an effort to deal with this problem in Dublin, the most unusual step was taken of calling all the members to a meeting in the Town Hall, Clontarf, where they were addressed by a priest from the American mission who argued, as Fr Lavelle had done many years before, that the I.R.B. was not banned by the church: he himself was a member of the sister oath-bound organisation in the United States, and made no difficulty about it.[67] I do not know whether the meeting achieved its purpose, but it gave the ordinary I.R.B. man in the city a chance to see who, outside his own confined circle, were in the business.

After the 1916 rising, the organisation proceeded to reform, but some former members dropped out because of the continuing church condemnation or for other reasons. De Valera's was an interesting case. He had joined because he found that Volunteer officers junior to him who were in the I.R.B. knew more about what was going on than he did. The contradictory orders at Easter exemplified for him the problems that arose between a public and a secret organisation; and he disliked swearing to obey an undisclosed executive.[68] He accordingly ceased all connection with

[64] S.P.O., C.S.O., R.P. 1895/10779/S.
[65] S.P.O., C.S.O., R.P., 1897/13217/S.
[66] Diarmuid Lynch, *The I.R.B. and the 1916 insurrection* (Cork, n.d.), pp 22–3.
[67] Earnán de Blaghd, *Trasna na Bóinne* (Dublin, 1957), p. 123.
[68] Earl of Longford and Thomas P. O'Neill, *Eamon de Valera* (London, 1970) (Arrow edition), p. 66.

the organisation and sought to persuade some close associates of his to do the same.

From its inception the I.R.B. was closely watched by the police, but after 1870 it rarely gave them any trouble. For many years the police paid particular attention to a group of Dublin workingmen within the organis- ation to whom they ascribed pretty well everything unpleasant that occurred in the city, including some dynamite explosions and the murder of a man suspected of being an informer.[69] To the fore in this group was the ex-boxer Jackie Nolan, of James's Street, who ended his Fenian career in a Canadian prison for his part in a bombing expedition that was aimed at disrupting supplies to the British army during the Boer war. The quality of police surveillance declined dramatically with the retirement at the end of 1901 of John Mallon, the head of the detective division of the Dublin Metropolitan Police, and the appointment in the chief secretary's office about the same time of a very untraditional under-secretary in the person of Antony MacDonnell. MacDonnnell, who displayed a frank and inde- pendent outlook on matters of general administration, was particularly suspicious of what civil servants and police had to say to him about the state of the country, and he made this so clear on the official files that it can only have caused the intelligence service to deteriorate. When he had been two and a half years in the job he made the devastating announcement that he had not seen a particle of substantial evidence to show that there was in Ireland any secret political activity of which the government needed to have the smallest apprehension.[70] Augustine Birrell, the chief secretary in the critical period before 1916, took the same line. In 1912 he told James Dougherty, who had succeeded MacDonnell, that he had read for more than five years those reports about secret societies without extracting much from them. He wished that the police would pay more attention to the north of Ireland where the secret orange societies were, for the moment at all events, of greater importance.[71] Dougherty agreed completely. In his opin- ion the resuscitation of the I.R.B. of which they heard in the Castle was, in the circumstances of that time, 'a hopeless proposal'.[72] An organisation that once boasted of having 200,000 members was now down to a thousand or two: it was a mere skeleton of its former self.[73]

Nevertheless, Dougherty could not have been farther off the mark. With the benefit of hindsight we can see that neither the politicians nor the senior civil servants had sufficiently taken into account the likelihood that things

[69] N.L.I., MS 94108, p. 30.
[70] S.P.O., C.S.O., R.P. 1905/29989/S.
[71] P.R.O., Colonial Office papers 904/13, July 1912.
[72] Ibid., 904/13, Nov.–Dec. 1912.
[73] See F. X. Martin, The scholar revolutionary (Dublin, 1973), p. 112 n.; J. Devoy, Recollections of an Irish rebel, p. 392; Ó Broin, Dublin Castle and the 1916 rising (Dublin, 1966), p. 35.

would change under the threat of the Ulster resistance to home rule, the involvement of Britain in a major war, and the stimulation of revolt that continued to come to Ireland from the United States. They could hardly be blamed for underestimating the revolutionary capability of John Devoy's disciple Tom Clarke, or of two younger Irishmen, Bulmer Hobson and Sean MacDermott; and a real source of trouble for the government arose from the blunting of an intelligence service that had given them a stranglehold over the I.R.B. in earlier times, and left them now incapable of anticipating

the use the secret organisation would make of an Irish Volunteer force in whose creation they were seen to be immensely active. The government did not really know what was going on, and Birrell, with astonishing frankness, said so publicly after the rising.[74]

What had been going on was the positioning, under the control of a military council or committee within the supreme council of the I.R.B., of as many I.R.B. men as possible in the officer ranks of the Volunteers. By that means essentially the rising was brought off; and the same technique was employed, and more efficiently, in the reorganisation after the rising of the Volunteers, and of Sinn Fein as it became accepted as the political wing of an expanding independence movement. In this work of reorganisation and consolidation Michael Collins, on his way to the top of the I.R.B., was the main driving force.

The 1873 constitution, as we said earlier, remained the fundamental law of the I.R.B. until 1917, although honoured more in the breach than in the observance in an important respect. The constitution then devised[75] dropped the first two of the new principles we mentioned before but retained the third, namely the determination to support movements calculated to advance the cause of independence. It added an intention to cooperate with all Irish military bodies towards the same end—this a necessary provision for an organisation which, in the Easter rising, had found allies in Labour's Citizen Army and in an independent volunteer corps associated with the American wing of the Ancient Order of Hibernians. It also introduced a social element by declaring that in the Republic there were to be no privileged persons or classes; all citizens were to enjoy equal rights. This was imported from the 1916 Proclamation which, in narrower and less trenchantly expressed terms than those of the proclamation of 1877, spoke of cherishing all the children of the nation equally,

---

[74] Ó Broin, *Dublin Castle and the 1916 rising*, p. 169.
[75] Printed as 'Constitution of the I.R.B. in 1914' in H. B. C. Pollard, *The secret societies of Ireland: their rise and progress* (London, 1922), pp 290–303.

and of eliminating the differences which an alien government had fostered in the past.

The 1916 men in announcing the establishment of a republic with a provisional government and president may perhaps have overlooked the fact that, through the constitution of 1873, a provisional republican government and president of the Republic already existed. On the other hand, the assignment to the provisional government of the administration of the civil and military affairs of the Republic until the whole people of Ireland could elect a permanent national government suggests that the I.R.B. constitutions of 1869 and 1873, which mentioned these matters in that specific form, as well as the provision for a military authority which was availed of in May 1915 to create the military committee or council that prepared the ground for the rising, were present to the mind of whoever drafted the proclamation. When the 1917 constitution came to be written, a clause was included in it specifically providing for a military council which was to be attached to, and at all times subject to, the supreme council. It was to have no power to direct or interfere with the policy of the government of the Republic or in any way to alter the constitution of the I.R.B. This possibly may have been intended retrospectively to clear up doubts about the 1916 position.

Incidentally, the 1917 constitution prescribed, in an addendum to the clause on the position and powers of the supreme council as the government of the Republic, including the power to make war and peace, that a declaration of war required the support of at least ten of the fifteen members thenceforth constituting the council. This was as near as the constitution got to the idea that there could be no war in the absence of popular approval; but, as has been pointed out recently, there was no definite inception of hostilities in what became known as the Anglo-Irish war of 1919–21. This just developed out of an initiative taken by some Volunteers without the prior authority of the democratically-elected Dail.[76] That authority was conferred *ex post facto* by the Dail, and, inferentially, by the I.R.B.

In September 1919 two significant amendments were written into the constitution as it then stood. A resolution had been carried at a private session of the Dail a month earlier requiring the deputies, the Irish Volunteers, and officers and clerks of the Dail to take an oath of allegiance to the government of the Irish Republic, which was stated to be the Dail itself.[77] This was an oath which converted the Irish Volunteers, whose origins went back no further than 1913, into the Irish Republican Army (I.R.A.) and distinguished that army from any predecessor of the same

[76] John A. Murphy, *Ireland in the twentieth century* (Dublin, 1975), p. 13.
[77] *Dáil Éireann, minutes of proceedings, 1919–21*, 20 Aug. 1919.

name that was built on membership of the I.R.B. or its American counterpart. The oath, of course, demanded a response from the I.R.B., many of whose members were affected by the resolution, and an effort was made to meet an obviously difficult situation by inserting in the constitution a new clause indicating that, as the organisation's policy had succeeded in establishing a duly elected public authority competent to declare the will and give expression to the desire of the Irish people to secure international recognition of the Irish Republic, and that this public authority had decreed that all servants and soldiers of the Republic should have a specified oath of allegiance, members might, in accordance with the terms and spirit of their own inception oath, loyally accept and obey this authority. The Dail was not mentioned by name; and the supreme council of the I.R.B. continued in its own constitution to be the sole government of the Irish Republic. A second amendment, however, suggested an intention to be generally subservient to the Dail by withdrawing from the president of the I.R.B. his status as president of the Irish Republic and leaving him solely to direct the working of the organisation subject to the control of the supreme council or its executive.[78]

That was the position when, by a substantial majority, the supreme council approved of, and recommended to the members, the Anglo-Irish treaty of 6 December 1921 in the negotiation of which Collins, the president of the council, had played a major part.[79] In doing so, it recalled that it had always been the policy of the organisation to make use of all instruments, political and otherwise, which were likely to aid in the attainment of a free, independent, republican government; and, whether they knew it or not, they were reacting to an offer of something less than a republic in the same way as the organisation had done in 1886. After 1921 the organisation appeared to die, but in 1923, as the civil war ended, an attempt was made to revive it and the constitution was once more rewritten—this time with a policy clause which pledged the I.R.B. to be the custodian of the republican ideal, the traditional expression of national independence, and to organise the maximum strength of the nation to achieve it.[80] But the objects of the I.R.B. no longer included the obligation to train and equip a military body for the purpose of securing an independent republican government by force of arms. This would have been inconsistent with the existence of the national army that had come into being as a result of the treaty.

The attempted revival occurred in the higher ranks of the national army at a time when large numbers of men were being disbanded from it, and when it was alleged that the republican ideal had been forsaken. A mutin-

[78] U.C.D. Archives, Mulcahy Papers, p. 7/C/42, P. 7/52
[79] Ibid., p. 7/52.
[80] Ibid., p. 7/C/42, P. 7/52.

ous situation led to a committee of inquiry and to a subsequent recommendation from the head of the government, W. T. Cosgrave, that the I.R.B. should be 'disembodied and discontinued'.[81] That was done in 1924, ending what for over sixty years had been, in the words of the last secretary of the executive, 'a living reality and a present force in shaping the destinies of the nation'.[82] In the same year the majority of county centres in service with the anti-treaty I.R.A. similarly decided to disband the I.R.B., in so far no doubt as they could do it.[83] The organisation thus died without reaching its objective, though surviving members were to claim that, through the rising of 1916, the establishment of Dail Eireann, and the treaty of 1921, the I.R.B. had opened up the way to the sovereign, independent, democratic[84] but territorially-limited, Republic in which we now live.

[81] Dáil Éireann Debates, vii, col. 3149.
[82] U.C.D. Archives, Mulcahy Papers, P. 7/52.
[83] Based on papers in possession of Maurice ('Moss') Twomey.
[84] Constitution of Ireland 1937, art. 5.

VI

Power politics, imperialism, and national emancipation, 1870–1914

Wolfgang J. Mommsen

The process of national emancipation must be considered the dominant feature of nineteenth-century European history. The first climax of this process was reached with the creation of an Italian nation-state in 1859 and the foundation of the German empire between 1867 and 1871. With the emergence of these two new nation-states, which from the start claimed to play a major rôle in European power-politics, not only was the balance of power in Europe substantially altered but also a new pattern of political organisation had been established which was to become a guideline for all those smaller European nations that still lacked a national political framework. Contemporaries hailed the formation of the German empire with great enthusiasm. Nowadays, however, we are no longer certain that the establishment of a German—albeit a 'klein-deutsch'—nation-state has been 'aller irdischen Güter höchstes', as Heinrich von Sybel expressed it in a letter to Hermann Baumgarten on the eve of the *Kaiserproklamation* at Versailles. The owls fly only at dawn, says Hegel; Germans of the later twentieth-century tend to prefer Nietzsche's admittedly rather harsh indictment that the foundation of the German empire amounted to the extirpation of the German spirit. But whatever our feeling may be on this point, the cases of Italy and Germany clearly served as a pattern for the further advance of the idea of national emancipation. The nation-state came to be universally considered both the telelogical end of the political processes of the age and the yardstick for practical politics. During the first world war all belligerent powers—with the sole exception of Austria-Hungary—eventually claimed that their policies were consonant with the principle of national self-determination, though they were rather disingenuous here, since their real intentions were to legitimise their respective war aims in the eyes of the world. The United States and the new Bolshevic Russia, which were about to displace Europe from her primacy in world affairs, also based their political programmes on the rigorous application of the principle of nationality; although with very different political objectives, as was very soon to become obvious. Consequently, the multi-national empires of the past could no longer be afforded a place in the modern world.

In the 1830s Guiseppe Mazzini had envisaged a Europe of free nations where the maintenance of peace would no longer be difficult, since there would be no more ambitious monarchs and selfish aristocrats. In this respect Woodrow Wilson was Mazzini's heir; although he was more realistic in other respects—in particular with regard to economic issues—he, like Mazzini, envisaged a peaceful world of free and democratic nations which would devote all their energies to the pursuit of economic progress and the happiness of all. We find it difficult to believe in these grand ideas; nonetheless we will readily admit that the process of national emancipation produced positive results despite its shortcomings. It might indeed be argued that the benefits of the process of national emancipation were substantially reduced by the fact that it was overshadowed by the rise of imperialism, in its later stages. Imperialism always tended to disregard the genuine national aspirations of others, and especially the interests of peoples and national groups directly or indirectly subjected to imperialist rule. Furthermore, the imperialist ideology substantially devalued the principle of nationality, that is to say, the idea that all peoples had a right to live in a state of their own as well as the right to develop their own autonomous national culture. In other words, power politics and the passion for imperialist rule distorted the Mazzinian ideal of a Europe of democratic nation-states and deflected from their original course the various processes of national emancipation which had been in progress all over Europe since the early nineteenth century.

Before we go into this problem in more detail we will have to investigate the meaning of the concept of nationality. Obviously nationality can no longer be considered an axiomatic element of history in the way in which most historians in the tradition of Herder tended to do well up to the present. We have learned that 'nation' can mean many things to many men. Historians used to distinguish between an 'objective' and a 'subjective' idea of 'nationality'. In the former case, nationality was associated with allegedly 'objective' criteria such as ethnic origin, language, and cultural tradition. In the latter case, nationality was determined by the subjective decision of individuals, as Renan argued in his famous definition according to which nationality is a 'plebiscite de tous les jours'. This distinction seems to be acceptable. But such subtle differentiations were meaningless for those who were late in embracing the ideal of national emancipation, and more especially for those who lived in regions with nationally mixed populations where neither ethnic, nor linguistic, nor cultural, nor socio-economic boundaries could be drawn clearly. Nowadays, there is universal agreement that ethnic origin, language, cultural heritage, religious denomination, common socio-economic interests, and a common political heritage—even in the form of subjugation to an oppressive system of foreign origin—are factors which, together or in part, can constitute the sort of group loyalty customarily described as nationality. To express it differently, the substantive content of the national idea can vary greatly according to time and circumstances. Closer analysis reveals the great fluidity of the concept despite the strident and self-assured language used by its champions. It is obvious from what has been said so far that the association of individuals with national groups is often determined along class lines. This phenomenon is familiar in all regions of mixed nationalities. As a rule, the socio-economic elites of national minorities were all too ready to join the ranks of the dominant national group, while the lower classes usually remained faithful to their specific national heritage, especially when in doing so they had the backing of their religious institutions. Only the intelligentsia did not easily assimilate in the respective dominant nationality, since the intelligentsia, according to Max Weber, is intent on defending particular 'ideal interests'. In view of these findings, the idea of an 'objective' as well as that of a 'subjective' principle of nationality appears artificial; most of the 'objective' factors are subject to subjective decisions by individuals or groups; conversely, the subjective decision in favour of a particular nationality, as Renan would have it, usually is largely determined by social and economic configurations outside the control of the respective individuals or groups. This conclusion is further corroborated by the observation that the propagation of a particular national ideology has often been part of manipulative strategies practised by authoritarian governments or small power-elites in order to achieve specific political or socio-economic objectives. An instructive case in point is the politics of 'Sammlung' against socialists and democrats inaugurated by Miquel in Prussia in 1893. This means that the democratic element inherent in the idea of nationality has in practice often been defeated by historical reality since Mazzini's days; one should therefore not be so rash as to assume an inseparable connection between the national idea and the principle of national self-determination, although we usually take this for granted. On the contrary, there have been many cases where the idea of nationality was used more or less effectively to check the emancipation of underprivileged classes or the advance of democracy.

In spite of these observations, it seems advisable to develop an 'ideal-typical' concept of 'national emancipation' which is definitely linked to substantive principles, in particular to the principle of democratic self-determination. Undoubtedly the phenomenon of nationalism is closely associated with the emergence of the modern egalitarian society, and in this social context the national idea often becomes an important instrument of politics. Graf Krockow, an eminent German political scientist, recently expressed it in the following manner:

In an age of progressive participation in politics nationalism and the nation-state have been, and still are,—as a matter of course—instruments of egalitarian policies designed to achieve solidarity, to mobilise the people at large and to bring about the integration of separate social groups into the political fabric.[1]

This definition, however, takes for granted the political organisation of social macro-groups in a state, whereas 'national emancipation' refers to a situation where this objective is still being pursued, usually under adverse conditions. In order to review processes of 'national emancipation' in a meaningful way one must confine the argument to such socio-political macro-groups as were already established as distinct cultural and political entities by the middle of the nineteenth century, regardless of the degree of their political autonomy and of their self-determination. Secondly, it is essential to apply this concept only to instances of the struggle of socio-political macro-groups *either* for liberation from domination by power-elites which belonged to different socio-political macro-groups with a more or less clearly defined national character, *or* against outside oppression with the ideal objective of establishing a political community where all citizens would be allowed equal participation in the political process. In other words, it is meaningless to speak of 'national' self-determination where this policy is not associated with the objective of implementing the principle of 'democratic' self-determination for the members of the respective socio-political macro-group.

This may appear a rather scholastic approach to the problem under discussion. However, unless the concept of 'national emancipation' is defined in accordance with certain substantive criteria the discussion will get hopelessly confused; it would be especially difficult to sustain a clearcut distinction between power-politics and imperialism on the one hand and legitimate national policies on the other. By 'legitimate national policies' we mean the struggle of socio-political macro-groups for their political as well as cultural—and in many cases also economic—emancipation from direct or indirect domination either by outside forces or by ruling elites of foreign origin. However, there can be no doubt that most processes of national emancipation—especially those in the second half of the nineteenth century—deviated widely from the ideal formulated by Guiseppe Mazzini. In fact, after the 1870s the national idea rapidly lost its original liberal content and became closely associated with crude power-politics which ignored the legitimate national interests of rival nations or

[1] Christian Graf Krockow, *Soziale und autoritäre Gewalt* (München, 1972), pp 72–3 (author's translation).

national groups. Jacob Burckhardt pointed to this in a remarkable passage of his *Reflections on universal history:*

in the first place the nation wishes to exert power more than anything else, whether it be pretended or real. To exist as a 'small state' is dismissed as if this were altogether a disgrace. The leading individuals are no longer satisfied with working for it. One wishes to belong to something really big, thereby demonstrating beyond doubt that power is the first objective while culture is only a secondary one. In particular one seeks to impose the general will on others outside one's own national boundaries in defiance of other nations.[2]

Burckhardt correctly predicted the fate of the principle of national self-determination. It became more and more imbued with mere power-politics in the interest of one's own nation; and consequently, although almost imperceptibly, its substantive content changed fundamentally. The socio-political and cultural ideas originally associated with the idea of nationality which had legitimised it as a widely accepted moral principle were pushed into the background and replaced by such pursuits as the exercise of power for the sake of power, display of military splendour in order to impress, demonstration of one's own power vis-a-vis rival nations and so forth. Eventually the idea of nationality became a straightforward ideological support of naked power-politics. In 1910 Max Lenz, then holder of Treitschke's chair at the University of Berlin, put it in the following words:

However independent and self-reliant the life of the state may be, it is after all only a modification of nationality as part of its very nature, and it cannot dissociate itself from the latter.[3]

Here the power-state and the national idea are viewed as two sides of the same coin; the one cannot exist without the other. The telelogical goal of the process of nation-building is the founding of a power-state which will enable the respective nationality to impose its will upon others. Almost imperceptibly the exertion of power, especially in the field of foreign policy, became the main content of the idea of nationality. The pursuit of 'Weltpolitik' came to be considered the very essence of the idea of nationality.

The final stage in the development of the concept of nationality was, of course, identification of nationalism with imperialism. Far from realising that, strictly speaking, the idea of nationality was incompatible with any sort of imperialist rule, by the 1880s the majority of the educated classes in Europe assumed that imperialism was—in Joseph Chamberlain's phrase—only 'a larger patriotism'. Henceforth and in the face of imperialist processes all over the world, imperialism appeared to many an essential

[2] Jakob Burckhardt, *Weltgeschichtliche Betrachtungen. Über geschichtliches Studium* (Darmstadt, 1956), p. 70 (author's translation).

[3] Max Lenz, *Die Großen Mächte. Ein Rückblick auf unser Jahrhundert* (Berlin, 1900), pp 21–2 (author's translation).

corollary to the idea of the sovereign nation-state. The idea that 'the future was with the great empires' which saw the smaller nations—those which did not acquire a colonial empire—destined to play only a 'secondary' rôle in world politics, soon became a universal obsession.[4] We find this view canvassed by such different men as Joseph Chamberlain, Paul Leroy-Beaulieu, Heinrich von Treitschke and Gabriele d'Annunzio. They all preached the doctrine that true nationalists—those who were dedicated to the idea of the sovereign nation-state—*had* now to become committed imperialists, since the possession of an empire was an essential precondition for the free development of one's own national culture in time to come. Max Weber, for instance, argued that it would have been better for the Germans to have abstained from the costly enterprise of founding the German empire if this was to be an end in itself and not the beginning of a vigorous German *'Weltpolitik'*.[5] In much the same manner, Paul Leroy-Beaulieu wrote that France, if she wished to retain her status as a great power in Europe, must build up a colonial empire; only the nations that grow will have a future at all, he told his readers.[6] Similarly, Joseph Chamberlain argued in 1897 in his 'Rectorial address' at the University of Glasgow that the consolidation and further extension of the British empire was an 'entirely popular sentiment not confined to individuals or classes, but identified inseparably with the national character' of the British.[7]

Thus we are faced with a dilemma. 'National emancipation' as an essentially liberalising process eventually negated itself by turning into an aggressive imperialist expansionism, which completely disregarded the principle of national self-determination. Moreover, the 'new imperialism', which the statesmen and ideologists justified by reference to nationalist arguments, soon turned into an irreversible process which was to have a devastating effect on the overseas world as well as on Europe.

One is forced to ask whether this was an inevitable development. I should rather say that under the impact of the new imperialism the processes of national emancipation were deflected from their original course everywhere in Europe. Most of the newly established nation-states were still in their infancy when the high tide of the new imperialism came in: the process of internal nation-building—i.e. the integration of the various social and economic sections and classes within the nation-state into the new socio-political fabric—had only just begun. While in the first half of the century and in the majority of cases the propertied classes had enjoyed the rôle of

4 Charles W. Boyd (ed.), *Mr Chamberlain's speeches* (London, 1914), i, 5.

5 Max Weber, *Gesammelte Politische Schriften*, ed. Johannes Winckelmann. (3rd ed., Tübingen, 1971), p. 23.

6 Paul Leroy-Beaulieu, *De la civilisation chez les peuples modernes* (3rd ed., Paris, 1886), pp 748–9.

7 Joseph Chamberlain, *Patriotism* (Glasgow, 1897), p. 28.

undisputed leadership in this process, the advance of industrialisation unleashed antagonistic forces within the social fabric that made it immensely difficult for the propertied classes to hold their own against their rivals both in the conservative aristocratic and in the newly-rising working-class camps. Thus the liberal impulses associated with the national idea—envisaging a Europe of sovereign nation-states—were decisively weakened. In other cases, notably in south-eastern Europe, the national movements could not count on reliable support from the numerically not very strong bourgeoisie; instead small groups of intellectuals took the lead. Consequently, the liberal-democratic ideas embodied in the national idea were largely supplanted by fervent, emotional national aims which were essentially elitist and did not refrain from employing subversive and even oppressive methods.

What was the impact of these changes in the substance of the national idea on the processes of national emancipation that were still in their initial stages when the high tide of the new imperialism set in? And what does this mean for the movements of national emancipation which had already succeeded in establishing independent nation-states? Until the early 1880s the processes of national emancipation had followed more or less the same pattern, although with many variations as to timing and speed. Everywhere the primary aim had been the establishment of nation states in accordance with constitutional principles which left the executive power to a monarchical head of state but which guaranteed the predominant political influence to the educated classes. The lower classes remained, as a matter of course, under-represented; however, the liberals assumed that, as time brought further educational progress, active participation in politics would eventually also be extended to the lower classes, without endangering the intellectual and moral predominance of the propertied and educated classes. Proper democratic conditions were looked upon as achievements of the distant future, but the idea that all classes of society would eventually enjoy an equal share in one and the same nation-state was still an unchallenged assumption.

By the earlier 1880s, however, the processses of national emancipation had split into two separate strands. In cases where the establishment of nation-states had been achieved, the political energies concentrated on the task of creating a maximum of internal cohesion, and secondly, on solving the problem of the integration of the working classes. Soon the democratic impulses were pushed into the background; instead, the national idea became an instrument for legitimising a policy of 'secondary integration' (Wolfgang Sauer) of the lower classes into the existing system;[8] and—as

[8] Wolfgang Sauer, 'Probleme des deutschen Nationalstaats' in Helmut Böhme (ed.), *Probleme der Reichsgründungszeit* (Köln-Berlin, 1968), pp 468–72.

has already been pointed out—this was often associated with policies of enforced assimilation of ethnic or religious minorities. These new trends were further intensified by the new imperialism. The enthusiasm of the middle classes for expansion overseas produced a new variety of national thinking which was primarily concerned with the grandeur of one's own nation and lost sight of the democratic dimension of the national idea altogether. At the same time the ruling elites were tempted to use this new imperialist version of national thinking for their own domestic objectives. The policy of 'social imperialism' became a useful tool for deflecting the attention of the rising middle classes from the constitutional issues and for reconciling them with the socio-political system of the day. From this point of view the imperialist ideology was essentially a defensive device of the ruling elites by which the privileged position of the upper classes was to be stabilised against the democratic forces and defended against the claims of the rising working classes.

The substantive changes which the concept of nationality had undergone became evident in these trends. It was also apparent that the national idea had adopted an entirely different social rôle. It could no longer be considered an emancipatory idea in any sense of the term. Nationalist arguments were now increasingly used as ideological weapons not only for justifying imperialist policies abroad but also for implementing conservative legislation at home. Of particular importance were three different applications of the national idea which must be singled out here.

1. The ruling elites as well as the bulk of the upper and upper-middle classes persuaded themselves that a maximum of national homogeneity was the indispensable precondition of a successful foreign policy. It therefore appeared to be no longer possible to allow national or other minority groups any substantial degree of autonomy within the nation-state. On the contrary, it seemed necessary to integrate all minority groups as rapidly as possible into the dominant nationality, in the last resort by political pressure or even by sheer force. The fate of the Poles under czarist rule is a striking example of this trend; similar phenomena could be found all over Europe.

2. The national idea was now increasingly used as a convenient ideological carrier by means of which the traditional political values of the aristocratic classes could be imposed on the rising middle classes. The integration of the British middle classes into the traditional constitutional system was effected under the banner of a 'Greater Britain'. Similarly the German ruling elites succeeded in imposing their militarist traditions—wrapped up in nationalist pathos—on the rising middle classes. Traditionally the German national movement had been devoted to the principle of the 'Landwehr', a democratic militia in sharp contrast with the standing

armies of the past. Since the early 1880s, however, the propertied and educated classes became increasingly impressed by the military splendour which was an essential element of Wilhelmine nationalism. Through the institution of the 'Reserveoffizier', the middle classes were allowed to participate indirectly in the semi-feudal symbolism of the German empire; and the acquisition of a 'Reserveoffizierspatent' became more and more popular among the educated classes, although this amounted to a break with their liberal traditions. This application of the idea of nationality was distinctly anti-liberal; undoubtedly it was an important factor in the defence of the existing socio-political order against the forces of democracy and modernisation.

3. In view of these changes in the content of the national idea which had no longer much in common with Mazzini's democratic nationalism, it is not difficult to see that the new nationalist ideology could also be used as an ideological weapon against the rising working-classes. Again, this development was most pronounced in Germany, but nationalist arguments were also used in other European countries as a means of checking the internationalism of the working classes and, indirectly, of combating their political and social objectives.

The changes in the substance of the idea of nationality were of great significance for the national movements in those regions of Europe where the process of nation-building was still in full swing. On the whole, the chances of the peoples still fighting for their national independence or living in incomplete nation-states—i.e. in states that had more or less justified claims on territories predominantly inhabited by co-nationals but belonging to neighbouring states—were substantially impaired by the growth of this new integral nationalism which was so directly associated with the imperialist zeal of the *beati possidentes*. In an age of imperialist rivalries of the great powers the idea of a democratic Europe of peaceful nation-states—big or small—appeared to be entirely outdated. The great powers in their relations with small nations insisted on their right to hegemonial control as a minimum concession. They had very little sympathy for the national movements still engaged in fighting for the fulfilment of their national objectives unless this fight could be exploited in the interest of their own imperialist designs. This is especially true of the policies of Russia and Austria-Hungary in the Balkans. Whenever they decided to back the national aspirations of particular peoples, they did so for reasons of their own which were directly or—as in the case of Pan-Slavism—indirectly related to their own far-reaching imperialist aspirations.

The European system of powers had always been reluctant to sanction territorial or other political changes, no matter how strongly they had been requested by the peoples concerned; now their reluctance became even greater unless the powers could expand their own sphere of influence under cover of supporting legitimate and morally justified claims of smaller nation-states or national minorities. The obstacles which national movements in Europe had to overcome in order to attain their cherished objectives rose higher the more the great powers became engaged in imperialist policies on a grand scale.

The position of the suppressed national groups or incomplete nations was further impaired by the rise of the modern industrial system. In the first instance, it must be pointed out that the social structures in advanced industrial societies were unfavourable to 'national emancipation'. The propertied classes—traditionally the main supporters of the principle of nationality—became increasingly divided into a variety of groups with diversified economic and political interests; therefore, their chances of directly influencing the political processes were generally reduced. Secondly, the gulf between the advanced industrial states and the bulk of the latecomers was greatly widened by the rapid industrial development. This rapid advance in industrialisation also placed powerful economic weapons in the hands of the established powers who could use them effectively to the disadvantage of movements for national emancipation which strove for independence and autonomy. Austria-Hungary, for instance, did not hesitate constantly to employ economic weapons against Serbia in order to reduce its attraction in the eyes of the Serbo-Croats living inside the Dual Monarchy.

On the other hand, these developments effected a radicalisation of the movements for national emancipation in the Balkans and elsewhere. The traditional intimacy between the propertied classes and the intelligentsia had declined; in some other cases it had never been established in the first place. Accordingly, parts of the intelligentsia increasingly resorted to national revolutionary strategies and the use of violence. Indeed, after the turn of the century, national movements all over Europe turned to more radical methods instead of using the legal, and in particular the parliamentary, means at their disposal to attain their goals. This is true not only of the peoples of the Balkans but also, for example, of the Irish national movement. The national revolutionary struggle was mainly carried on by comparatively small and often marginal elitist groups which did not hesitate to turn to conspiratorial devices wherever necessary. However, even under such adverse conditions the principle of national self-determination proved so powerful an idea that it could no longer be suppressed. But it was also clear that the processes of national emancipation were substantially slowed down—and in some cases entirely extinguished—by the changes within the social systems and the mounting imperialist rivalries between the powers. This will be demonstrated in greater detail by analysing a few case-studies which deal with the fate of the smaller European nations during the latter half of the nineteenth and the earlier decades of the twentieth centuries.

The fate of the Polish people is perhaps one of the most conspicuous cases to be taken into account in this analysis. Unlike the Southern Slav peoples the Poles could look back to a great historical past, although rich in vicissitudes and suffering. Since 1793 their territory had been divided between Russia and the central powers; initially both the Russians and the Austrians—to a lesser degree also the Prussians—had conceded a certain measure of autonomy to the Poles under their control. However, the realisation of the national aspirations of the Polish people—the re-establishment of a sovereign Polish nation-state—was unthinkable without a major upheaval in the European system of powers. Thus Adam Mickiewitz had every reason to pray to God that he might send a general European war in order to deliver the Poles from their yoke.

Unfortunate as the position of the Poles was, it deteriorated even further in the age of high imperialism. It should be remembered that Bismarck had succeeded in gaining Russia's goodwill for his German policies by assisting the czarist autocracy in the suppression of the Polish national uprising of 1863. This case is notable, because here German national emancipation had worked against Polish national emancipation, although the German liberal movement—the main popular force behind the policy of German unification—had always supported the Polish struggle for national emancipation. It is therefore not very surprising that the czarist autocracy no longer respected the status of autonomy which had been assigned to the Polish people within the czarist empire by the congress of Vienna, after Bismarck had so substantially changed the political conditions in central Europe as to make the stipulations of the congress with regard to Poland obsolete.

It may be said that the conflict between the German and the Polish peoples, which was to overshadow European politics for more than a century, was in a sense the inevitable corollary to the foundation of the German empire. After the early 1880s this became all the more apparent, when in the German empire and in Russia the nationalists insisted on a greater degree of centralisation and requested that national homogeneity must be achieved, if necessary by a forcible policy of assimilation. Accordingly, both governments began to implement various laws and administrative regulations—especially relating to the educational sector—that were designed gradually to reduce the national autonomy of the Polish minorities under their control. In the beginning Bismarck restricted such governmental action to the Polish clergy and the Polish aristocracy; after 1883 the National Liberals successfully pleaded for much more comprehensive measures. Eventually the Prussian government even forbade the use of the Polish language in political gatherings; it also implemented legislation authorising the government to nationalise Polish estates—if necessary—in order to turn them into small German peasant holdings. The policies of assimilation adopted by the czarist autocracy were—at least until 1905—even harsher; they sought, though on the whole with limited success, to reverse the process of polonisation of the lower classes of the population in the eastern provinces of Russian Poland. It was only in Galicia that the Poles enjoyed a moderate degree of autonomy; this gave rise to the hope that Galicia might play the rôle of a Polish Piedmont, which was the point of orientation in Pilsudski's skilful policies during the first world war. In general it must be concluded that the rise of nation-states in central Europe and the intensification of the rivalries between the great powers had only negative consequences for the status of the Polish people, whether they lived under Russian or German rule. The rising tide of nationalism—as such a by-product of the general process of greater participation of the masses in politics—was another factor which proved unfavourable to the cause of the Polish national movement.

Perhaps even more conspicuous in our present context is the history of the Balkan peoples. Here the political scene had long been dominated by two disintegrating, but still strong multi-national empires, which for centuries had shared control over the Balkans. In the earlier nineteenth century, however, Russia had begun to challenge the predominance of these two empires in this region. Russia's historical goal—the control of Constantinople and the Straits—gathered momentum in the 1850s, and later it became a substantial part of Russia's imperialist objectives. Since the fifteenth century the czars had exercised the historic right of protectors of the Christians within the Ottoman empire. This right was a convenient, if not always effective, pretext for exerting a degree of informal influence on Ottoman politics; moreover, it could be used to justify massive political interference and even military intervention in the Ottoman empire whenever general political considerations seemed to necessitate such a move. In addition, Russia did everything in her power to support the Southern Slav national movements which amounted to a two-pronged attack against Turkish rule and against the hegemonial claims of Austria-Hungary in the Balkans. Russia did so for sentimental reasons—embodied in the so called Pan-Slavist ideology—and for very real power interests. However, it must be conceded that she did not wish for any sudden changes that might result in the complete collapse of the fragile balance of power in the Balkans; neither had the Russian statesmen any particular liking for the radical methods of the rival national revolutionary movements in the Balkans. Nonetheless, the Russian statesmen were always inclined to exploit, albeit cautiously, the national movements to their advantage. This meant, however, that one had to slow down the dynamism of these processes in order not to lose control over them. Indeed, the complete independence of all Southern Slav nations in the Balkans would have terminated Russian hegemonial control at a blow. Russia was therefore vitally interested simultaneously to encourage and keep at bay the national aspirations of the various Balkan peoples, and all the more so because their respective territorial claims were mutually incompatible.

For the Ottoman empire and the Hapsburg monarchy the situation was very different. Both were vitally interested—although for different reasons—in suppressing the national revolutionary processes. The Ottoman empire had, however, reached a stage of disintegration that made the development of a rational policy toward the subjected Balkan peoples virtually impossible; the great powers were therefore repeatedly forced to press administrative reforms on the Ottoman empire in order to relieve the non-Moslems from the worst excesses of Turkish rule. In doing so they effectively slowed down the processes of national emancipation; and indirectly they rescued Ottoman rule in the Balkans from a complete breakdown. Austria-Hungary had a specific interest in all this; she could neither welcome the establishment of independent nation-states in this region nor could she tolerate an extension of informal Russian control at the expense of the Ottoman empire. Austria-Hungary soon had to realise that there was little chance of pursuing an expansionist policy in the Balkans; instead she worked hard for the consolidation of the *status quo*, trying her utmost to prevent the emergence of any strong Balkan state.

Great Britain and France had strong sympathies with the nascent national movements in the Balkans. The romantic enthusiasm for the liberation of Greece in the 1820s was by no means forgotten; and the idea that it was a moral duty to deliver the Southern Slav peoples from Turkish yoke gained greater currency the more Ottoman misgovernment resulted in widespread rebellion and upheaval. Gladstone's famous speeches against what he called 'the Bulgarian atrocities' did count in British politics. It is worth noting, however, that Disraeli—in the wake of his becoming a champion of the new imperialism—did not hesitate to put British imperial interests first and sympathy for the suppressed European minorities second. The preservation of the Ottoman empire in the face of constant Russian encroachments was to remain one of the fundamental principles of British foreign policy until 1915; in the first instance, in order to check Russian aspirations in these regions, and, secondly, because any other policy might have meant a European war. Consequently, reforms were forced on the Ottoman government only in so far as they did not endanger the delicate fabric of this decaying political system. Bismarck was at times less hesitant in these matters. He declared that the German empire was not interested in the Balkans; they were, as he put it, not worth the bones of a single Pomeranian grenadier. Already in 1876 he remarked that, provided he was given a decisive say in this matter, he would try to preserve peace in Europe at the expense of the Ottoman empire, which appeared to him to be no longer a viable institution.[9] But this did not mean that he cared in the least about the fate of the suppressed nationalities. When the congress of Berlin met in June 1878 in order to revise the oppressive peace of San Stefano, which Russia had imposed upon a helpless Turkey three months before, Bismarck encouraged the powers to draw new boundaries in the Balkans according to the principles of traditional power-diplomacy, rather than to pay any attention to the national aspirations of the peoples directly concerned. It is no mere coincidence that he encouraged France at the same time to occupy Tunisia, and that he told the British that the German empire had no objection to a British occupation of Egypt.

It is therefore not surprising that the congress of Berlin yielded very meagre results in terms of the national aspirations of the Balkan peoples. The informal Austro-Hungarian annexation of Bosnia and the so-called sanjak of Novi-Bazar (the latter was considered useful in view of the projected railway line to Valona, which was intended as the axis of Austro-Hungarian informal imperialism in the Balkans) was even a retrograde step; the hopes of the Serbo-Croats that sooner or later they would be united in one national state were severely disappointed. Clearly, the Bosnians did not consider the exchange of inefficient Ottoman for bureaucratic Austro-Hungarian rule a good bargain.

The future development of the Balkans was largely determined by the fact that the great powers acted on the assumption that any changes in this region were incompatible with the preservation of peace in Europe. This was maintained the more adamantly the more the powers became entangled in imperialist conflicts among themselves. Hence the struggle of the Balkan peoples for national independence was fraught with enormous difficulties. Their chances were further reduced by the fact that some of the Balkan peoples themselves turned imperialist once they had attained their independence. Greece, Bulgaria, Rumania and Serbia did not content themselves with fighting against Ottoman rule or Austro-Hungarian predominance; they soon began to look out for territorial conquests at the expense of one of the others.

It must be admitted, however, that this dynamic process which pushed the Balkan peoples beyond the boundaries of what may be described as the pursuit of legitimate national interests was partly initiated by the Young

[9] *Die Große Politik der Europäischen Kabinette* (Berlin, 1922), ii, no. 250, pp 71–2; 'Diktat' of October 20, 1876.

Turk revolution; this was essentially a rebellion against the rule of Ottoman puppet regimes dependent on the will of the European creditors and the instructions of the ambassadors of the European powers. Furthermore, the vicious circle of fratricidal nationalist wars was set in motion by the indirect impact of the new wave of European imperialism started by the 'Panthersprung nach Agadir' in 1911 and followed immediately by the Italian invasion of Libya early in 1912. When Italy had demonstrated that the powers were prepared to tolerate limited warfare against the time-honoured Ottoman empire, the Balkan states were quick to found a Balkan League in preparation for a military assault on European Turkey. Russia watched these developments with sympathy and granted indirect assistance, all the more energetically since she hoped to divert the aggressive energies of the Balkan League against Austria-Hungary once the Turks had been driven from European soil. But at the same time the Russian diplomats advised the Balkan League to proceed slowly, because they feared that their action might otherwise initiate a general European conflagration. When the Balkan nations embarked on what may be called sub-imperialist policies of their own, they in fact discredited the principle of national self-determination to such an extent that a permanently unstable situation was created in the Balkans. From now on nationalist extremists in Bosnia and Serbia came to consider statesmen like Francis Ferdinand, who favoured a moderate course on the nationalities question, a greater obstacle to the eventual triumph of the national revolutionary aspirations of the Southern Slavs than those politicians who opposed any concessions to the Slav nationalities.

Winding up this somewhat sweeping analysis of the developments in the Balkans, we can observe that the chances of a timely solution of the intense nationality conflicts in this region had been impaired to no small degree by the policies of the great powers; and this tendency increased the more the great powers pursued their massive imperialist interests. For reasons which had originally little to do with the Balkan peoples the powers for a long time blocked all major changes there, and whenever they accepted change they did so in the hope of furthering their own imperialist objectives. The German empire, for one, considered it imperative to support Austria-Hungary at any price on the Balkan issues in order to prevent her political collapse, although Germany herself had few direct interests in the Balkans. For reasons of general policy the German empire believed that she could not afford to do otherwise, despite the warnings of the German ambassador in Vienna, von Tschirschky, not to tie the future of the German empire to the fate of a rapidly disintegrating empire. Great Britain, France and to some extent also the German empire were for a long time primarily interested in keeping alive the 'sick man' at the Bosphorus, as this was the necessary precondition of the policies of economic penetration on which they had embarked increasingly since the 1880s. The processes of national emancipation in the Balkans were on the whole viewed with sympathy; but the activities of the national movements were tolerated only in so far as they did not endanger informal European imperialism in the Ottoman empire or disturb the precarious balance of power.

This is in some ways true for the Arab nations also: a fact which is rarely given sufficient attention by historians when they deal with the question of national emancipation. In the middle east, European imperialist penetration had in particular one lasting effect: it obstructed for almost a century the emergence and expansion of an Arab nationalism. The European nations had already interfered in Arab affairs well before the period which is our main concern here. Already in 1831, and again ten years later, the powers had rescued the Sublime Porte from the assault of the victorious armies of Mehemet Ali. They had thus prevented a radical reconstruction of the political order in the near east which might well have brought about a more suitable framework for the development of Arab national movements than the time-honoured vilayets of the Ottoman empire, or later the artificial mandate territories on which the powers agreed in the Paris treaties after the first world war.

It may be added that formal imperialist rule in Egypt, Tunisia and Morocco was established only with the assistance of indigenous elites, often of different national origin from the bulk of the populations, who were collaborating with the European powers. On the whole, European imperialist rule tended to perpetuate the extremely privileged social positions of these small, traditionalist ruling elites, provided that they accepted European control. In a number of cases the powers intervened with military force whenever the positions of these indigenous elites were threatened by nationalist rebellions from within; as in Egypt in 1882 or in Morocco in 1910. None of the imperialist powers was particularly interested in training the indigenous intelligentsia in order to prepare it for a greater degree of participation in the respective country's affairs. Though Arab nationalism had its roots in religious, rather than in political traditions, it might have matured much earlier, had it been given more opportunities for a free and spontaneous political development.

A less direct case illustrating the fundamental dichotomy of imperialist and national movements is that of Ireland. The rising tide of imperialist emotions in the aftermath of the British occupation of Egypt and the death of General Gordon at Kartoum in 1885 had a direct bearing upon the Irish question. When Gladstone decided upon military intervention in Egypt, he did not foresee that in so doing he was to initiate an accelerated process of territorial aggrandisement overseas that was to alter fundamentallly not only international but also British domestic policies. Measured by present standards, which consider formal and informal imperialism as merely two sides of the same coin, Gladstone was perhaps no anti-imperialist. But there is no doubt that he preferred the indirect strategies of indirect influence which could be implemented with a minimum of formal political control. Within the limits of British paramount control, Gladstone believed sincerely in national emancipation, and this was particularly the case in the Irish question, which had harassed British politics at least since the end of the eighteenth century. The 'Kilmainham treaty', which Gladstone had negotiated with Parnell in 1882, might well have become the initial stage of an evolutionary process which might eventually have brought about an all-Irish nation-state, though perhaps within the British commonwealth. This great historic opportunity was lost, primarily because the larger issue of the future of the British empire doomed the initiative. Under the influence of the new imperialist fervour, the British public came to consider the formulas 'Greater Britain' on the one hand, and 'Home Rule' for the Irish on the other as incompatible. Soon the home rulers were slandered as 'Little Englanders', and *vice versa*. Furthermore, the rising tide of imperialism destroyed the unity within the liberal party, and broke its political backbone. Thus the domestic rationale for an alliance between Irish constitutional nationalism—as represented by Parnell—and the British liberal party was jeopardised.

The split within the liberal party in 1886 over the issue of 'home rule' was perhaps the most important juncture in British domestic politics since the repeal of the corn laws. The liberals lost control over British policies for almost two decades, with the nominal exception of the Gladstone-Rosebery administration which was handicapped by severe internal rifts. The main engineer of the split had been Joseph Chamberlain, who was later to become the foremost British imperialist statesman next to Cecil Rhodes.[10] The reason for Chamberlain's desertion of the 'grand old man' was his opposition to Gladstone's comprehensive plan for 'home rule'. In making this decision, Chamberlain had been guided by a new, more stringent concept of empire which would have been jeopardised by granting such a high degree of autonomy to an Irish parliament. Already in 1885 Chamberlain had argued that he 'did not believe it to be possible to reconcile conditions as to the security of the empire, and the supremacy of parliament, with the establishment of a legislative body in Dublin'.[11] Chamberlain's vigorous opposition to any scheme of Irish self-government came as a surprise to most of his contemporaries, as he had previously advocated a rather liberal Irish policy. His abrupt change of mind can be accounted

[10] Cf. William E. Strauss, *Chamberlain and the theory of imperialism* (Washington, 1942), p. 38 ff.
[11] John Morley, *Life of Gladstone* (London, 1903), iii, 295.

for only by his conversion to the new imperialism: he considered the maintenance of the integrity, and the greater integration, of the British empire as a first priority, to which the Irish question had to be subordinated. The general elections in July 1886 not only buried Irish hopes of self-government within the near future but also marked the beginning of a new era of conservative rule under the banner of popular imperialism.

In such conditions, the Irish constitutional nationalists who sought to attain their objectives by legal and constitutional means were bound to fail. Indeed, the conservative government of Lord Salisbury was far from contemplating the possibility of a constitutional deal with the Irish people. Salisbury argued that Ireland consisted not of one but of 'two nations', and seemed to liken the Irish to 'races like the Hottentots . . . incapable of self-government'.[12] This equation of the Irish with African tribes is in itself a symptom of the prevailing contemporary prejudices surrounding the Irish question; it also throws indirect light on the hidden connection between the Irish problem and the imperialist issues. Under given conditions few people in Great Britain could remain aloof from the cluster of prejudices and political traditions associated with the idea of a 'Greater Britain'. Largely for reasons which had little or nothing to do with Irish politics, the majority of the British electorate consistently voted against any appreciable concessions to the Irish national movement. Only in the wake of the anti-imperialist era which began after the first world war were the Irish people eventually granted national independence. The Irish case corroborates our observation that the processes of national emancipation heading for the creation of sovereign nation-states with the political participation of all social groups were substantially deflected from their course, or at any rate considerably slowed down, by the impact of the new imperialism which dominated European politics between the 1880s and 1918.

The effect of the new imperialism on the secular process of national emancipation, which in a way found its eventual fulfilment in the reconstruction of Europe after the first world war according to the principle of nationality, may now be summed up.

First, the imperialist ideology in its various versions resulted in a grave mutilation of the principle of national self-determination. In cases where the establishment of nation-states had already been accomplished the processes of internal 'nation-building' were substantially distorted, largely in an anti-democratic sense. Instead of promoting a high degree of sociopolitical homogeneity by means of a gradual extension of active political participation to the lower strata of the population the national idea in its imperialist version served as an instrument of 'secondary integration' (Wolfgang Sauer). The national ideology became a convenient means not

12 Ibid., p. 317.

only of justifying an agressive policy of expansion overseas but also of taming the democratic and social forces within the nation-state itself. In particular, it was used as far as possible to block the full emancipation of the working classes within the given socio-political order.

Secondly, the new imperialism jeopardised the chances of political emancipation of nationalities that were still subjected to foreign domination, e.g. the Polish people and parts of the Southern Slav peoples. It increased the reluctance of the great powers to accommodate the wishes of national movements unless these could be exploited in the interest of their own imperialist objectives. Parts of the intelligentsia therefore did not see any other way to promote the cherished cause of national emancipation than to resort to strategies of guerilla warfare. At the same time, national revolutionary movements were themselves affected by imperialist fervour wherever the chance offered itself; for instance, the smaller Balkan nations developed sub-imperialisms of their own in the decade preceding the first world war.

In view of the various deformations of the principle of national emancipation during the period of high imperialism, the first world war may be interpreted as the eventual climax of the collision of two essentially different strands of national thinking. In the case of the established nation-states the idea of nationality had deteriorated into a spirit of imperialist aggrandisement, often associated with an aggressive militarism and prestige-hunting by the dominant elites. In the 'unredeemed' territories of the incomplete or subjected nations, however, there emerged an extreme revolutionary nationalism which at times—as in the case of Serbia in 1914—attempted to force the hands of the statesmen by resorting to political murder and guerilla warfare.

The first world war ended with the final breakdown of the traditional European system of powers. The lofty expectations of the previously subjected nations were accomplished overnight, although inevitably not always in full. The 'Völkerkerker' Austria-Hungary fell apart, and the Ottoman empire was totally dismantled. The old Mazzinian idea of a free Europe of democratic nation-states appeared to have triumphed at last. However, the satisfaction with the eventual victory of the principle of nationality over the older traditions of European statecraft had been somewhat premature. For one thing, some of the liberated nations—small or big—at once launched imperialist campaigns of their own in order to capture as much territory as possible from their neighbours. Poland's invasion of the still defenceless Bolshevik Russia in 1920 was only the most conspicuous case. Furthermore, the new nation-states in east central Europe were soon to realise that national independence in itself did nothing to solve the pressing social and economic problems with which they were confronted in the 1920s. And they began to realise that membership of larger multi-national units, like the Austro-Hungarian monarchy, had also had positive aspects.

Accordingly, the triumph of the principle of national self-determination was soon followed by disenchantment. The new frameworks for international cooperation which appeared necessary to overcome the economic and social difficulties in Europe could not be created at once. The League of Nations did its best to foster the development of an expanding international economic system and to grant assistance to the new nations, directly or indirectly, but its lack of real power soon became all too apparent. It took Europe another quarter of a century to learn the new lesson that national independence was not the key to the solution of all problems, and that it must be accompanied by intensive international cooperation in order to be successful in the long run. Some nations, like the Germans and the Italians, learned this lesson only after another desperate attempt to turn the wheels of history back: Ernst Nolte has aptly defined fascism as the 'life-and-death struggle of the sovereign, martial, inwardly antagonistic group' against the universal trends of the modern age.[13] In historical perspective, the age of nationalism has definitely passed its climax, even though a great many people are not yet prepared to acknowledge this truth. Perhaps it is one of the tasks of the historical profession to analyse rationally the nature of European nationalism in order finally to break its spell over the present age.

[13] Ernst Nolte, *Three faces of fascism. Action française, Italian fascism, national socialism*, translated from the German by Leila Vennewitz (New York, 1969), p. 537.

VII

Britain and the independence of the dominions: the 1921 crossroads

David Harkness

There is this to be said for them (the representatives of the British Government), that they are always ready to abandon a position when they think the time has come when they can no longer safely hold it.[1]

The variety of routes taken by self-conscious peoples towards the goal of national independence has already been demonstrated in the preceding papers. This paper will concentrate upon another variation on the same theme, that peculiar case of the British colonies of white settlement which, having grown at least to adolescent status in the century before the first world war, entered into mature statehood, as fully-recognised, sovereign nations, between 1918 and the outbreak of the second world war. They did so through the device of 'dominion status', and although this device was purposely vague in expression, although the separate dominions had moved at different paces, although they had acquired their domestic responsibilities at different times, and although they retained very different conceptions of their national interests, they now made their final movement towards the acquisition of all the attributes of sovereignty in some measure of unison. The process of evolution from say 1917, to 1939, was swift. But at the start its direction was far from certain, and for a time it may have seemed that the dominions were preparing to settle for something less than independence, as it was then understood: to deny themselves the sovereign right to unfettered individual decision in foreign affairs, in the pursuit of an alternative form of common security, based upon common policy-making. In the year 1921 two conferences forced dominion and British leaders to commit their views of the future to paper, and the emergence of these views now from the British records adds some fresh insight to a debate which is already familiar to historians. How nearly was there established an imperial cabinet that would give central directives to the empire in its dealing with other nations, thus blocking the dominions' road to independence just short of its goal?

The road these settlement colonies had already travelled is worth recap-

[1] J. W. Dafoe, editor, *Manitoba Free Press*, quoted in H. Blair Neatby, *W. L. M. King*, ii, 187.

ping, the peculiar aspect of their travel worth stating. They differ from the peoples of Europe who had in the past slowly overcome anarchy, or fragmentation, or unwieldy agglomeration or the humiliating domination of a strong neighbour or neighbours, to forge their nation states; and they are unlike the more recently independent Asians and Africans, often grouped in arbitrary territorial units, who, having shrugged off the domination of Europeans are now, after the event, striving to fit out their states with national consciousness. For they assumed from very early on in their settlement certain rights of local decision-making, shared many interests and assumptions of the mother country, and they did, in the course of time, and through the impact of distance, lose any fear of the forceful application of the metropolitan will. They moved at their own pace, in other words, towards assuming full self-government, without troubling too much about the timing of arrival at their destination, but increasingly confident and increasingly competent.

Generalisations about colonies of settlement so diverse in size, in situation, in tradition and above all in the composition of their populations, however, cannot proceed very far. The considerable French minority within, and the vast American Republic without, together heavily influenced Canadian development, which in turn affected that of the other settlement colonies. New Zealand, with its distinctive Maori minority, shared with Australia a loneliness on the rim of Asia, and a dependence on British migrants, British markets and British arms which contributed to a solid acceptance of British identity; much more so, certainly, than the deeply divided Boer and British communities of South Africa, heavily outnumbered within their eventual union as they both were by indigenous African peoples. Yet the growth of these settlement colonies followed a similar and, of course, well-known pattern. After the stirring of democratic sentiment in Britain, representative institutions were established amongst Englishmen overseas; in time these institutions became not merely representative of, but responsible to, the settler communities. Opinion in Britain reacted variously to this process, from those who, like Turgot before them, expected with complacence that their colonies would ripen and fall from the metropolitan tree—the 'pomological view'[2] as the Canadian historian, Professor D. G. Creighton, has dubbed it—to those who thought that the process should be resisted, and to others who felt that only in a federal union of mother and daughter nations could British greatness persist into the twentieth century. This spectrum, partly chronological in that federal determination grew to prominence towards the end of the nineteenth century, has been described memorably by Professor Man-

[2] D. G. Creighton, 'The Victorians and the empire' in *Canadian Historical Review*, xix, (1935), p. 144.

sergh. Noting the surge of imperial jingoism that coincided with Victoria's jubilees, he commented of the imperial enthusiasts: 'no longer ripeness but greatness was all'.[3]

It would be a mistake to imply any single 'British' viewpoint at any stage of this process of development. British financial, trading and agricultural interests, for example, as well as various colonial lobbyists brought their often conflicting pressures to bear upon those in authority. British governments were influenced in turn, to varying degrees, by domestic public opinion, international circumstances and the pressures of military or naval advisers. Home politicians, home civil servants and overseas officials often sought their own solutions to problems and were not always in accord. Thus, for example, it suited the British treasury that Canadians and New Zealanders should be given more control over their internal affairs: then they could be required to pay for their own defences. That this degree of autonomy might lead also to the imposition of tariffs upon British exports to the colonies had to be weighed in the balance. But the weighing was pragmatic, *ad hoc;* and the evolution of Canadian or New Zealand responsibilities followed more the development of their own self-confidence than any preconceived British plan.[4] That colonial leaders began to meet together in London with their British counterparts was largely fortuitous, at first irregular, and only through shared awareness of the value of such gatherings given institutional form. Thus the jubilee get-together of 1887 became the first colonial conference, which, through further jubilee and coronation meetings in 1897 and 1902, and the creation of the Australian Commomwealth in 1900 and the South African Union in 1909, matured from 1911 into the imperial conference system. To imperial conferences came the prime ministers of the British 'dominions' to confer on matters of mutual interest, and in the course of time, to claim the attributes of national sovereignty. It was perhaps a process lacking in drama, though there were dramatic enought events in the individual territories; their common business at first may indeed have been 'prosaic', to use Professor Mansergh's apt description. But a unique road to national independence was in fact being followed. The nature of its foundations have been summarised admirably by Sir Charles Jennings in an aside to his study of British policy towards the non-settlement empire; an aside which ties in well with at least one previous paper:

The American revolution of 1783 made it virtually certain that, in other places where British colonists settled, the right to independence would be claimed, and

[3] P. N. S. Mansergh, *The Commonwealth experience* (London, 1969), p. 126.

[4] For a concise reappraisal of analyses of nineteenth-century British imperial policy see C. C. Eldridge, *England's mission: the imperial idea in the age of Gladstone and Disraeli, 1868–1880* (London, 1973); but see also B. A. Knox, 'Reconsidering mid-Victorian imperialism' in *Journal of Imperial and Commonwealth History*, i, no 2 (Jan. 1973), pp 155–72.

conceded, when the people concerned felt themselves to be capable of standing on their own feet. It would be too much to say that this became anything like a 'purpose' of British colonial policy; the purpose, if there was one, was not so much to create new states as to find some way of keeping in the family the new states which insisted on being created. It was touch and go, but a way was found to solve the problem of Canada, and so the concept of 'dominion status' became established, to be applied, as time went on, to the new nations in Australia, New Zealand and South Africa.[5]

There was, in short, no consistent British policy, and so far as there was policy from the dominions themselves, Canada was the pioneer. In this context the influence of MacDonald, Laurier, and Borden upon Canadian and hence upon 'dominion' development is well charted. It was the colonial conference of 1907 which decided to formalise the conventions already practised at these 'summit' meetings, to lay down agreed rules and a regular timetable for future 'imperial' conferences and to call into being a new dominions department in the colonial office. Trade and defence also featured high on its agenda, cooperation in the latter at least being advanced by the further recognition and expansion of the committee of imperial defence, which had emerged late in 1902 and which was now augmented by an imperial general staff.[6] These matters were taken further at the imperial conference of 1911, which was distinguished by a comprehensive survey of foreign affairs by the British foreign secretary, Sir Edward Grey. Prime Minister Asquith averred, however, that while foreign policy could be discussed, Britain's responsibility for its determination could not be shared.[7]

The unsatisfactory implications for the dominions of this position became clear all too suddenly in 1914. Although they all supported Britain, to whose cause they were automatically committed by the war declaration of their sovereign, King George V, they quickly had their worst fears of embroilment in 'the vortex of militarism which is now the curse and the blight of Europe',[8] as Laurier had put it in 1902, amply confirmed. In 1916, therefore, the dominion leaders readily agreed to accept a summons to confer in imperial conference, and, more importantly, in imperial war cabinet to oversee the direction of this war.

Time had almost arrived, they soon asserted in the now famous resolution ix, of their conference of 1917, when the status of the dominions and the relations between them and the mother country should be clarified. On the cessation of hostilities a 'special imperial conference' should be called to

---

[5] Sir Charles Jennings, *Transfer of power* (London, 1960), pp 15–16.
[6] See Denis Judd, *Balfour and the British Empire* (London, 1968), i, for the story of the committee of imperial defence.
[7] See *Report of the imperial conference 1911, précis of the proceedings* [Cd 5741], 1911.
[8] *Canada, parliamentary debates (commons)*, lvii, 4726 (12 May 1902).

make necessary adjustments and these would have as their starting point 'a full recognition of the dominions as autonomous nations of an imperial commonwealth'. They would require also 'an adequate voice in foreign policy and in foreign relations, and . . . effective arrangements for continuous consultation in all important matters of common imperial concern, and for such necessary concerted action, founded on consultation, as the several governments may determine'.[9] Peace, participation in the Versailles negotiations, and membership of the League of Nations strengthened the international character of the emerging dominions, but still left their actual status ambiguous, open to misunderstanding from within, and also by the international community at large. They had, after all, participated in the peacemaking as part of a British Empire delegation, and they had joined the league as component parts of that same empire. Furthermore, the Geneva body (and their own imperial conference) had admitted also the far from autonomous India, in recognition of the great Indian contribution to victory.

The dominions, poised for independence, at this point seemed to hesitate. Was it really the moment to stand on their own feet? They began to doubt and Britain encouraged their uncertainty. Put simply, the members of the imperial association faced a dilemma 'the two horns of which were autonomy and unity'.[10] The *Round Table* caught the mood well:

how the orthodox believer of today is to worship the diversity in unity and the unity in diversity of the British Commonwealth, neither confounding the persons by undue centralisation nor dividing the substance to the point of the complete independence of its parts, is a question which awaits solution by some Athanasius of empire who has not yet appeared and would probably find himself *contra mundum* if he did.[11]

Analysed at greater depth, the direction of dominion advance was seen to impinge upon both their international security and their national unity. As Gwendolen Carter, looking back after the second world war observed:

The pervading question after 1918 was: how could the security of the period before 1914 be regained? Was it by avoiding responsibilities or by assuming them? If by assuming them, within what type of organisation should it be—in the British Empire, now being transformed into a British Commonwealth of Nations, or in the new international organisation, the League of Nations? Could either one or a combination of these offer the reestablishment of world security and a framework within which the dominions could continue their normal lines of development?[12]

Hitherto, they had been able to get the best of both worlds, for the flexibility

[9] *Report of the imperial war conference 1917* [Cd 8566], 1917, pp 4–5.

[10] H. Duncan Hall, *Commonwealth: a history of the British Commonwealth of Nations* (London, 1971), p. 366.

[11] *Round Table*, xi, no. 43 (June, 1921), p. 542.

[12] Gwendolen M. Carter, *The British Commonwealth and international security: the role of the dominions, 1919–39* (Toronto, 1947), p. xvii.

of the commonwealth had 'enabled the dominions to pursue cooperation without specific commitments, to act like small states which their populations indicated them to be yet to have the share in world affairs to which their area and resources entitled them'.[13] But might there not come a time when the demands of autonomy and of unity would be in conflict—when the peoples of the dominions might themselves be divided over these very priorities? In terms of national unity—and above all in the pursuit of national independence—membership of a commonwealth emphasising united action in foreign affairs might prove a more divisive than a consolidating force. Certainly in retrospect this appears to have been the case, for, although on the one hand, the commonwealth helped in the dominions to raise public interest beyond merely local considerations, on the other hand 'economic, social, or racial divisions in Canada, Australia and South Africa were accentuated in times of extreme stress by the division between those who interpreted their country's interest in local terms and those who believed it was best served by group action'.[14]

The dominions were at a crossroads in their journey towards sovereignty, and because they were by no means of one mind, they paused and allowed events to help decide for them. Thus, when the proposed 'special imperial conference' met from 20 June to 5 August 1921, it decided not to attempt to write down the mysteries of the status of its members or the constitutional relations betweeen them. It reached this decision, however, only after considerable argument and not a little thoughtful comment. Where, after all, did the dominions stand? How, in the circumstances did Great Britain view the course of their evolution? The answers are now a little clearer even though the outlines have long been familiar enough.

General Smuts, amongst the dominion prime ministers, had taken most trouble to explore the way ahead and he had aired his views with Leopold Amery, who, as chairman of the British cabinet's interdepartmental committee preparing for the conference, was coordinating the agenda in London. At the same time the young Australian enthusiast of dominion evolution, H. Duncan Hall, was writing a long historical account of dominion history coupled with some forthright recommendations, the chief of which was the necessity of a constitutional declaration of dominion equality within an association to be called, officially, the 'British Commonwealth of Nations'. His treatise, the conclusions of which appeared in a pamphlet in the summer of 1920, was published as a book that November[15] and gained the approval of Smuts in his correspondence with Amery. This correspondence, first revealed in an article written more than forty years later

---

[13] Ibid., p. 314.
[14] Ibid.
[15] *The British Commonwealth of Nations* (London, 1920).

by Duncan Hall himself, may now also be found summarised in Keith Hancock's biography of Smuts.[16] It reveals specific suggestions for enhancing dominion autonomy and improving dominion co-operation, suggestions which were to inspire Smuts's successor, Hertzog, to action in 1926. But the suggestions were not endorsed at the conference, in the event, owing mainly to the hostility of Prime Minister Hughes of Australia to any tinkering with inter-imperial relationships, and also to the obvious unwillingness of Canada and New Zealand to innovate. Instead the prime ministers agreed only that communications must be improved, that meetings should be annual if possible and that direct communication between the U.K. and dominion prime ministers should continue. As to the proposed 'special' meeting, 'no advantage was to be gained by holding a constitutional conference'.[17]

Yet this decision not to decide merely reinforced the uncertainties of dominion development and it is only now that the records of informal meetings between the prime ministers during the conference are yielding up the division of opinion that lay behind their bland pronouncement. The records, at the same time, spell out as never before the imperial cabinet ideal favoured by Britain in the troubled post-war era; an ideal which editorials and occasional ministerial statements in *The Times* had kept alive since the end of the war.[18] The conference report left the matter undecided, so that it was possible to claim that this cabinet, created in war, was to continue in peace, with all that might imply for central direction of joint strategy in international affairs. What lay behind this indecision?

The answer in the first place, was the forceful personality of Hughes. He emphasised from the beginning of the confidential prime ministerial discussions that he regarded the 1921 imperial conference as being charged at most with the task of drawing up an agenda for any 'special' constitutional conference that might be held in the future, though he personally felt that there was no call for such an exercise. Smuts, who had expected to conduct the constitutional debate there and then, perhaps sensed that the moment was not right to introduce his progressive ideas. He felt, however, that, if they were not going to overhaul inter-imperial relations then, the public, which was expecting such action, should be so informed. In the meantime he asked consideration of the following muted proposals:

(I)   There should be a declaration of equal partnership within the empire and of equality between the governments and parliaments of the empire.

(II)   The imperial conference as it had existed hitherto should be continued for the discussion not of the policy of the empire, but of inter-empire questions.

[16] W. K. Hancock, *Smuts: ii, The sanguine years* (London, 1968).
[17] *Report of the conference of prime ministers, 1921, summary of proceedings*, [Cmd 1474], 1921, p. 10.
[18] *The Times*, 2 Jan 1919; 17, 18, 19 Nov. 1920. See also Hall, *Commonwealth*, pp 340–2.

Then [the minute continues] there should, in addition, be a prime ministers' conference. He did not like the phrase 'imperial cabinet', which exposed him and his colleagues to attack in the dominions. The object of this prime ministers' conference should be to discuss empire policy and foreign policy, and defence. It should meet yearly, and, in the absence of those prime ministers who could not attend, other ministers should be sent in their place.[19]

The first round of discussion then broke up, resuming later in the same day, when the British attitude to the pursuit of full dominion autonomy was revealed in the form of a draft prepared by Sir Edward Grigg, but also incorporating the views of Massey of New Zealand. There is little evidence here of British favour for the process of devolution and autonomy that the dominions were in practice so soon to adopt.

The Grigg-Massey paper took the form of a declaration of principles, set out in eight paragraphs:

(I)   The governments of the British self-governing dominions and of the Indian empire, with those of the crown colonies and protectorates, are all equally the governments of his majesty the king, and are united in allegiance to his throne.

(II)   The aims of the British Empire are:
(a) to maintain its unity as a Commonwealth of Nations;
(b) to provide for the free political development of all the nations composing it in accordance with their respective traditions and ideals;
(c) to keep the peoples of the empire a united power for right, security and peace in all relations with other powers.

(III)   A single foreign policy for the whole British Empire, combined with a cooperative system of organisation for defence, is essential both to guarantee the national liberties of the self-governing peoples of the empire, the security and progress of the dependent peoples, and the unity of the whole.

(IV)   In order that the king as sovereign of the empire may speak with one voice in all matters of imperial concern, and that his constitutional position may be safeguarded against strain, it is essential that he should be advised in such matters by a single set of ministers. This responsibility lies naturally upon the government of the United Kingdom.

(V)   Since, however, the policy of the British Empire cannot be adequately representative of democratic opinion throughout the Commonwealth unless representatives of the British self-governing dominions and of the Indian empire are associated with those of the United Kingdom in considering and deciding the advice to be tendered to his majesty in matters of imperial concern, it is advisable that ministers of the self-governing dominions and representatives of India should sit with ministers of the United Kingdom for the consideration of the main issues of imperial and foreign affairs.

(VI)   These sittings will be known as meetings of the imperial cabinet, since all the ministers and representatives present, while severally responsible to their own parliaments and peoples for the advice which they give, are associated as a single cabinet advising the king.

[19] P.R.O., CAB 32/4: 'Imperial conference 1921, meetings of prime ministers, secret E 24, 'Notes of informal conversations', p. 31 (22 July 1921).

(VII) It is desirable that the prime ministers of the empire and the representatives of India should meet in London or some overseas centre as an imperial cabinet if possible once in each year.

(VIII) It is also desirable, though not compulsory, in order that the dominions and India may have a voice adequate to their status in the conduct of imperial and foreign affairs, that ministers of the dominions and representatives of India should be appointed to reside in England in the periods between the meetings of prime ministers. Such ministers and representatives shall be summoned when necessary to sit with ministers of the United Kingdom as an imperial cabinet for the consideration of matters of imperial concern. They will also at all times have access to the necessary information regarding imperial and foreign affairs.[20]

Britain seemed reluctant to depart from its *primus inter pares* position traditional within the imperial fold. But although Hughes must have been sympathetic to the main principle on foreign policy, of unity under British direction, too much was written down here in black and white for his essentially pragmatic preference. He would have no part in it. He did not favour reducing 'the constitution of the British Empire to writing'. Were their governments not, as Smuts had said, 'equal and coordinate governments of his majesty the king, united by allegiance to the throne?'.[21] No one was challenging their rights, he pointed out, so why write them down, an exercise that might do much harm? The dominions were evolving, acquiring powers formerly vested in Westminster and in recent time acquiring them at a more rapid rate. Adopting any set of principles or proposals would be a mistake, he asserted, reinforcing his point by reading from his own prepared submission:

It has never been the practice to attempt to set out in writing the precise limits of the powers surrendered by Britain to the dominions or of those retained by her. The reasons against any attempt to delimit the respective spheres of power and to define the constitutional relations between Britain and the dominions are obvious and overwhelming. The great merit of the constitutional relationship existing between Britain and the dominions is and always has been its elasticity. To this is due its wonderful adaptation to changing circumstances arising from the growth and development of the dominions. To attempt to substitute for this a rigid constitution or to define or set out in writing the relationship between the dominions and Britain is most undesirable. . . . The plasticity of the structure satisfies those who contend that we have the status of nations and who look with suspicion upon every attempt to create machinery to ensure unity in foreign affairs and naval defence, as well as those who regard unity of empire as more important than dominion self-government. . . . Conflict between the theory and practice of the constitution, between the sovereignty of Britain, the autonomy of the dominions, and the unity of the empire, has been avoided; because it has seemed that there were no limits which would exhaust the reserve of powers which Britain granted to the dominions as and when the circumstances seemed to demand them. Apparent inconsistencies evoked little criticism because there were, or seemed to be, no limits to modification,

[20] Ibid., p. 64.
[21] Ibid., p. 47 (E 31B, 27 July 1921).

expansion or readjustment. But if the constitution were reduced to writing the position would be very different. Any attempt to enumerate the powers or rights of the dominions must necessarily exclude all those omitted.

Hughes had one further point, a qualification upon the unfettered development of dominion autonomy, which brought him more in line with British thinking:

There remains, however, a somewhat vague but very wide sphere over which Britain still retains her sovereign powers. Amongst these are the powers necessary to determine the policy of the empire with foreign nations.

The basis upon which the British Empire rests is unity of action in foreign policy. The surrender by Britain to the dominions of all these powers necessary for complete autonomy is in theory consistent and has been found in practice to be compatible with that fundamental principle of unity without which there can be no empire. But it is clear that no further surrender of her powers can be made without fear of impairing that principle. . . . If it is to be accepted that unity is the basis of empire, then it is clear that on foreign policy the empire must speak with one voice. And it follows from this that Britain cannot waive any one of her rights to speak for the empire without the consent of all the self-governing dominions. . . . The right of the dominions to an effective voice in moulding the foreign policy of the empire is incidental to their autonomous powers over domestic affairs. . . . Clearly then, once it is admitted that the dominions have a right to an effective voice in directing foreign policy, it follows that Britain cannot entrust to any one dominion the power to take any action in regard to foreign affairs except as and to the extent agreed upon by the representatives of the whole empire.[22]

It was thus that Hughes, to use his own phrase, 'soldered up the constitutional tinkers in their own can'.[23] He prevented a definition of dominion status or a clarification of inter-imperial relationships, hoping no doubt to continue his own practice of assuming Australian rights when convenient and relying on British or empire protection when necessary. But he was skating over the central dilemma of an evolving association seeking to combine unfettered individual decision-making with collective security. His smokescreen suited British preference well enough. Lloyd George had agreed with Hughes in the discussions that nothing should be done 'in the direction of defining the position of the dominions towards the mother country', and the records also find the British prime minister in accord with Massey:

Mr Massey said that in effect what Mr Lloyd George said was that although it was termed a conference it acted as a cabinet. Mr Lloyd George replied in the affirmative. The decisions taken here had been the decisions that a cabinet would take. A

[22] Ibid., pp 66–7 (E31 B app. 4). This memorandum is reproduced in Hall, *Commonwealth*, app. A3, pp 976–8.
[23] For expansion and references see D. W. Harkness, *The restless dominion; the Irish Free State and the British Commonwealth of Nations, 1921–31* (London, 1969), pp 1–13; also Hall, *Commonwealth*, p. 393.

cabinet was a consultative body. . . . It did not really matter what the body was called, for the present conference had carried the weight of a cabinet.[24]

In parliament, later, Lloyd George reported his satisfaction that all the dominions would now be helping to formulate a foreign policy, the machinery for the execution of which would, of course, remain in British hands.[25] His foreign secretary, Lord Curzon, was reported at the same time as expressing the renewed confidence that such a decision implied: 'it will readily be seen what enormous strength it adds to the position of the foreign secretary. He feels now that he is not only speaking for Downing Street or for the British Isles but for the state which constitutes the British Empire.'[26]

If the representatives of Britain and Australia and New Zealand saw no conflict between the equality of domestically autonomous dominions, along with the mother country, and their joint participation in an imperial foreign policy which, inevitably, would in practice be dominated by Britain, the same could not be said for widespread opinion in Canada and South Africa. From the former, even the conservative Meighen had demanded at the conference specific recognition of Canadian rights and a clear distinction between matters affecting the empire as a whole and those arising between Canada and the United States, upon which Canada must be granted the final word.[27] Mackenzie King was soon to go much further than this as Canadian prime minister, while in South Africa the more nationalistic Hertzog, on succeeding Smuts in 1924, quickly joined the resistance against any commitment of the dominions by British foreign-policy decisions.

The immediate purpose in this paper of going into the 1921 conference discussions in such detail, however, falls short of these developments. It must be remembered that while the debates on the nature of dominion status in the summer of 1921 were in progress, the British government was deciding to offer that status, whatever it might be, to certain republican nationalists nearer home, who were striving to assert the independence of Ireland. That this decision was to be taken by Britain alone is surely significant commentary on the 'equal' status of the other partners of the association. But once the British did offer dominion status to de Valera on 20 July 1921, it might well be asked what was their understanding of what they were giving, and, by the same token, what did the Irish imagine they were getting? The answers to these questions help to delineate still further the crossroads position of the empire commonwealth in 1921.

[24] P.R.O., CAB 32/4, as above, p. 59.

[25] D. Lloyd George, in *Hansard 5 (commons)*, cxlix,, 29 (14 Dec., 1921).

[26] R. McG. Dawson (ed.), *The development of dominion status, 1900–36* (London, 1937) p. 216, where Curzon is quoted in an article by J. W. Dafoe.

[27] Ibid., p. 210, where the *Montreal Gazette*, covering Meighen's speech at the conference, is quoted.

The dominion status solution to the Irish question had not sprung to Lloyd George's mind from out of a void. This idea, confused by the alternative terminology 'dominion home rule', difficult to define owing to the rapid advances made by the dominions, and further obscured by a variety of qualifications assumed or denied by its proponents in Britain and Ireland, had been gathering momentum at least since 1917. Earlier than that, Ireland had been recognised as an imperial problem by British statesmen, one of interest in, and significance for, the dominions. In the 1890s A. J. Balfour had recognised Irish autonomy, within or without the empire, as the only alternative to killing home rule with kindness.[28] The home rule bill debates from 1912 had contained many imperial references, while in 1911 Erskine Childers had actually written a book which advocated dominion home rule, on the then relatively undeveloped Canadian precedent.[29] During the Irish convention, in 1917, two dominion home rule schemes had been submitted and Sir Horace Plunkett had kept the idea alive afterwards by founding, in July 1919, his Irish Dominion Party. He had also talked dominion status with Smuts in 1918, and again earlier in 1921.[30] Meanwhile H. H. Asquith, not long after surrendering the premiership to Lloyd George, had urged his successor to seek dominion help in settling the post-rising problem of Irish nationalism. It was he who had later made the first public statement by a prominent British leader urging dominion home rule, most notably during his Paisley campaign, on 2 February 1920.[31] Lloyd George himself had discussed a qualified version with C. P. Scott, as early as February 1919,[32] and during that year the suggestion had been propagated in America (where Plunkett toured), raised by Smuts and even aired by Northcliffe in *The Times*.[33]

Discussion of Lloyd George's controversial Government of Ireland Bill gave further opportunities, in lords and commons, for advancing the dominion solution, and the cabinet had discussed the matter in July 1920, not long after Lord Monteagle had launched a dominion scheme in the

[28] C. K. Young, *Arthur James Balfour* (London, 1963), p. 120. The best chronicle of the emergence of the dominion solution for Ireland is contained in D. G. Boyce, *Englishmen and Irish troubles: British public opinion and the making of Irish policy, 1918–22* (London, 1972). See also his 'How to settle the Irish question: Lloyd George and Ireland, 1916–21' in A. J. P. Taylor (ed.), *Lloyd George: twelve essays* (London, 1971). Many, though not all, the references in this section are also given by Boyce.

[29] Erskine Childers, *The framework of home rule* (London, 1911).

[30] M. Digby, *Horace Plunkett, an Anglo-American Irishman* (Oxford, 1949). See also R. B. McDowell, *The Irish convention, 1917–18* (London, 1970), and J. Van der Poel, *Selections from the Smuts papers*, v, 85–8.

[31] See S. D. Waley, *Edwin Montagu* (London, 1964), p. 125, and J. A. Spender and Cyril Asquith, *Life of Lord Oxford and Asquith* (London, 1932), pp 331–7. P. N. S. Mansergh, op. cit., p. 205, places Asquith's pioneering role in 1919.

[32] Trevor Wilson (ed.), *The political diaries of C. P. Scott, 1911–28* (London, 1970), p. 372.

[33] Thomas Jones, *Whitehall diary*, iii, 12.

lords. At the same time the officials in Dublin castle had been recommending a dominion solution, and Thomas Jones, of the cabinet secretariat, had presented his own, similar, conclusions to Lloyd George.[34] Delegations from Ireland had reiterated the message, while Plunkett's party had held a Dublin peace conference in its support in August 1920.[35] In September, Lord Grey had pushed the idea in the *Westminster Gazette,* and early in October Asquith had again taken up the cause in *The Times,* before Lloyd George had been driven on 9 October, in a speech at Carnarvon, to denounce the dominion solution, arguing a nightmare vision of Irish militarism and asserting an absence of responsible Irishmen with whom to deal.[36] Yet the following month had found Lloyd George expressing cautious approval of dominion home rule, plus safeguards, though he was reluctant to declare himself publicly without evidence that the scheme might be acceptable to the Irish.[37]

Meanwhile the Government of Ireland Bill had proceeded on its way through parliament, to become law on 23 December, and the working out of its provisions had given new stimulus to the debate during the earlier part of 1921. The relatively small circle of enthusiasts had conferred, refined their proposals, and burst into voice and print, while an equal volume of warning had surfaced about the dangers of granting dominion powers so near to home, and of denunciations of the vague meaninglessness of such phrases as 'dominion status' and 'dominion home rule'. A. B. Keith had contributed to this exercise[38] and had been followed by H. Duncan Hall whose book, published on 15 November 1920, has been referred to above. He had added to this an article on 'The meaning of dominion status' in *The Nation,* on 27 November 1920, and had contributed further articles to *The Times* in June 1921 as the imperial conference drew near.[39] All these arguments, together with the approach of the conference, had made good newspaper and periodical copy, and there can have been little excuse on either side of the Irish sea for complete ignorance of the issues. General Smuts had been active, after his arrival in Britain on 11 June, and his contribution to the king's speech at the opening of the Belfast parliament on 22 June, and his visit to enlighten de Valera on 5 July[40] are well known precursors to the eventual offer by Lloyd George to de Valera on 20 July.

[34] *Hansard 5 (lords),* xl, 1113(1 July 1920); Thomas Jones, op. cit., pp 25–32; R. B. McDowell, op. cit., p. 210; Boyce, *Lloyd George,* pp 151–2.

[35] Thomas Jones, op. cit., p. 34; Digby, op. cit., p. 250.

[36] *Westminster Gazette,* 29 Sept. 1920; *The Times,* 5 Oct. 1920; Boyce, in *Lloyd George,* p. 153.

[37] Stanley Salvidge, *Salvidge of Liverpool* (London, 1934), p. 187.

[38] See for example, his letter to *The Scotsman,* 18 Aug. 1920.

[39] *The Times,* 11, 14, 16, 21 and 22 June 1921 (series of 5 articles entitled 'Horizon of empire').

[40] W. K. Hancock, *Smuts,* ii, 51–60; Dorothy Macardle, *The Irish republic* (London, 1937), p. 490.

After de Valera's rejection of this offer on 10 August, Lloyd George published on the 15th their correspondence,[41] heralding another burst of advice and analysis in the national press designed to enlighten and encourage the intransigent Irish. There was, therefore, considerable evidence upon which both sides could draw when their negotiating teams finally came together around the table on 11 October 1921. Even so, it was realised by the British that they would have to spell out fully to the Irish what it was, in practice, that was being offered. Dominion status had already been equated by some with full independence, even carrying within it the right of secession from the imperial association; others had emphasised the obligations of allegiance and the common responsibilities of membership. During the preliminary soundings the British, while making it perfectly clear that any dominion settlement would have to be supplemented by defence guarantees to safeguard British, and by implication Irish, interests, had made their own attempt to summarise the 'powers and privileges' attaching to the 'free nations which compose the British Empire', asserting for Ireland 'complete autonomy' in taxation, finance, law, home defence, education and agriculture—indeed, the whole gamut of government responsibilities (subject only to listed conditions relating to international defence, trade and debt).[42] But now, as Lloyd George and his team met to consider the negotiations ahead, a more authoritative definition of dominion status was required. It was decided, therefore, 'that Mr Curtis should prepare a memorandum on the meaning of "dominion status" with special reference to recent imperial developments'.[43]

Lionel Curtis, who, with Tom Jones and Sir Edward Grigg, made up the British secretariat at the negotiations, had been a member of Milner's kindergarten, but had in recent years been preoccupied with the Indian side of his great imperial enthusiasms. Earlier in 1921, however, he had made a tour of Ireland with the editor of the imperial journal, *Round Table*, and together they had made in its June issue a penetrating study of Ireland's historical development and its current needs and opportunities.[44] A convinced believer in the higher claims of the empire as a whole over those of its constituent members, Curtis nevertheless approached his task with a sympathy for Ireland and a recognition of the damage caused by centuries of the denial to Irishmen of their right to govern themselves. When his survey was presented to the British delegation on 15 October, however, it was quickly realised that, owing to the delicate nature of

---

[41] *Correspondence relating to the proposals of his majesty's government for an Irish settlement* [Cmd 1470], 1921. These are conveniently reproduced in Macardle, op. cit., pp 499–503.
[42] Ibid.
[43] P.R.O., CAB 43/3, S.F.C. 2, conclusion 5 (11 Oct. 1921).
[44] *Round Table*, xi, no. 43 (June 1921), pp 465–534. See also comment in Frank Pakenham, *Peace by ordeal* (New English Library ed., 1967), p. 116.

dominion evolution, not to mention the recent decision of the imperial conference, they had placed themselves in a difficult position. In the words of the official minute:

Strong objection was . . . taken to the proposal to hand to the Irish representatives, in the name of his majesty's government, a document purporting to set forth the constitution of the empire in law and practice. Such a document if disclosed would become of supreme constitutional importance and have permanent and far-reaching significance, not only in the Irish controversy, but in the determination of imperial relations.[45]

It was decided, instead, therefore, to instruct Curtis to prepare a new draft 'written in untechnical language', stressing 'the great range of powers enjoyed by the dominions' and having 'regard to the ardent desire of the Irish representatives that Ireland should be free to develop her industries and commerce'.[46]

When, on 18 October, Tom Jones passed to his opposite number, Erskine Childers, the ensuing twenty-page memorandum, in 'non-legal and un-technical language', it now bore, not the imprimatur of his majesty's government, but merely that of 'Mr Lionel Curtis, an acknowledged authority on the subject'. On the edge of one of the copies of this document, Sir Charles Dixon, later legal adviser to the colonial office, has pencilled the comment 'this is interesting'.[47] It is. It is also an eloquent request, written in a personal and informal style, for Irish appreciation of the imperial association as it then stood and also for what it might become.

Curtis could not 'define' but only 'describe' dominion status, in view of the imperial conference decision, and he chose to do so by asserting first the domestic powers of the dominion parliaments which were 'commensurate with those of the British parliament over the United Kingdom'. Then he embarked upon a sweeping tour, dominion by dominion, stressing the variety of their individual economic, social and commercial preoccupations, appropriate to their diverse circumstances. But status was fundamental and to this he soon returned:

If I am asked then, to say what the status of a dominion is so far as matters domestic to itself are concerned, I am forced to answer that it is exactly the same as the status of the United Kingdom.

Should he be challenged on the powers of Westminster to revoke or amend dominion constitutions, he would, he went on, draw the distinction between law and fact that was central to the imperial story of devolution:

Law itself rests on something more potent than law. In law the king can veto a measure passed by lords and commons. In fact, he can do no such thing. Custom,

45 P.R.O., CAB 43/4, S.F.B. (15 Oct. 1921).
46 Ibid.
47 In P.R.O., CAB 43/3.

based on experience has abolished that right, and custom is the ultimate basis of law. . . . I am bound to say, therefore, that a dominion constitution is no more liable to be changed except at its own instance than that of Great Britain.

Dominions, too, he proceeded, can conduct commercial treaties, have their own armed forces, and now, recently, participate in foreign affairs.

At last, Curtis had reached the crux of the contemporary dilemma: the conflict between a concept of dominion autonomy and that of imperial unity. Describing the management of the war in inspirational terms, Curtis gave his own version of how 'the ministers of each dominion sitting with those of Great Britain directed the war policy of the whole British Commonwealth as one state',[48] before quoting Lloyd George's own flight of rhetoric proclaiming the double advantage, during the peace negotiations, that attached to the dominions, at once small powers with independent rights, and also members of an imperial association giving them representation at the highest councils, whereby 'each dominion exercised influence which was infinitely greater as being part of the British Empire than it would have exercised if it had stood absolutely alone'.[49] Membership of the League of Nations (Curtis asserted here their yet unclear eligibility 'as minor powers for election to the council in their separate capacity')[50] and of the imperial conference ('the final repository of those traditions which safeguard the autonomy of all the dominions, their equality of status with Britain in the councils of the commonwealth, and also of the unity which these nations together present in matters affecting themselves in common and the world at large')[51] completed their international standing and cemented their national security.

Yet even though it was now evident that 'the dominions and Britain are now once and for all on a footing of formal equality in external as well as in domestic affairs' this was only the current stage of development and Curtis would not 'conjecture what it may become'. He would merely conclude by repeating the necessity of presenting a united face to the world at large:

It is recognised that, in matters common to all, the empire must speak with one voice and the foreign office in Whitehall is the mouthpiece through which that voice is heard. That office is the agent which all the dominions recognise as speaking for all. Each government is free to take any action it chooses, but each is expected to consult the others before taking action which affects the unity of the commonwealth as a whole. And if the imperial conference is of opinion that the action proposed would affect that unity, the government proposing it is expected to abstain. That is actually how the system works. It depends entirely on the willingness of each to refrain from doing what it is free to do, but which, if done, would limit the freedom of all the rest.[52]

[48] P.R.O., CAB 43/4, secret S.F.C. 13: memorandum on dominion status, pp 1–14.
[49] Ibid., p. 17.
[50] Ibid., p. 18.
[51] Ibid.
[52] Ibid., pp 19–20.

Here Curtis once again opts for the whole over the parts, for unity above autonomy. But before the Irish interpretation of the same 'recent imperial developments', is noted, one other expression of the British government's view of the trend of dominion evolution, as outlined during these negotiations should be recorded. The circumstances were rather different, the statement was for a more limited audience, being contained in a letter to Sir James Craig, who had written on 11 November his 'refusal to discuss the participation of Northern Ireland in an all-Ireland parliament', and countered with a proposal 'that Southern Ireland and Northern Ireland should be constituted two separate dominions'. This, it seems, struck the British as offending against 'broad imperial principle':

The status of the dominions, both nationally and internationally, is based on the gradual amalgamation of large territories and scattered colonies into natural units of self-government. To make a dominion of Ireland as a whole is in itself a reversal of the normal process of imperial development. We have proposed it because Ireland is one of the parent-islands of the commonwealth and comparable to existing dominions as a natural unit of self-government.[53]

The Irish delegates, however, were not invited to grapple with 'broad imperial principles' of this nature. Given freedom to choose, they would hardly have interested themselves even in the vision of Curtis. Rather, they preferred to present their own plan of 'external association' with the commonwealth group, arguing that the undoubted freedoms claimed for Canada and the other overseas dominions would hardly apply to an Irish dominion so close to Britain. Because the existing dominions lay thousands of miles away, they claimed:

Great Britain . . . has neither desire nor temptation to interfere in their home affairs. The crown to them is a symbol of the internal unity of equal states, not of the internal repression of subordinate states. Ireland, on the contrary, lies beside the shores of Great Britain, which has been accustomed for generations to interfere, in the name of the crown, in every detail of Ireland's life. The desire and temptation to continue interference will remain if the crown remains, as it cannot be the symbolic crown that the dominions know, but will continue to possess the real power of repression and veto which Ireland knows.[54]

Presented late in the negotiations and argued with conviction, this plea stood little chance in the face of British strength, negotiating skill and, it must be admitted also, timely concession. When Ireland was offered, as a clause in the first article of the treaty, 'the same constitutional status in the community of nations known as the British Empire as the Dominion of

[53] P.R.O., CAB 43/4 'Conference on Ireland: letter in reply to Sir James Craig's letter of November 11 1921', p. 1. See also Cmd 1561: *Correspondence between his majesty's government and the prime minister of Northern Ireland relating to the proposals for an Irish settlement.*
[54] P.R.O., CAB 43/4, 'Conference on Ireland: memorandum by the Irish delegates on their proposal for the association of Ireland with the British Commonwealth', pp 1–2.

Canada', Collins and Griffith at least, if not Childers, were prepared to risk the hazards of geographical propinquity, and to posit a view of the emerging commonwealth that offered even an Irish dominion both the promise of genuine freedom and the security of numbers while this promise was being fulfilled.

Collins put on paper such a view,[55] and there can be no doubt from reading this that he and his colleagues had benefited from the mass of public debate which had risen to a crescendo in 1920 and 1921. In particular the voice of Smuts and the pen of Duncan Hall were crucial, though the legal arguments of A. B. Keith, then as later, were also useful. Frank Pakenham has stressed the value to Collins of Duncan Hall's *The British Commonwealth of Nations,* amongst other authorities, adding, significantly, that Collins 'drew from them lessons very different from those drawn by Childers, the dominions expert of the delegation—or indeed by the authors themselves'.[56] Hall has revealed subsequently that every member of the Irish delegation had a copy of his book, and has pointed out that its particular virtue was its insistence upon 'a maximum interpretation of dominion status—not the limited interpretations that still coloured British thinking'.[57] He quotes the appreciation later expressed to him by two of the Irish officials, J. A. Costello and Alfred O'Rahilly, while the latter, in his pamphlet urging support for the treaty at the time, made much of South African precedent and general dominion potential, quoting directly from both Hall's book and the letter written to de Valera by General Smuts prior to his departure at the close of the imperial conference.[58] The publication of Thomas Jones's *Whitehall diary* makes it clear that Gavan Duffy, too, made use of Hall's book as a working document during the negotiations.[59]

The Irish vision emerged, then, of a dynamic dominion status that would ensure full national independence without recourse to further bloodshed. National sovereignty, it was claimed, could be harmonised with international association but national sovereignty must be fully recognised and the commonwealth association, if it was to be accepted, must

be based not on the present technical, legal status of the dominions, but on the real position they claim, and have in fact secured. . . . It is essential that the present *de facto* position should be recognised *de jure,* and that all its implications as regards sovereignty, allegiance, constitutional independence of the governments should be acknowledged.[60]

[55] Reproduced in F. W. F. Smith, *Frederick Edwin, earl of Birkenhead* (London, 1959), pp 382–4.
[56] Frank Pakenham, op. cit., p. 226.
[57] *Commonwealth*, p. 198.
[58] Alfred O'Rahilly, *The case for the treaty* (?1922).
[59] Thomas Jones, op. cit., p. 122.
[60] F. W. F. Smith, op. cit., p. 383. This passage is also contained in D. W. Harkness, op. cit., p. 16.

Though reluctant to settle for such a compromise of their republican ideal, the Irish delegates, on 6 December 1921, did accept, under threat of immediate and terrible war, the proffered membership of this free association of equal states. Collins did not live to argue through his conception of dominion status, but the Irish position had been stated, and FitzGerald, O'Higgins and McGilligan, successive external affairs ministers, lent Ireland's weight to the enthusiasts of dominion independence, in Canada and South Africa in particular, helping thus to ensure the sweeping away in the next two decades of both the united empire foreign policy and that body of anachronisms and anomalies—survivals of a colonial past—that together obscured before the world the reality of the several dominion sovereignties.

The British, albeit with some reluctance, reacted characteristically by facing up to dominion pressure and adjusting their concept of commonwealth to accommodate increasing, and then complete, independence.[61] By 1931 in effect, and by 1939 visibly to all the world, the dominion status road to national independence had been followed to the end, a matter which was to be of some significance to Britain and its non-settlement colonies as they sought to arrange independence, with continuing association, in the post second-world-war era.

Even at the beginning of 1921, it must be admitted, the development of dominion status to equate with independence was already well advanced. But early in that summer, as the dominions had paused, reluctant to hazard their common security in the pursuit of full sovereignty, British statesmen had urged upon them caution, propagating a contemporary wisdom of joint policy in an uncertain world. As always, British interests were foremost in the minds of these statesmen, and in the course of action they recommended. Yet by July, when these interests nearer home demanded an accommodation with, but curtailment of, Irish nationalist ambition, the dominion solution they devised could not but impinge upon the delicate dominion balance. By thus creating an Irish dominion, the British government unwittingly influenced all the dominions still pausing at the crossroads, helping to push them along the open road to independence, away from the *cul de sac* of a centralised imperial authority.

[61] See D. W. Harkness, op. cit., and also 'Mr de Valera's dominion: Irish relations with Britain and the Commonwealth, 1932–8' in *Journal of Commonwealth Political Studies*, viii, no. 3 (1970), pp 206–28.

VIII

The pursuit of national independence in Botswana and Nigeria: a study in contrasts

John Blake

The peoples of Nigeria, after struggling for many years to recover their independence, reached their goal in October 1960. At that moment, the Batswana were just beginning to think seriously of independence and yet within the short span of six years they also had become free as citizens of the republic of Botswana. The colony and protectorate of Nigeria, on the eve of independence, with a population of some 40 millions and an area of 341,000 square miles, was one of the largest, most populous, potentially rich and best-known of all the colonial dependencies of sub-saharan Africa which were liberated during the historic decade 1957–66. In contrast, the Bechuanaland Protectorate (the B.P.), with a Texan-sized territory (275,000 square miles) but a tiny population of half a million, was one of the poorest, most sparsely peopled, and least-known countries in the world: indeed, the B.P. was widely, though inaccurately, regarded as a semi-arid wasteland set in the eastern part of the Kalahari desert. The two colonial dependencies were very different; and the purpose of this paper is to attempt a critical comparison of the respective independence movements in them, and also to suggest that along the road to national freedom sharply contrasting factors determined the attitudes and actions of their respective peoples from the inception of British rule to the achievement of independence.

At the root of future divergence was the hard fact that the circumstances in which alien rule was established in these territories differed profoundly. This (I suspect) permanently coloured the attitudes and responses of the indigenous inhabitants. It proved in the long run to be crucial in shaping African reactions to colonial administration. It goes a long way to explain the contrast between Botswana's smooth, amicable and relatively swift transition from protectorate to republic, and Nigeria's more troubled and turbulent, long, stormy and even violent path to the 'threshold of paradise'.[1] Setting aside the question of British motivation, it is broadly true to

[1] The picturesque, if optimistic, description used by the Yoruba leader, Obafemi Awolowo, in his *Autobiography* (London, 1960), p. 299.

argue that, whereas the Batswana through their leading chiefs repeatedly asked for British protection, the very many different peoples of what we today call Nigeria were mostly subjected to British rule piecemeal and by force. The tribes of Bechuanaland wanted to come under the secure umbrella of the 'great white queen'. In contrast, nearly all the ethnic groups of Nigeria—Delta and river folk, Yoruba in the west, Edo of the middle west, Ibo or Ibibio of the east, Tiv of the pagan middle belt, Hausa-Fulani-Kanuri of the moslem north, and scores of others—resisting alien penetration as best they could, had to be deliberately hammered before they would submit to British rule. Indeed, the introduction of foreign rule was conditioned by entirely different situations, which from the beginning provoked contrasting reactions from the indigenous Africans. Let us consider the Batswana first and then the peoples of Nigeria.

The Batswana, with the important exceptions of the Shona Kalanga[2] in the north and the wandering Bushmen,[2] are all substantially of the same stock and members of the western Sotho branch of the Bantu. Though still grouped in tribes—Ngwato, Ngwaketse, Kwena, Kgatla, Tlokwa, Tswana, Lete[3] and Rolong—they are essentially one people in language and culture. In this respect, when British rule came, their basic homogeneity contrasted strongly with the ethnic, religious and linguistic diversity of the peoples of Nigeria; and in the future, when the restoration of independence could be contemplated, the task of nation-building was to prove less formidable and the divisiveness of tribalism less acute than for the Nigerians. In the era of aggressive European imperialism, then, this circumstance among the Batswana allowed for a degree of cooperation between the leading chiefs which contributed to the survival of their people and the effective preservation of their own way of life. In point of fact, their livelihood was gravely imperilled from the middle of the nineteenth century by trekboers, mostly from the Transvaal, who coveted their lands, their cattle and particularly their water supplies. Their position, especially that of the southern tribes, the Tlhaping and the Rolong, already thus exposed, deteriorated still further with the discovery of diamonds in the Kimberley area and the inrush of miners, freebooters and white riff-raff. As John Brown of the London Missionary Society, writing of the desperate plight of the Batlhaping in 1878, vividly put it:

They saw the country in which they had been born and brought up, and over which their chiefs had exercised undisputed authority for years past, taken out of their hands. . . . They saw strangers come and take possession of fountains at which their own cattle had hitherto drunk unhindered.[4]

---

[2] The Botswana government regards all inhabitants of the republic as citizens, and there is no legal discrimination.
[3] Of Ndebele origin but assimilated.
[4] Quoted in A. Sillery, *John Mackenzie* (Cape Town, 1971), p. 43.

The response of some of their leading chiefs, at this stage especially of the tribes of the Tlhaping, Rolong and Ngwaketse, was to seek British protection. In doing this, they were influenced partly by the advice of friendly missionaries but also by the example of their cousins in Basutoland then recovering under Moshoeshoe I from the disruptive effects of the Mfecane.[5] True, it was a case of Hobson's choice; but the protection of Queen Victoria was infinitely preferable to subjection to boer farmers of the Transvaal and the Orange Free State, whose biblical calvinism, for all its sincerity, could bring no comfort to those who would become 'hewers of wood and drawers of water'. Sir Henry Barkly, the high commissioner at the Cape, knowing in 1871 that boer encroachments on Tswana lands had been taking place 'for upwards of twenty years', reported the situation to Whitehall: 'One and all of the chiefs . . . under whatever influence they may be, are most anxious that their country should be taken under her majesty's protection'.[6] Then, in 1876, chief Khama III, of the powerful Ngwato, added his considerable weight to the rising pleas for British protection.[7] But a reluctant British government remained unmoved until, in 1884, a direct threat to the security of the 'missionary road to the north' suddenly erupted. Following the proclamation in that year of a German protectorate over Namaqua-Damaraland (i.e., South-West Africa or Namibia), this vital northern route from Mafeking through Bechuanaland to the heart of Africa could be closed in the event of a Transvaal-German link-up;[8] and this alarming prospect at last galvanised the British government into action. By order-in-council of 27 January 1885, British jurisdiction was extended northwards over a vast region from the Cape frontier to the 22nd latitudinal parallel and westwards from the Transvaal border to 20°E. If the southern part of this area, inhabited by the Tlhaping tribe and some divisions of the Rolong, and known as British Bechuanaland, was subsequently (1895) incorporated within Cape Colony to become today a part of the Bantu homeland of the Tswana, the northern sector beyond the Molopo river, where the more powerful Tswana tribes lived, remained under the direct protection of the crown. Though British policy was not dictated primarily by concern for the Batswana, it is significant that the leading chiefs, notably Khama III, welcomed the news of the protectorate as an answer to their prayers. Chief Khama's one criticism was that the northern boundary line—22°S.—cut

[5] The Mfecane (Zulu for 'marauding') or Difaquane (Sotho for 'hammering') is the term commonly used to describe the devastation and partial depopulation of the high veld particularly north of the Orange river, resulting from Zulu wars and raids initiated by Shaka and occurring during the years, *c.* 1822–37.

[6] Barkly to Pretorius, 25 Jan. 1871, in [C 459], H.C. 1871, xlvii, 397. Barkly to Kimberley, 18 Dec. 1871, [C 508], H.C. 1872, xliii, 163.

[7] Ibid., [C 4227], H.C. 1876.

[8] *Cambridge history of e British Empire,* viii (Cambridge, 1963), pp 524–9.

his lands in half, because his territorial claims, though disputed by the Ndebele, extended as far north as the Chobe river. His claim was recognised in 1891, which may be regarded as the year when the boundaries of the present republic of Botswana, with only minor subsequent modifications, were determined.[9]

Thereafter, until the restoration of their independence, the Batswana and their chiefs, despite occasional internal crises, appear to have been reasonably content under the British dispensation. Indeed, British protection, though in the course of time entailing some erosion of the traditional powers of the chiefs, proved to be effective against all external threats. Thus, in 1895, chiefs Khama of the Ngwata, Bathoen of the Ngwaketse, and Sebele of the Kwena, having visited London to lodge a vigorous protest against a proposal to transfer the administration of their lands to the British South African Company, returned home in triumph. They had met the 'great white queen' at Windsor castle, and seem to have been deeply moved. As Sebele said:

Her majesty is a very charming old lady. . . . But I had no idea that she was so small. The corridors and the magnificent palace where she lives are all lined with stalwart soldiers. as big as I am, in glittering uniforms. None ever moved. They all stood erect and motionless like the marble statues in the streets of London. While passing along their line I boldly tested one of these giants. I thrust my finger almost into his eye to make certain that he was a living being, and not a statue placed there to add to the grandeur of the palace. To my great surprise he never flinched, but merely rewarded me with a smile. When I was in one of her majesty's splendid apartments, I was greatly astonished to see an ordinary, tiny house-fly! It was a puzzle to me to know how it got there, for I could hardly believe that even death could enter such a palace.[10]

They had also met Joseph Chamberlain, the colonial secretary, and received his personal assurance that the status of the Bechuanaland Protectorate would not be changed.

Even more significant, however, was the survival of the protectorate after 1910 when the Union (now the Republic) of South Africa was formed. All the efforts of successive Pretoria governments to incorporate Bechuanaland, along with the two other former High Commission territories (Basutoland and Swaziland), proved abortive; and this despite the general expectation, as reflected in section 151 of the Union act and its schedule, that transfer to South Africa would be only a matter of time.[11] British

[9] For details of the northward extension of British jurisdiction, see A. Sillery, *Founding a protectorate* (London, 1965), pp 144–58.

[10] Quoted in J. Mockford, *Seretse Khama* (London, 1950), p. 129.

[11] *Basutoland, the Bechuanaland protectorate and Swaziland: history of discussions with the Union of South Africa, 1909–39*, [Cmd 8707], H.C. 1952–3, xxiii, 169–309. See also, Lord Hailey, *The republic of South Africa and the High Commission Territories* (London, 1963); M. Perham and L. Curtis, *The protectorates of South Africa* (London, 1935); and R. Hyam, *The failure of South African expansion, 1908–48* (London, 1972).

insistence that African opinion must be consulted before incorporation tended to harden, as time passed, into the view that a pre-condition for any transfer must be, not merely consultation, but also the positive consent of the indigenous peoples; and, as it happened, Tswana opinion seems always to have been strongly against incorporation within the union. Chief Sekgoma of the Ngwato was adamant on this point in 1924:

I am not one of the chiefs who, according to the deputation to General Hertzog, support the idea of including the Bechuanaland Protectorate in the Union. My father[12] before me and now I myself have always been treated with the greatest consideration and thoughtfulness by the imperial government and, owing to this, we are still a united and happy people. It is my earnest wish to live and die under the imperial government, as my father did. We are a contented people, not like those who are under the Union government. There the native people are oppressed and crying. They have practically lost the identity of their different tribes. We would strongly oppose any effort to include the Bamangwato reserve in the Union. We are a free people. We have our cattle and our lands.[13]

Because relations between the protecting power and the tribal rulers of the B.P. had from the outset been established on a basis of mutual goodwill, British governments came to be increasingly unwilling to take, or encourage, any step prejudicial to the peace and stability of the existing regime. Is it surprising, therefore, that in the fulness of time the transition to independence was also effected, not only expeditiously, but also with remarkable harmony? The first president of the republic of Botswana, Sir Seretse Khama, using language reminiscent of his father's, Sekgoma's, comments, testified to this on independence day:

It would be wrong of me not at the outset to state again, as I have done so frequently before, the great gratitude of my people for the protection and assistance which have been given to Botswana by the United Kingdom during the long period of our dependence.[14]

But what a contrast we find when we come to examine the circumstances of British penetration and rule in Nigeria! Here the pattern of events is much more complicated—indeed, more complex than this paper will suggest. What is clear is that the extension of British rule over the land provoked continuous tension, occasional acts of treachery, murder and violence, and a series of wars of conquest. The use of force was characteristic from the bombardment of Lagos in 1851 to the conquest of the northern emirates in 1903, and for nearly twenty years thereafter the British had to deal with isolated risings against them. The reason was simple: Nigerians, like Africans everywhere along the west coast from the first advent of Europeans, though welcoming trade, always made plain their

[12] Khama III.
[13] Quoted in Mockford, *Seretse Khama*, pp 182–3.
[14] Quoted in A. Sillery, *Botswana* (London, 1974), p. 161.

desire to remain independent. Thus, for example, just as in 1482 Caramansa, the Elmina chief, had doggedly resisted the building of a Portuguese fort on his land, so more than four hundred years later in 1888 the Yoruba chiefs of Abeokuta were still refusing to surrender their freedom: when an Egba deputation from Lagos asked about a rumoured treaty with Frenchmen from Porto Novo, they repled categorically: 'we thank you for your anxious care, but neither to the French nor to the English are we giving our country.[15] Memories of dealings with the strangers who came from the sea stretched back over centuries, and it had always been the Africans who had dictated the terms of trade. There had never been much love for the white man, and experience had taught caution and suspicion. Even the Fulani emirs of the Sudan, though remote and apparently immune from attack, were from the start deeply suspicious of white explorers, white traders and Christian missionaries. The unspoken anxiety behind the remark of the percipient Sultan Mohammed Bello, conversing with Hugh Clapperton, the explorer, in Sokoto 1824, is revealing: 'You [English] are a strange people, the strongest of all Christian nations; you have subjugated all India'.[16]

If this was the attitude before the partition of Africa, antagonism sharpened thereafter as the British, particularly following the foundation of the Royal Niger Company, gradually imposed their rule upon the Nigerians. Admittedly, the desire to enforce the ending of the slave trade and then to stamp out slavery was genuine enough, and this led to the beginnings of direct British rule: the occupation of Lagos and its annexation as a crown colony in 1861. But there were other British aims too, less disinterested and more mercenary: the development and control of the palm oil trade; domination of the trade routes to, and access to the markets of, the hinterland of the Niger Delta, which, when implemented, resulted in many instances in the forcible displacement of the African middlemen; the pursuit of direct trade far up the Niger to its confluence with the Benue, involving the founding of a trading base at Lokoja;[17] and, in the closing years of the nineteenth century, the diversion southwards of the trade of the Fulani-Hausa-Kanuri complex, much of which previously had passed north and north-east along the old trans-saharan caravan routes. It was in pursuance of these aims that, whenever rival French or German missions threatened the British position, or seemed to threaten it, the response of British consuls, British merchants, Sir George Goldie, and officials of the company was to step up the effort to dominate and control the interior and not to tolerate African resistance.

[15] S. Johnson, *History of the Yoruba*, ed. O. Johnson, (London, 1963), pp 571–2.
[16] E. W. Bovill (ed.), *Missions to the Niger*, iv (Hakluyt Society, London, 1966), p. 688.
[17] H. J. Pedraza, *Borrioboola-Gha: the story of Lokoja.* (London, 1960).

This story of power politics, 'gunboat' diplomacy, and wars of conquest needs no elaboration. It has been well told by scholars such as Onwuka Dike, John Flint, Margery Perham, John Hargreaves, and Michael Crowder.[18] Its relevance here is that the violent methods frequently used to impose British rule were not forgotten by Nigerian patriots. The Sardauna of Sokoto, Alhaji Ahmadu Bello, a great-grandson of Mohammed Bello and one whose life spanned almost the whole period of the British regime in northern Nigeria, recorded his view with the restrained and dignified generosity which comes naturally to a scion of a distinguished dynasty:

Whatever the rights and wrongs of the attack on Kano and Sokoto may be, the British were the instrument of destiny and were fulfilling the will of God. . . . But we did not like the soldiers: they were our own people and had conquered us for strangers and had defeated our people on the plain just before us.[19]

Nnamdi Azikiwe, the vigorous Ibo leader of the nationalist movement in southern Nigeria, was much more outspoken, and in his inaugural speech as premier of the Eastern Region (1954) recalled those who had suffered for opposing the British lion: 'Let us not forget those who, among others, made the foundations of liberty in Nigeria secure—William Pepple, Ovonramwon, Jaja of Opobo, Herbert Macaulay, Horatio Jackson, names for ever enshrined in our national pantheon'.[20] If such emotive language was also propaganda aimed at rallying mass support for the independence campaign, it reflected the old spirit of determined resistance to the colonial regime. The road to defeat and humiliation, as Nigerian patriots fought vainly to defend their birthright, had been littered with scenes of violence: the Jaja 'kidnapping' (1887),[21] the 'sordid' Nana affair (1894),[22] Goldie's 'gambler's fling' with the maxim gun in conquering Bida and Ilorin (1897),[23] and, in the same year, the burning and the looting of the ancient city of Benin, were but the more notorious.

A surprising feature in this sorry story of aggression is that the criticisms of most Nigerian nationalists, during the generation between world war II

[18] K. O. Dike, *Trade and politics in the Niger Delta* (Oxford, 1956); J. E. Flint, *Sir George Goldie* (London, 1960); M. Perham, *Lord Lugard* (London, 2 vols, 1956, 1960); J. D. Hargreaves, *Prelude to the partition of West Africa* (London, 1963) and *West Africa partitioned* (London, 1974); M. Crowder (ed.), *West African resistance* (London, 1971); and many other monographs.

[19] Ahmadu Bello, *My life* (London, 1962), pp 19, 23.

[20] *Zik: selected speeches* (Cambridge, 1961), p. 89. William (Dappa) Pepple, Delta chief, deposed by consul John Beecroft in 1854 and exiled to Fernando Po; Ovonramwon, Oba of Benin, exiled after the conquest of Benin by consul general Ralph Moor to Calabar; Jaja of Opobo, Delta 'king', allegedly 'kidnapped' by acting consul (Sir) Harry Johnston in 1877 and then deported to the West Indies; Herbert Macaulay, sometimes called the 'father of Nigerian nationalism', editor of the *Lagos Daily News* and twice imprisoned; Thomas Horatius Jackson, editor of the *Lagos Weekly Record*, which his father John P. Jackson founded.

[21] See R. Oliver, *Sir Harry Johnston* (London, 1957), pp 104–23.

[22] Lord Salisbury's description of the deposition and exile in 1894 of Nana, chief of the Itsekiri. See O. Ikime, *Niger Delta rivalry* (London, 1969).

[23] Flint, op. cit., p. 246.

and the achievement of independence, were by and large so restrained and moderate. But it is also interesting to observe how, after independence, the tone changed; and the new school of young African historians is now far more direct and blunt. As Dr A. E. Afigbo, himself a Nigerian, puts it:

The post-partition reversal of the traditional roles by which the former [African] 'protectors' became the 'protected', with all its implications for the sovereignty and independence of the people, was totally unacceptable and was contested at every turn with all the means at their disposal.[24]

What is more, Lugard's conquest of the northern emirates in 1903 did not end the period of violence. In contrast to Tswana attitudes towards the protectorate administration of Bechuanaland, in Nigeria resentment and resistance persisted through the era of colonial occupation. This expressed itself at first and until 1919 in the form of fitful and isolated uprisings. As time passed, however, the mood changed: the sense of hopeless frustration resulting from the failure of repeated efforts to reject alien domination gave way to a mood of calculated optimism leading to direct pressure on the British authorities, first for a share in the control and direction of public affairs and, secondly, after world war II, for the restoration of independence.

If for the Batswana, then, security under the British crown was an acceptable role, among many of the peoples of Nigeria the passion for independence, fuelled by unrelenting resistance to British rule, always burned fiercely. It would be an error, however, to sharpen this contrast to the point of total difference. Everyone dreamed of freedom. But while Nigerians, especially the educated elite, were often openly outspoken and sometimes ready to risk all in rebellion, the Tswana chiefs and their advisers were realists enough to recognise that, in face of the continuing threat from white South Africa, the umbrella of Britain was the best available guarantee of their lands and their cattle.

But when Batswana and Nigerians dreamed of freedom, what exactly did they envisage? If British rule should end, would there be, or indeed could there be, a reversion to the old order? Would the pre-colonial authorities be restored intact? Or had the passage of time so altered expectations that some kind of new order would have to be set up?

In this context, two inter-related developments occurring under British rule went far to determine the future. The first was that the Tswana chiefs and at least the younger generation of Nigerian intelligentsia gradually came to recognise that the post-partition territorial boundaries, however artificial in historical or ethnic terms and though arbitrarily dictated by the colonial powers in the era of the 'scramble', were probably going to survive; in any case, these frontiers were likely to prove not less advantageous than other possible options, and—more importantly—arguments about fron-

[24] J. F. A. Ajayi and M. Crowder (eds), *History of West Africa*, ii (London, 1974), p. 425.

tiers must not be allowed to divert attention from the major issue of independence. Or so at least it seemed to ardent Nigerian nationalists of the calibre of Nnamdi Azikiwe or Obafemi Awolowo. But it was not a simple issue. Even for the Batswana, to accept the partition boundaries meant tragic separation from their Rolong and Tlhaping kinsmen in the Transvaal and the northern Cape province. For Nigerians the issue was to prove much more complex, not least for the northerners: indeed, the effort to adjust to the new territorial horizons proved to be only marginally possible. As it happened, sixty years of colonial rule, with territory-wide transport, communications, coinage, taxation and administrative machinery, helped to accustom the deeply-divided peoples of Nigeria to the new frontiers and in this way contributed to the educational process of nation-building. Moreover, the generation of nationalist leaders which directed the final campaign for independence had all grown up under the British dispensation, and this must have influenced northerners as well as southerners. Indeed, the new attitude, at least of southern nationalists, was indicated by 'Zik' in a speech in the legislative council, on 4 March 1958, delivered significantly in the northern capital, Kaduna:

This country, Nigeria, can no longer be regarded as a mere geographical expression. It is also an historical expression. . . . It is essential that ill-will be not created in order to encourage a Pakistan in this country. The north and south are one, whether we wish it or not. The forces of history have made it so. We have a common destiny; so, too have the east and the west. Any attempt from any source to create dissension and make the north feel that it is different from the south and the west from the east . . . should be deprecated.[25]

A second and much more important development under colonial rule was the genesis of popular nationalist movements. The leaders of these movements by and large either, like Seretse Khama in the Bechuanaland Protectorate, took the new boundaries in their stride, or, as with Nnamdi Azikiwe in Nigeria, urged their compatriots to uphold them as an integral part of the struggle for national independence.

However, when we come to look more closely at the growth of nationalism in the two countries as a factor in the pursuit of national independence, many contrasts emerge. Nationalism as a mass movement among the Batswana came late in the era of 'the wind of change': not till the late fifties, indeed as some would argue not till the early sixties, of this century, was it of any account; and no nationalist party was formed in the

[25] *Zik*, p. 102. This paper does not attempt to deal with contrasts in constitutional reforms leading to self-government in Botswana and Nigeria. In Nigeria, the Richard's quasi-federal constitution had involved (1946) the setting up of assemblies for the east, the west and the north. The trend towards a federal structure persisted, with the establishment of regions (1951) and regional premiers (1954), despite warnings from 'Zik'. The standard work on the boundaries of Nigeria is J. C. Anene, *The international boundaries of Nigeria, 1885–1960* (London, 1970).

protectorate before 1961. Still, when its power was eventually felt, and particularly after the foundation early in 1962 of the Bechuanaland Democratic Party (BDP) with Seretse Khama as leader, it easily encompassed the partition frontiers, relatively easily transcended tribal allegiances, telescoped the slow and painful stages of constitutional change on the road to freedom experienced by the peoples of other colonial dependencies—and Nigeria more than most—and carried the protectorate to statehood within not much more than a single quinquennium.

In striking contrast, the nationalist ideology took root in Nigeria even before world war II. Admittedly, its adherents, mostly the younger generation of western-education elite, mainly Lagos-based or members of the largely Yoruba-dominated Nigerian Youth Movement, founded in 1936, did not at that time command much popular support and had virtually no roots in the north. But their strength grew, particularly after the return to Nigeria of 'Zik' in 1938. Six years later, the first truly nationalist party was founded—the National Council of Nigeria and the Cameroons (the NCNC), with Herbert Macaulay as president and 'Zik' as general secretary, and the party's ambitious aim was 'to weld the heterogeneous masses of Nigeria into one single block'. But unlike the BDP of the protectorate, the NCNC never really enjoyed the nation-wide support which it claimed. Though it gathered up members from among non-Yoruba elements in the west and some non-Hausa-Fulani from the middle belt of the north, it always remained, perhaps because of organisational defects, essentially the party of the Ibo-speaking people of the east. Indeed, its efforts to capture the allegiance of the west were frustrated in 1951 by the formation of the Yoruba-controlled Action Group (the AG) headed by Awolowo. In the moslem north, the success of the NCNC was even more limited; and the foundation of the Northern People's Congress (NPC) in 1949 was possibly a more decisive moment in the history of the pursuit of independence in Nigeria than has been generally realised.[26]

The powerful northern emirs, who began to take control of the NPC in 1951 after its more radical members had seceded, were cautious, conservative and autocratic. They did not like what they saw of southern

[26] See J. S. Coleman, *Nigeria: background to nationalism* (Los Angeles, 1958), the pioneer and still-standard work on the subject to which this paper is heavily indebted. G. O. Olusanya, in 'Political awakening in the north' in *Journal of the Historical Society of Nigeria*, iv, 1 (Dec. 1967), pp 125–34, challenges Coleman's thesis that northern nationalism came late and was primarily the product of reaction to fears of southern domination: he argues that northern nationalism was locally-born and, as exemplified in 1945 in the foundation of the Northern Elements Progressive Association (NEPA), was as much an expression of reformist criticism of the autocratic and conservative regime of the emirs as a desire for freedom from colonial rule. It seems to the present writer, however, that northern nationalism was insignificant until the formation of the NPC which the emirs soon controlled.

nationalists, some of whom they regarded as little better than rabble-raising Gracchi. Ahmadu Bello put it thus:

It has become the fashion in other regions to regard the north as backward and hidebound by tradition. . . . We [Northerners who attended the early meetings of the house of representatives under the Macpherson constitution] all found it very strange and did not care for our stays in Lagos. The whole place was alien to our ideas of life, and we found that the members for the other regions might well belong to another world. . . . I was very glad not to be a member of the council of ministers.[27]

The attitudes of the northern emirs were also motivated by fears, not only of southern domination, but also of social revolution. So they took over leadership of the NPC with the deliberate purpose of preserving the distinctive cultural and religious character of the north intact; and, despite the alleged backwardness of northern education,[28] the power and influence of the emirs, combined with political know-how deriving from generations of experience in their own kind of imperial government, enabled them in some respects to dictate the course of events during the critical decade immediately preceding independence and, indeed, to some extent thereafter. There were moments in that decade when, on the one side, impatient southern leaders were tempted to seek independence unilaterally with or without the north, and, on the other, northern leaders seriously considered secession. The internal crisis between north and south reached its peak in 1953 when Chief Anthony Enahoro of the AG moved in the house of representatives that the primary target should be 'self-government for Nigeria in 1956'. The northerners, appalled at such precipitancy, quietly countered with the proposition 'self-government as soon as practicable', and, with the AG and most of the NCNC members walking out, carried the day. The fact was that the cautious northerners would not allow haste in the pursuit of the dream of freedom to outpace its feasibility. In the end, having gained vital time, they settled for 1960, and the path to independence was at last effectively cleared. But they had made their point: southerners had been reminded that they should not underestimate the 'inscrutable' north.[29]

The tide of nationalism in Nigeria, then, if in contrast to the Bechuanaland Protectorate, rising earlier and mounting faster, failed nevertheless to

---

[27] *My life*, pp 79, 85. It is possibly significant that the emirs took control of the NPC following reports of the riots, violence and trials, mostly in the east (the Enugu strike among coal-miners and the ensuing riots in Port Harcourt, Onitsha and Calabar), which were associated with the Zikist-stimulated violent phase of militant nationalism, 1949–50.

[28] Dr Coleman points out that no northerner went abroad for higher studies until 1945. One of the first to go overseas was Alhaji Abubakar Tafawa Balewa, afterwards the first prime minister of the Federation of Nigeria. However, he was not a Fulani aristocrat, but the son of a district head of the Jere tribe.

[29] The story of this crisis, told from the northern viewpoint, is set out in *My life*, chs 10 and 11.

unite all the peoples of that country in one single purpose. Nationalist leaders might talk of 'unity in diversity'; in fact, however, nationalism was always compounded with regionalism and even tribalism; and the leadership, often split, reflected the deep divisions. Whereas in the B.P. one leader—Seretse Khama—stood out above all others in directing the course of events, and was able always—as he still does[30]—to rally overwhelming support for the moderate policies of the BDP, in Nigeria the leadership was the subject of bitter personal rivalry and wide policy disagreement. Indeed, there is even some truth in the view that, in the infinitely complex story of the pursuit of independence in Nigeria, nationalist leaders, in striving for control and preeminence, actually aggravated the old ethnic and cultural divisions within the embryonic nation.

The divergent paths followed by nationalists in the two countries to achieve freedom can in one respect be explained very simply. Nigerians and, above all, Nnamdi Azikiwe, were pioneers in the movement for independence in English-speaking Africa south of the Sahara. As Dr. James S. Coleman writes:

During the fifteen-year period 1934–1945, Nnamdi Azikiwe was undoubtedly the most important and celebrated nationalist leader on the west coast of Africa, if not in all tropical Africa. To the outside world 'Zikism' and African nationalism appeared to be synonymous.[31]

Because Nigerians were pioneers, indeed, the wind blew hot and cold for them, and they experienced all the trials and tribulations that go with a crusade. Contrariwise, by the time the Batswana became interested in independence, the essential battle was over, the signposts along the road thither had come to be familiar, and the goal could be reached with a minimum of tension.

Nevertheless, the two nationalist movements did have some common features. In both the B.P. and Nigeria, there were always those who dreamed of determining in their own way their own political destinies. In both, inspiration was drawn from the heroic resistance of Abyssinian forces in face of Italian aggression in 1935–6. During the years 1939–45, wartime experiences, not least among some 10,000 Nigerian soldiers in East Africa, the middle east, India and Burma, immensely widened horizons and did much to destroy the old myths about white men and white superiority. Each, too, could learn from clause 3 of the Atlantic charter which endorsed 'the right of all peoples to choose the form of government under which they will live'; and in 1947 the model of Indian independence showed the way. What is more, the weakening in world war II of the European colonial

[30] In the most recent general election in Botswana (1974), the BDP won 27 of the 32 elective seats in the assembly.

[31] Coleman, op. cit., p. 220.

powers in general and of Britain in particular, did not go unnoticed. Nor did changing British attitudes towards colonial responsibilities: if Harold Macmillan's speech on 'the wind of change' was delivered (summer of 1960) after Nigeria had won her battle for freedom, it climaxed the new thinking and was not without influence among black southern Africans.

But the differences were more striking, and these arose, not just from contrasting experiences when European imperialism was rampant, nor only from the contrast between Nigerian heterogeneity and Tswana homogeneity. They derived, too, from the relative isolation, even rural insulation, of the Batswana from the changing currents of mid-twentieth-century world opinion contrasted with Nigeria's more central situation on the world stage and the world contacts and experiences of many of her more prominent leaders. The B.P., on the eve of African independence, with eyes rivetted as in the past on the vortex of South African politics and distracted by the storm over Seretse Khama's marriage, was educationally very backward and could boast virtually no educated elite: the number of its graduates, mostly from Fort Hare College at the Cape, was very small. Nigeria was more fortunate: she could claim, save in the north, an old and strong tradition of western education and, after world war II, especially in the teeming, bustling, urban centres of the south (Lagos, Abeokuta, Onitsha, Enugu, etc.), a whole new generation of men who were better educated and with wider horizons than their predecessors. The new elitist leadership included Nnamdi Azikiwe, Obafemi Awolowo, Hezekiah Oladipo Davies, Samuel Ladoke Akintola and the Zikist extremist Anthony Enahoro. 'Zik' himself, by education and outlook, personified the new leadership. Educated in the U.S.A., he had come under the influence of various strands in Afro-American thinking, notably Marcus Garvey's 'back to Africa' movement and W. E. B. Dubois's pan-Africanism. Beyond that, while in the United States, he had observed the importance of political organisation and the power of the popular press. These lessons he applied on his return to Nigeria; and they were reflected in both his editorship of the *West African Pilot* and his leadership of the NCNC. Speeches, press propaganda, recruitment tours, mass party rallies, the exploitation of discontent in the powerful labour unions, and appeals to the youth of the nation were all used, often somewhat unscrupulously, as instruments to work up popular support for the nationalist cause.[32] With such skilful and energetic leadership, the nationalist movement rapidly built up to such a pitch that no British government could ignore it. If 'Zik'

[32] An NCNC deputation, visiting London in 1947 to protest against the Richards constitution, also went to Dublin where the lord mayor told them that 'the Irish people were always on the side of all peoples struggling for national independence regardless of race, colour or creed' (Coleman, op. cit., p. 293).

partly lost his grip on the leadership as independence drew near, particularly in face of the rivalry of Awolowo and the AG and the powerful intervention of the northerners, his unique contribution was recognised when he became the first president of the republic of Nigeria.

In conclusion, we may observe that in the Bechuanaland Protectorate the run-up to independence, so different from that in Nigeria, was remarkably smooth. If nationalists in Nigeria, as we have seen, in some sense pioneered the pursuit of independence in English-speaking Africa and consequently experienced all its pangs, the Batswana, entering late in the race, took it in their stride. With the victory for the principle already effectively won in Ghana and Nigeria, they were encouraged to seek freedom, not in face of opposition from the protecting power but with its active cooperation. Again, if the changing climate of world opinion and such powerful influences as Afro-Americanism and pan-Africanism contributed importantly to the genesis of mass nationalism in Nigeria, nationalism, in the Protectorate at least in its more extreme form, was more the product of factors peculiar to southern Africa. By 1960, with anxiety about incorporation within South Africa now only a spectre from the past, independence could be seriously contemplated. Sharpeville was possibly decisive in the birth of Tswana nationalism.[33] South African refugees, seeking shelter in the Protectorate from Afrikanerdom, joined with local Tswana patriots—returned Rand miners among them—to form small nationalist parties. Their hero was, not Marcus Garvey nor W. E. B. Dubois, but Kwame Nkrumah of Ghana and his Convention Peoples Party which had helped to finance the struggles of the pan-African and African Congress movements in South Africa. But though urban-based, in Francistown and Lobatse, like the first Nigerian nationalists many years before in Lagos, they signally failed, unlike the latter, to win wide popular support. Their radical condemnation of both white rule and chiefly authority, coupled with demands for immediate independence, inspired a strong reaction among moderate Batswana, and it was this which led to the formation in 1962 of the BDP, whose members, drawn from all parts of the country, persuaded Seretse Khama to accept the leadership. Seretse, born in 1921 at Serowe, schooled at Lovedale, graduated at Fort Hare and educated at Balliol College, Oxford, and the London School of Economics, had been exiled during the marriage and succession crisis, and had in a hard, even callous, world ripened in knowledge and been toughened by experience. The leadership of the BDP, which he now assumed, was to prove decisive for his country: Seretse himself, wise and moderate, gentle but firm, was to bring prestige and statesmanship of a singularly high order to the task of

---

[33] On the Sharpeville 'massacre' and its background, see M. Wilson and L. Thompson (eds), *Oxford history of South Africa*, ii (London, 1971), ch. 9.

nation-building. Furthermore, his party, as Sillery explains, was 'the party of the countryside, of the farmers, cattle-owners, herdsmen, the men of the tribes, who form the great majority of the people of the territory. In the towns the party appeals to the moderates, the professional and middle classes'.[34] More than that, the party he now led also had the backing of nearly all the principal chiefs.

The intervention of the BDP, indeed, did prove decisive, much more so than that of the northern emirs in the turbulent struggle for Nigerian independence. In contrast to Nigeria, where divisions among the national-ists ran very deep and were at times chaotic, the BDP commanded enthusiastic and overwhelmingly united support; and there was never any question of partition or secession. Indeed, the concept of an unitary state was from the start accepted and assured, and this was symbolised by the building of a brand new capital out of the bush at Gaborone. Seretse Khama, like the emirs of northern Nigeria, sought independence 'as soon as practicable'. Unlike them, he did not have to compromise with more radical and less patient extremists. There was no violence, as there was in Nigeria; and trade unionism was never the power in the politics of inde-pendence in the B.P. that it was in Nigeria. Seretse's BDP, indeed, dictated the terms of the quick transition to independence, with only one year of intervening, internal self-government. In striking contrast to Nigeria's long and stormy passage to freedom, the Protectorate's experience was an exhibition model.

[34] *Botswana*, pp 156–7.

Maps of Botswana and Nigeria showing peoples and places mentioned in the text; kindly prepared by Miss Shirley Keeley in the drawing office of The New University of Ulster

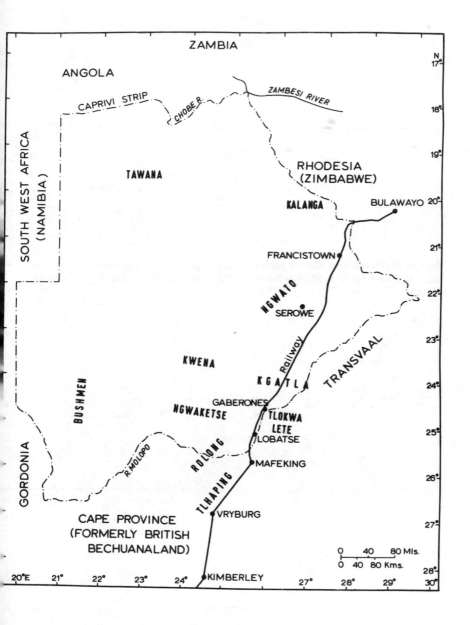

Botswana

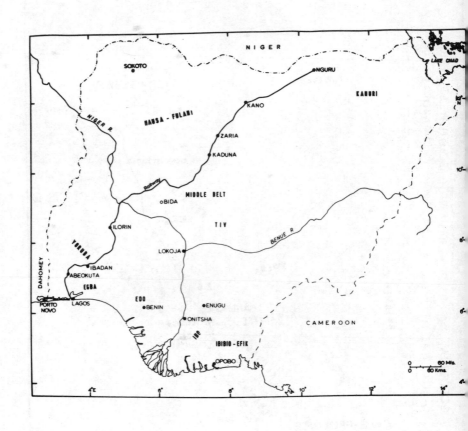

Nigeria